POLYNESIAN TATTOO DESIGNS

VOL. I

Ocean Legacy

TattooTribes.com

2014

ISBN-13: 978-8890601668

ISBN-10: 8890601663

All images by TattooTribes based on traditional motifs

CONTENTS

MANTAS

Mantas are amazing animals usually associated to several different meanings, some depending on their nature and behaviour, some inherited from legends and stories.

They symbolize beauty and elegance, freedom and voyage and they are related to knowledge and wisdom too.

Mantas are also associated to flying and their tail is often used as a symbol of sexuality representing the male.

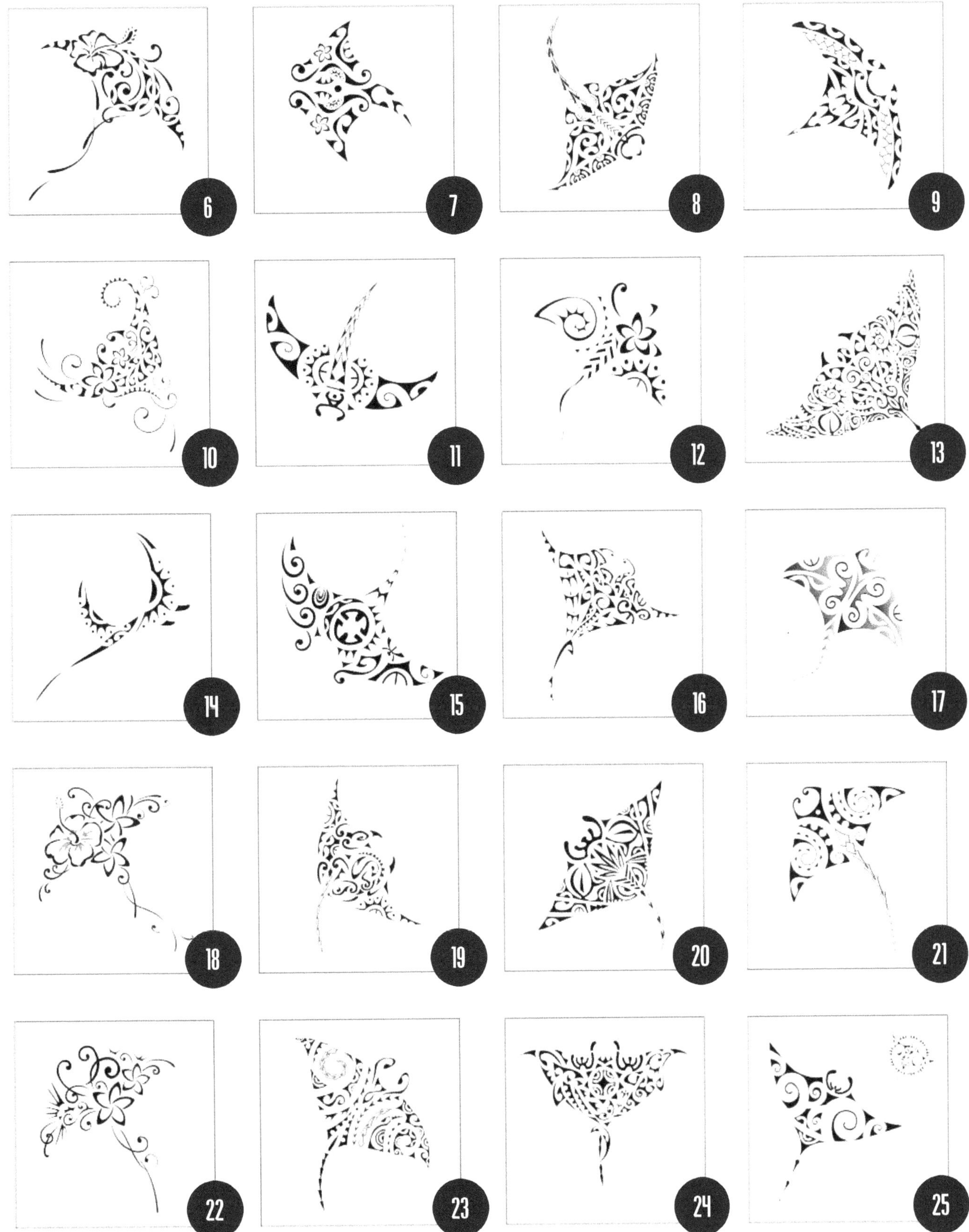
6
7
8
9
10
11
12
13
14
15
16
17
18
19
20
21
22
23
24
25

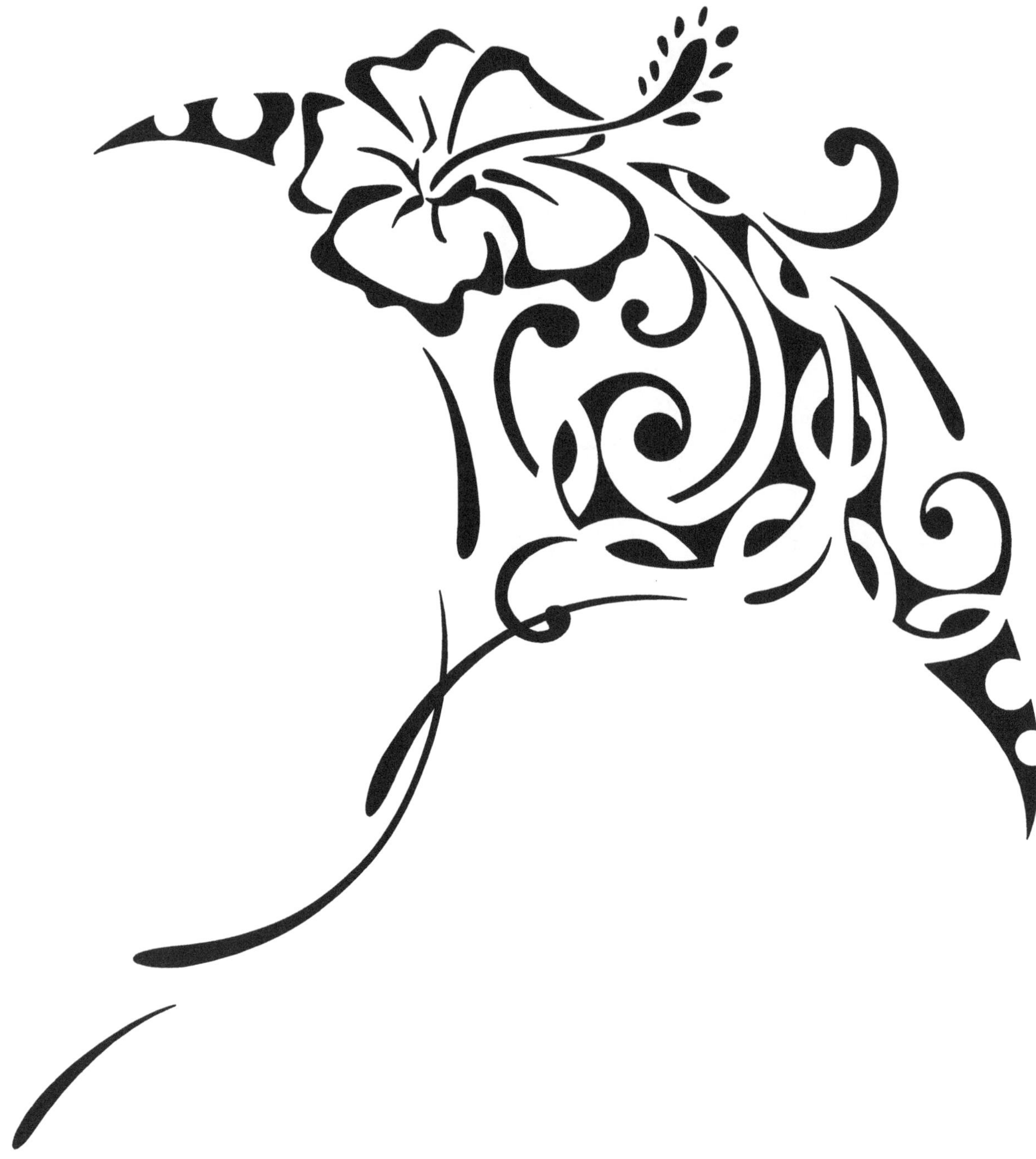

FEMININITY

Flowers of hibiscus grow mainly on tropical islands and thus perfectly symbolize their relaxed and laid back way of living. They are symbols of femininity and beauty, associated here with waves since water too is related to fertility and femininity in all cultures.

STENCIL: t001

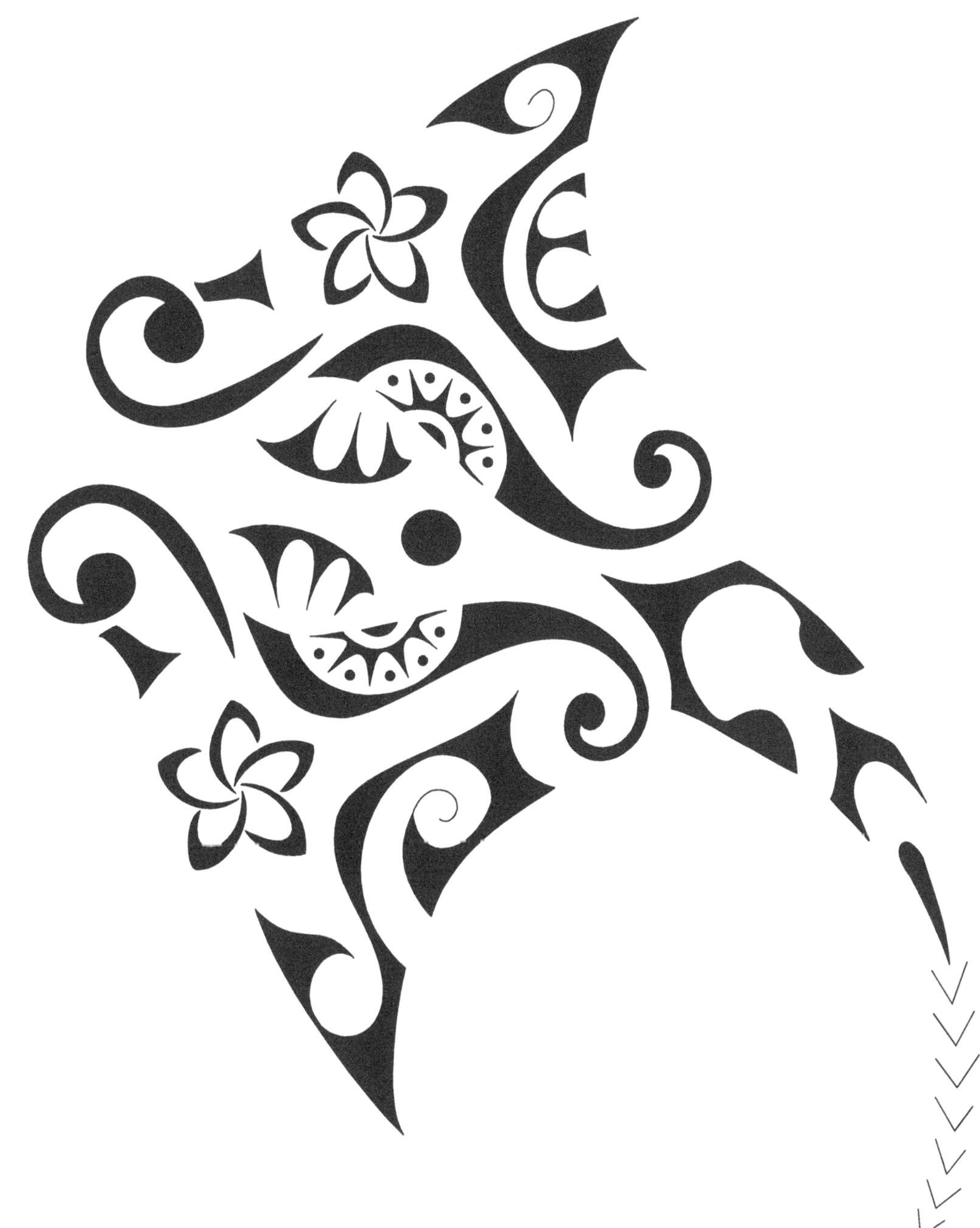

PROTECTION

In this design, Frangipani flowers symbolize two children, guarded and protected by the two seahorses, which have a dual symbolism: father and maternal love (male seahorses carry the eggs provided by the females).
The sun, hand of *tiki* and fish hook are symbols for joy, protection and prosperity.

STENCIL: t002

FIGHTER

This manta is shaped to recall the face of a warrior with his tongue stretched out to symbolize defiance and facing every challenge with valiance. Elements like the centipede and spear heads symbolize a fighting spirit whilst the upside-down *enata* represent here defeated enemies.

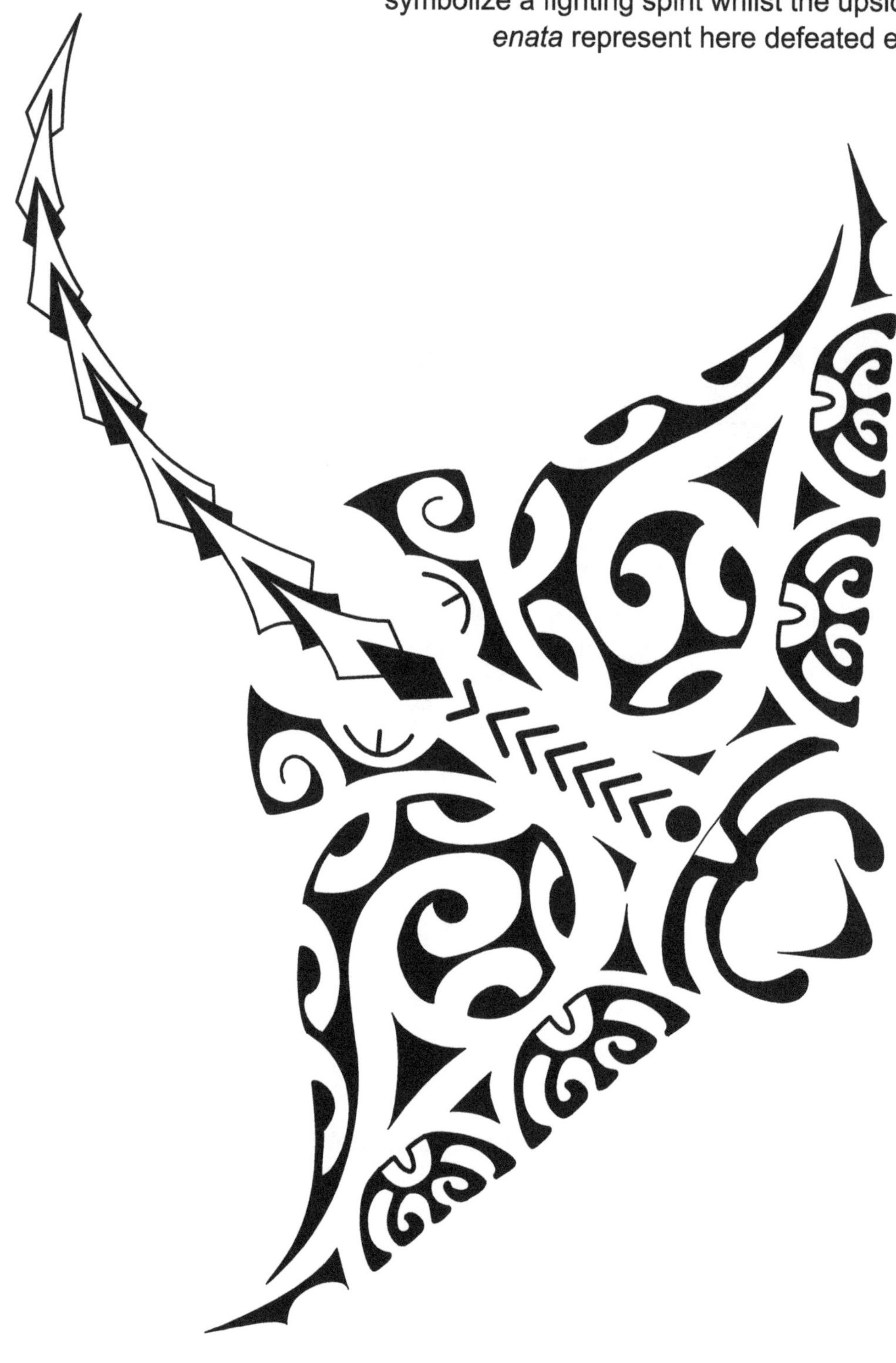

STENCIL: t003

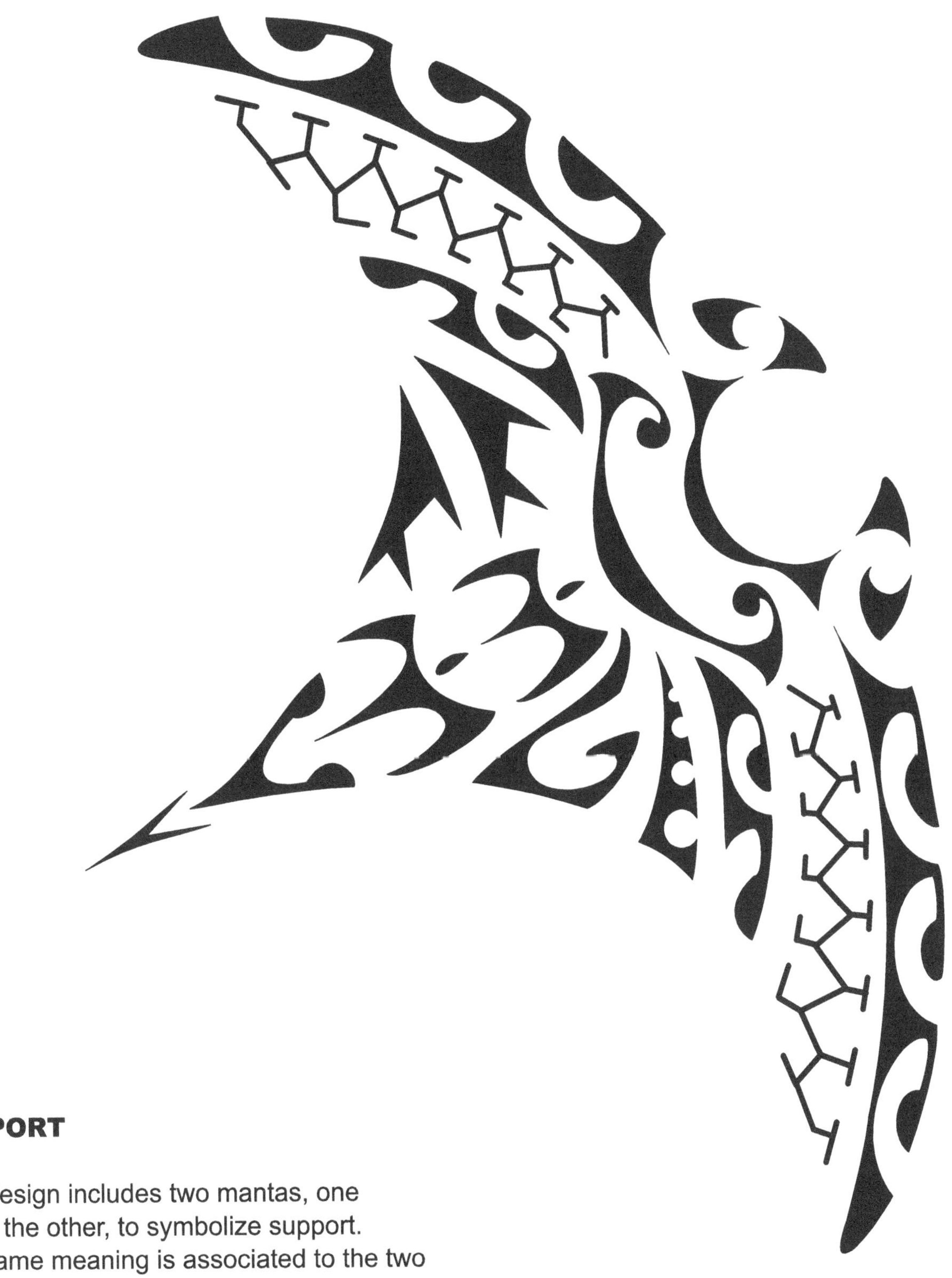

SUPPORT

This design includes two mantas, one inside the other, to symbolize support. The same meaning is associated to the two chasing birds and to the pattern representing the ancestors that embraces the smaller manta.

STENCIL: t004

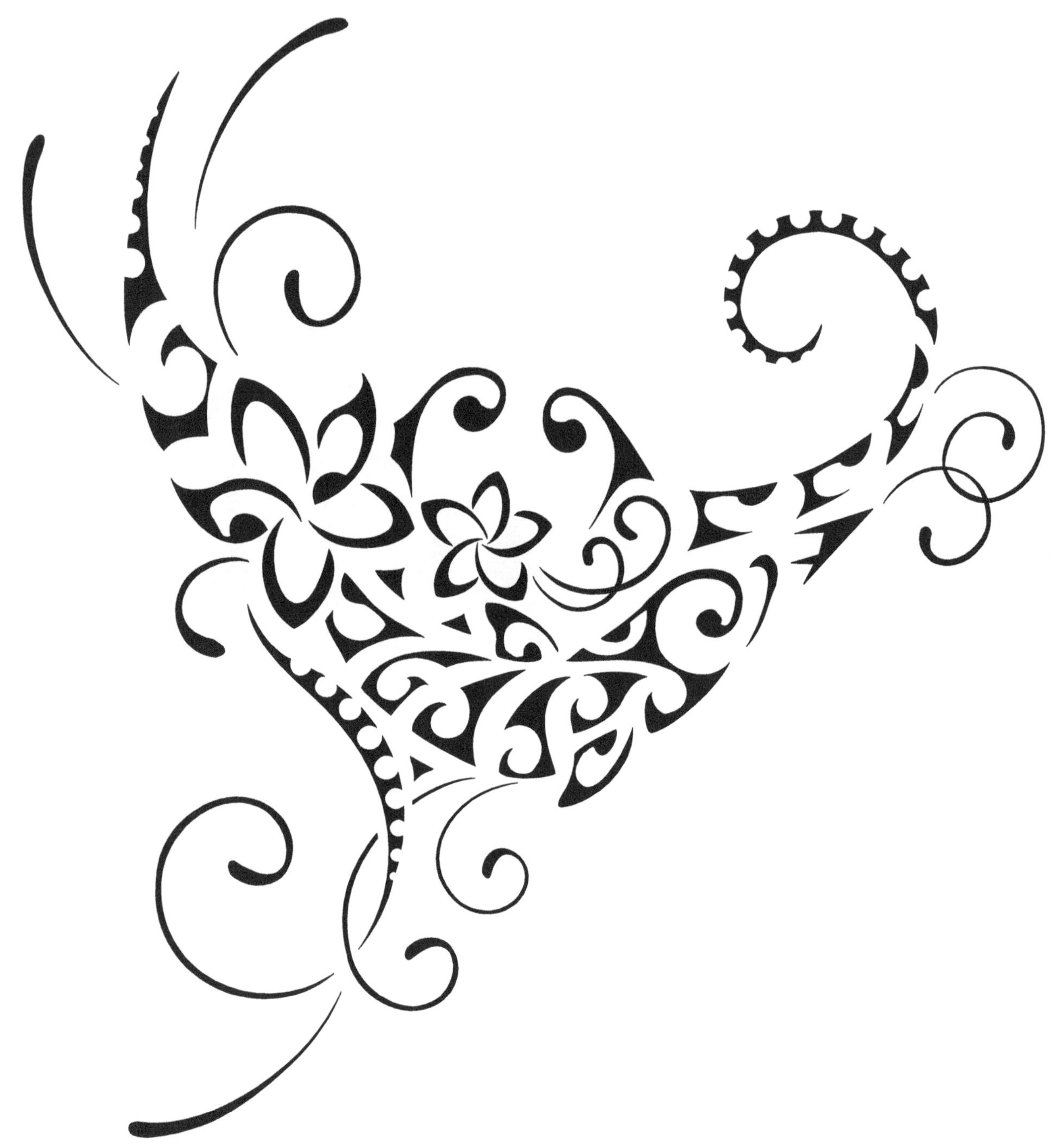

JOY, PASSION

This manta design was shaped to resemble a scorpion because scorpions are associated to love in several cultures; the bite of a scorpion shares similar symptoms with passion: shortened breath, feverish state, accelerated heartbeat and pain if not reciprocated. Dolphin, flowers and *koru* are symbols for joy, beauty and life.

STENCIL: t005

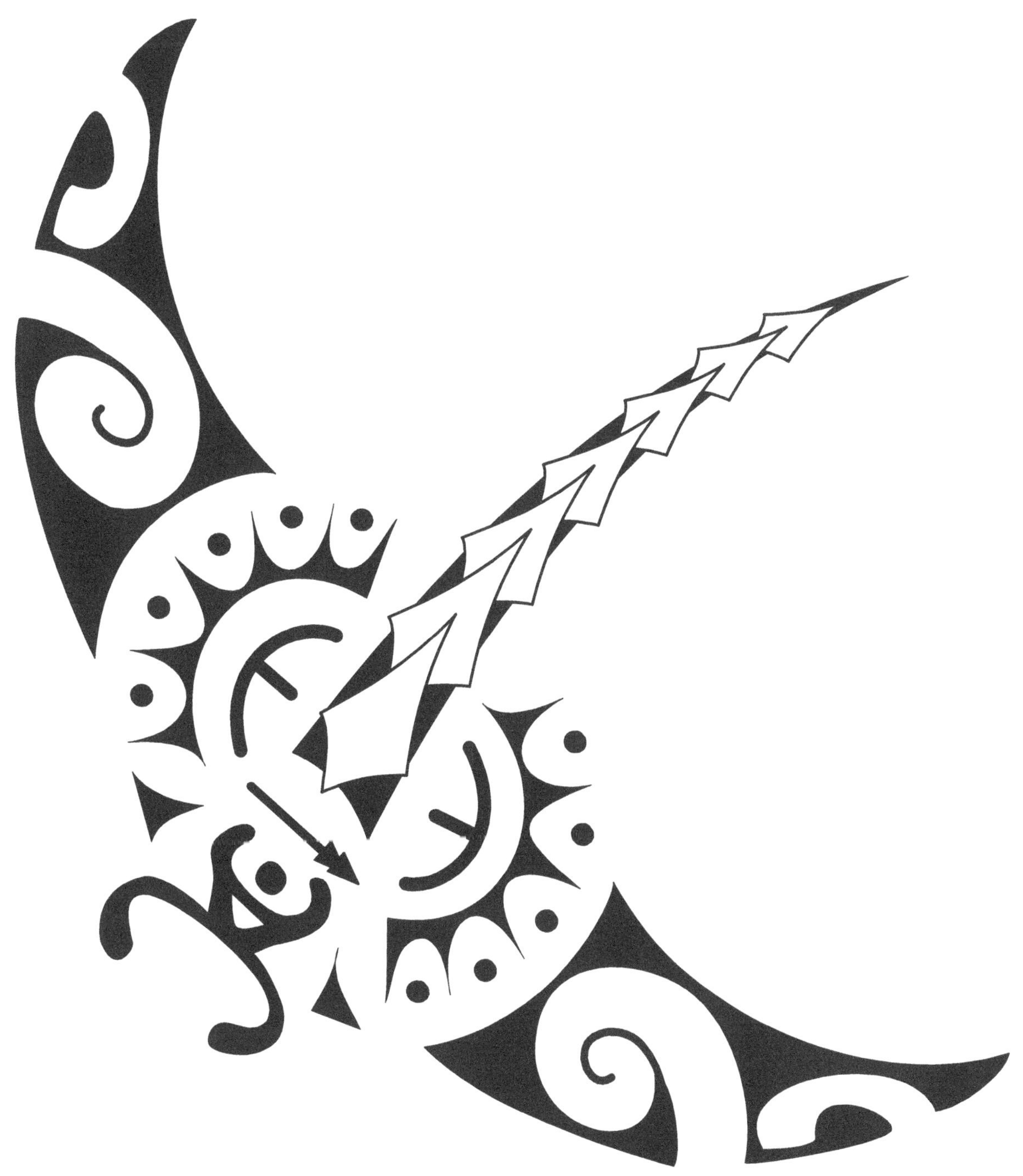

WARRIOR

This manta represents the warrior facing every challenge with courage and strength (the spear heads) to reach for success.

STENCIL: t006

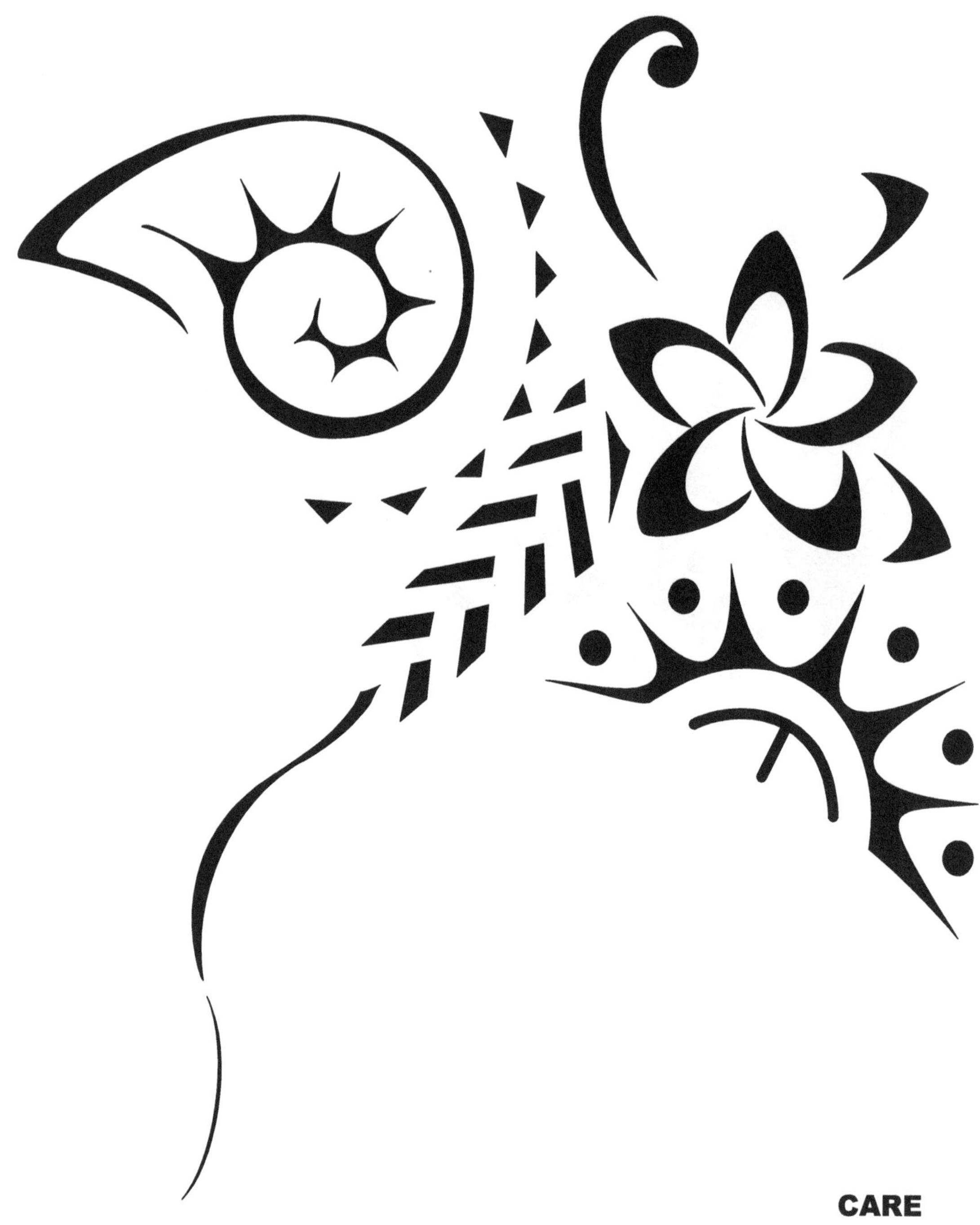

CARE

The seashell is a symbol for safe shelter, similar to the frangipani, and love. The *koru* is a new life, the sun is for joy and the braid is a symbol for family union.

STENCIL: t007

FAMILY PROTECTION

Central in this design is a turtle representing family, enclosed and guarded between two *tiki* faces, protecting family on all sides.
The lizard in the tail of the manta is a bringer of good luck while other symbols such as suns and fish hooks are for joy, positivity and prosperity.

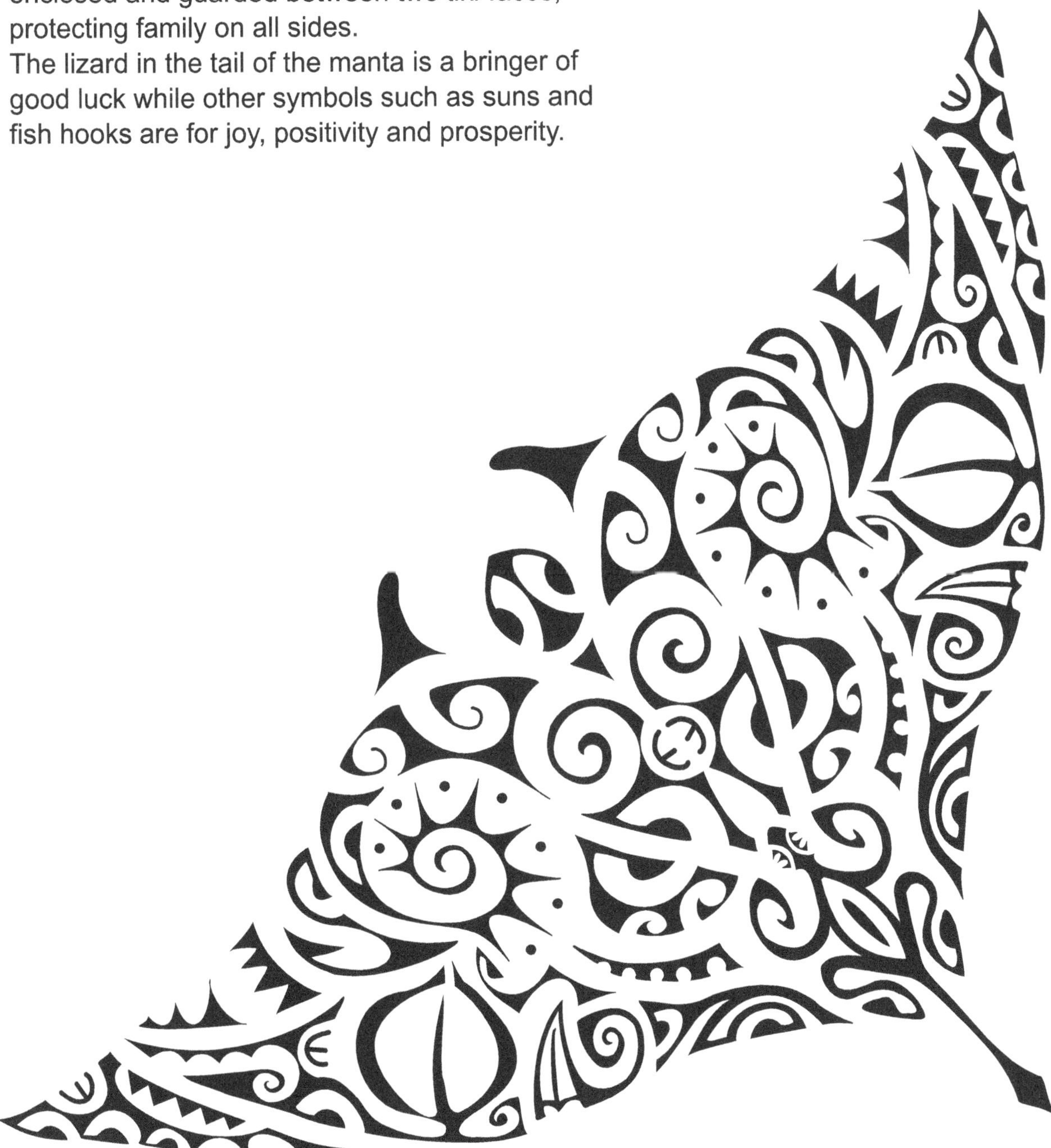

STENCIL: t008

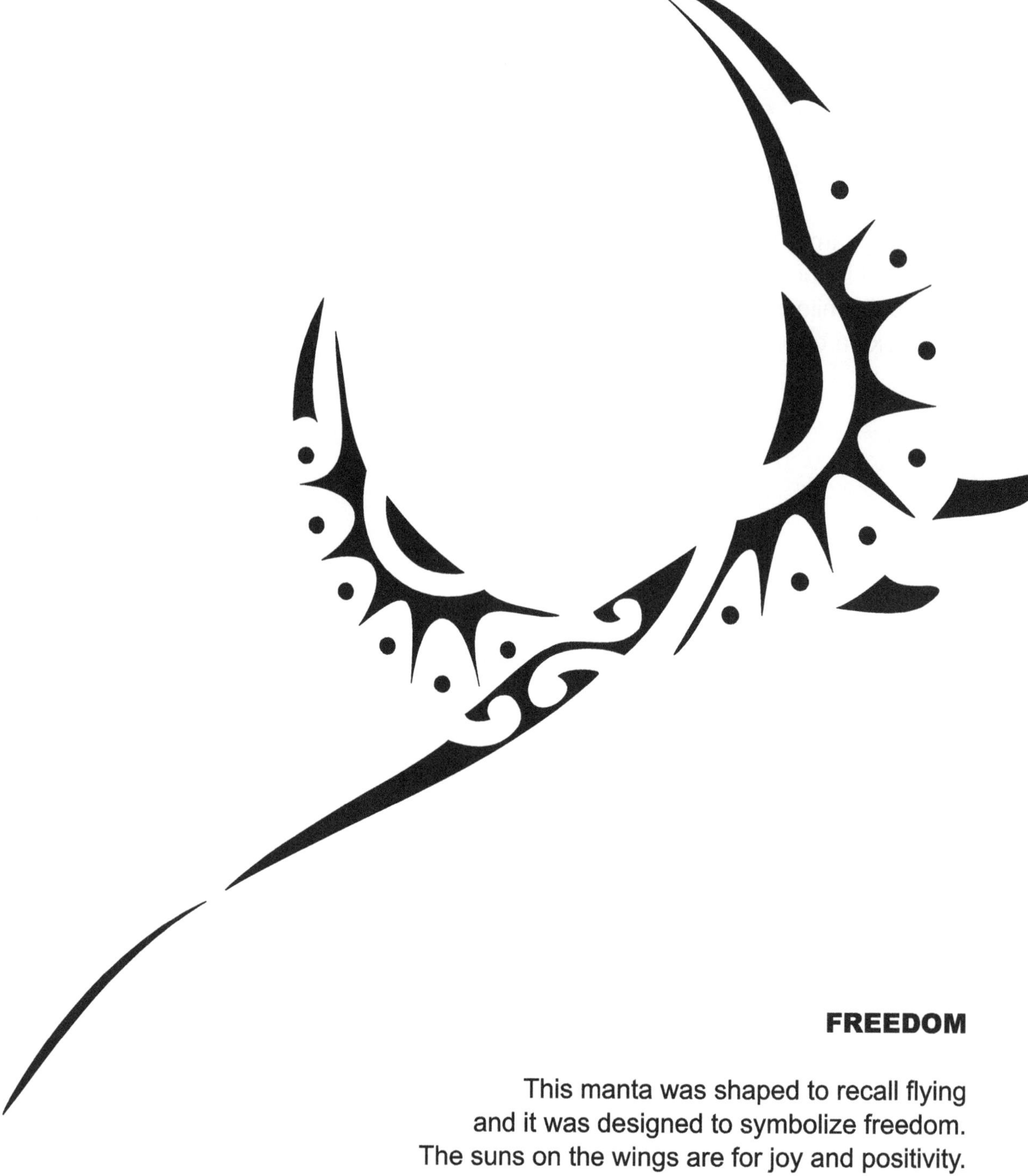

FREEDOM

This manta was shaped to recall flying
and it was designed to symbolize freedom.
The suns on the wings are for joy and positivity.

STENCIL: t009

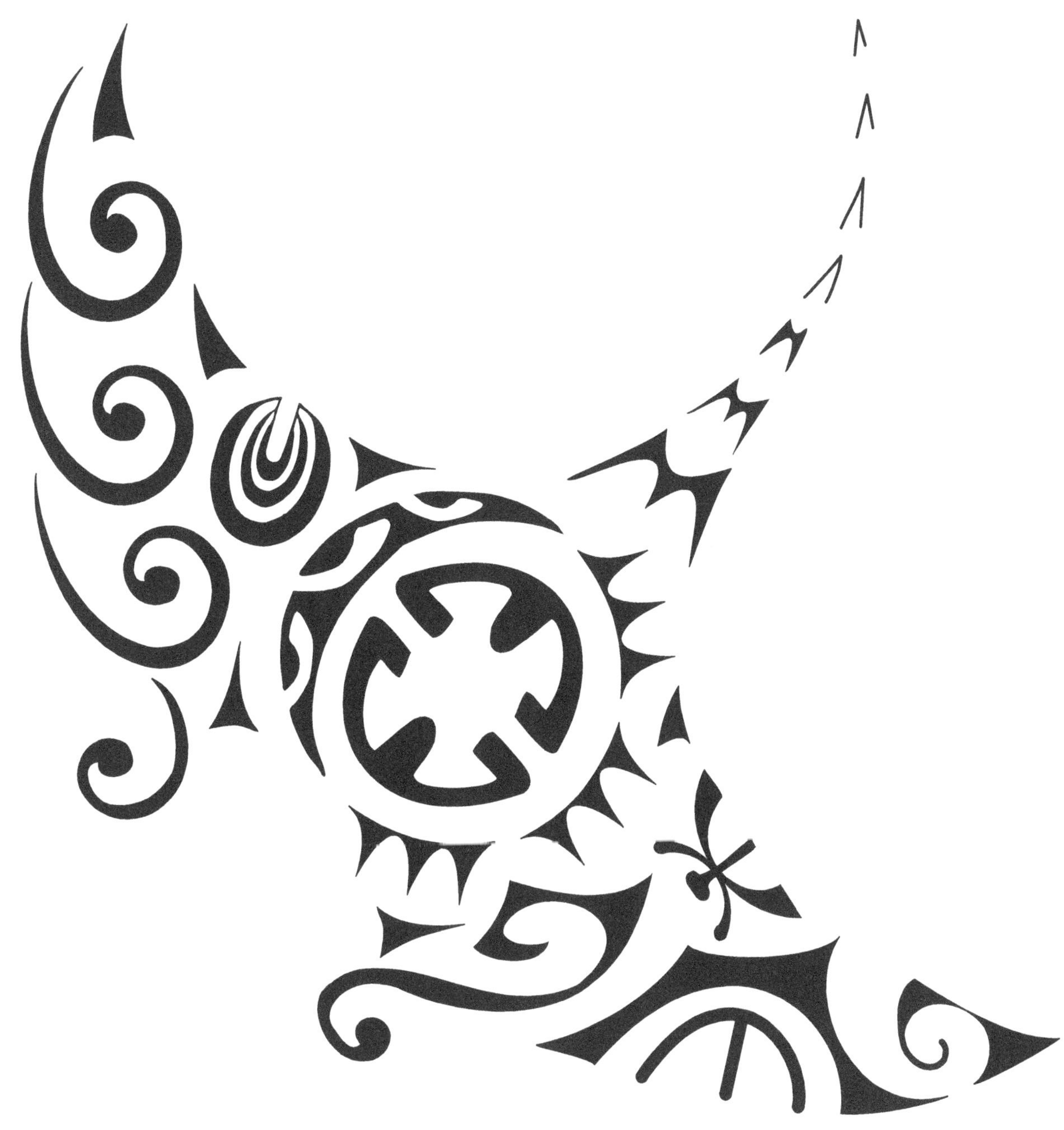

MARRIAGE

The central element represents a couple, the union between man and woman, surrounded by a sun and a moon (impossible that becomes possible), male and female and by other elements symbolizing the union of opposites and the help that will always be granted between them.

STENCIL: t010

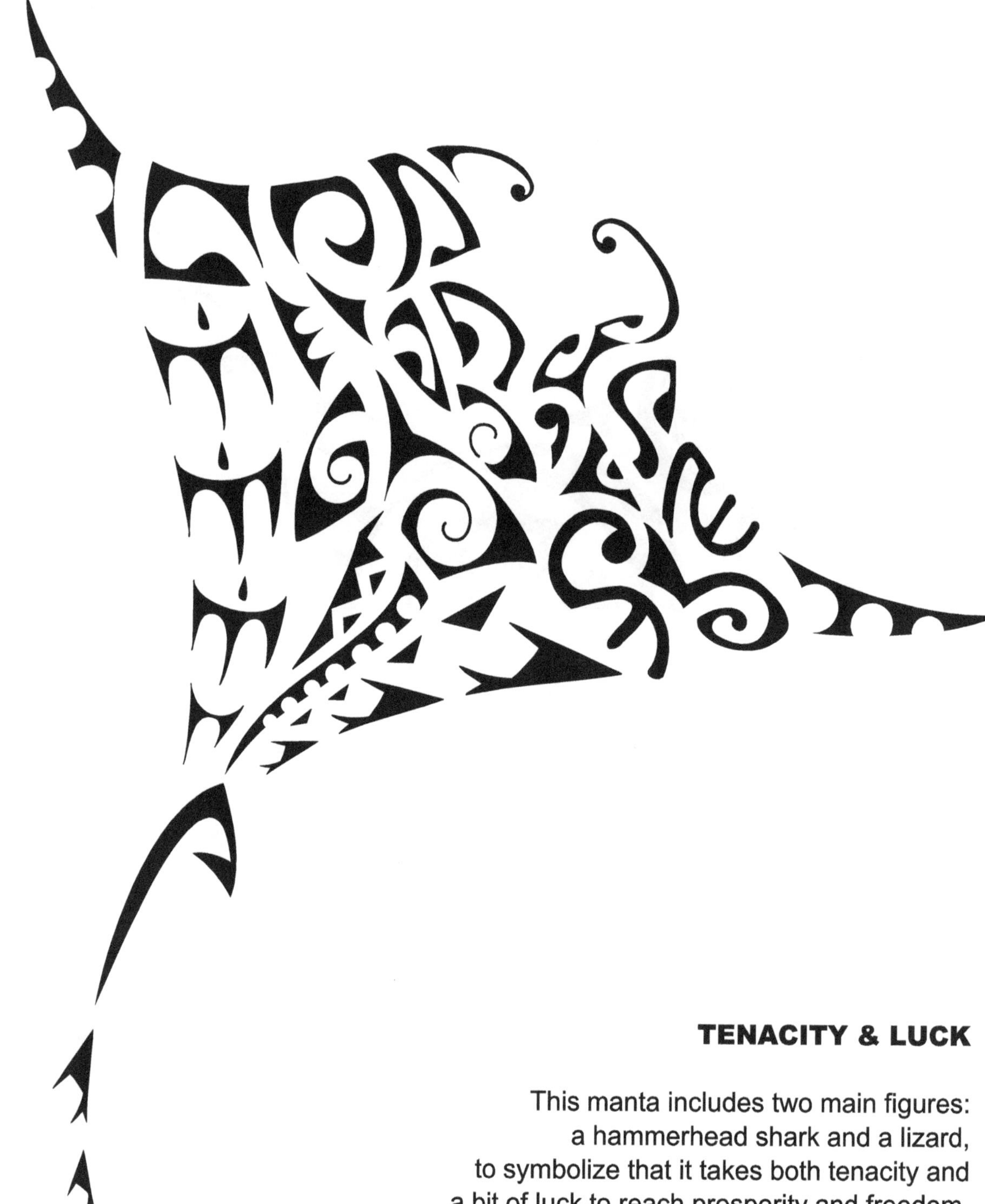

TENACITY & LUCK

This manta includes two main figures:
a hammerhead shark and a lizard,
to symbolize that it takes both tenacity and
a bit of luck to reach prosperity and freedom.

STENCIL: t011

REBIRTH

Koru symbolize new life, new beginning.
This manta includes several *koru* laid out
to resemble a butterfly, which is yet another symbol
for rebirth, transformation and freedom.

STENCIL: t012

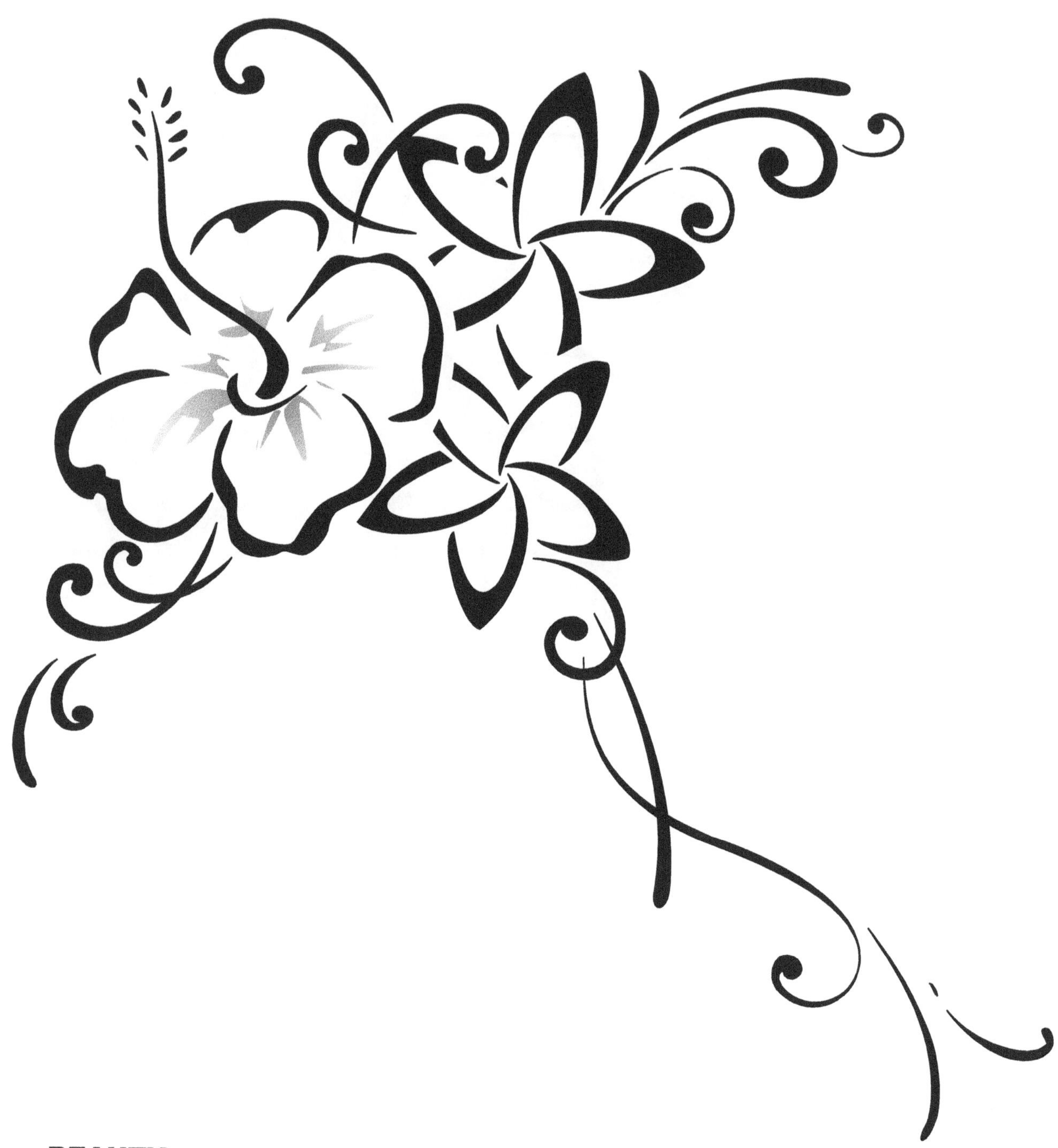

BEAUTY

This feminine manta is entirely shaped by flowers to symbolize beauty and femininity.

STENCIL: t013

GOOD LUCK & HEALTH

Two lizards following each other are the main elements of this design, surrounded by a sun and a moon to represent good luck, health and protection under any circumstances.

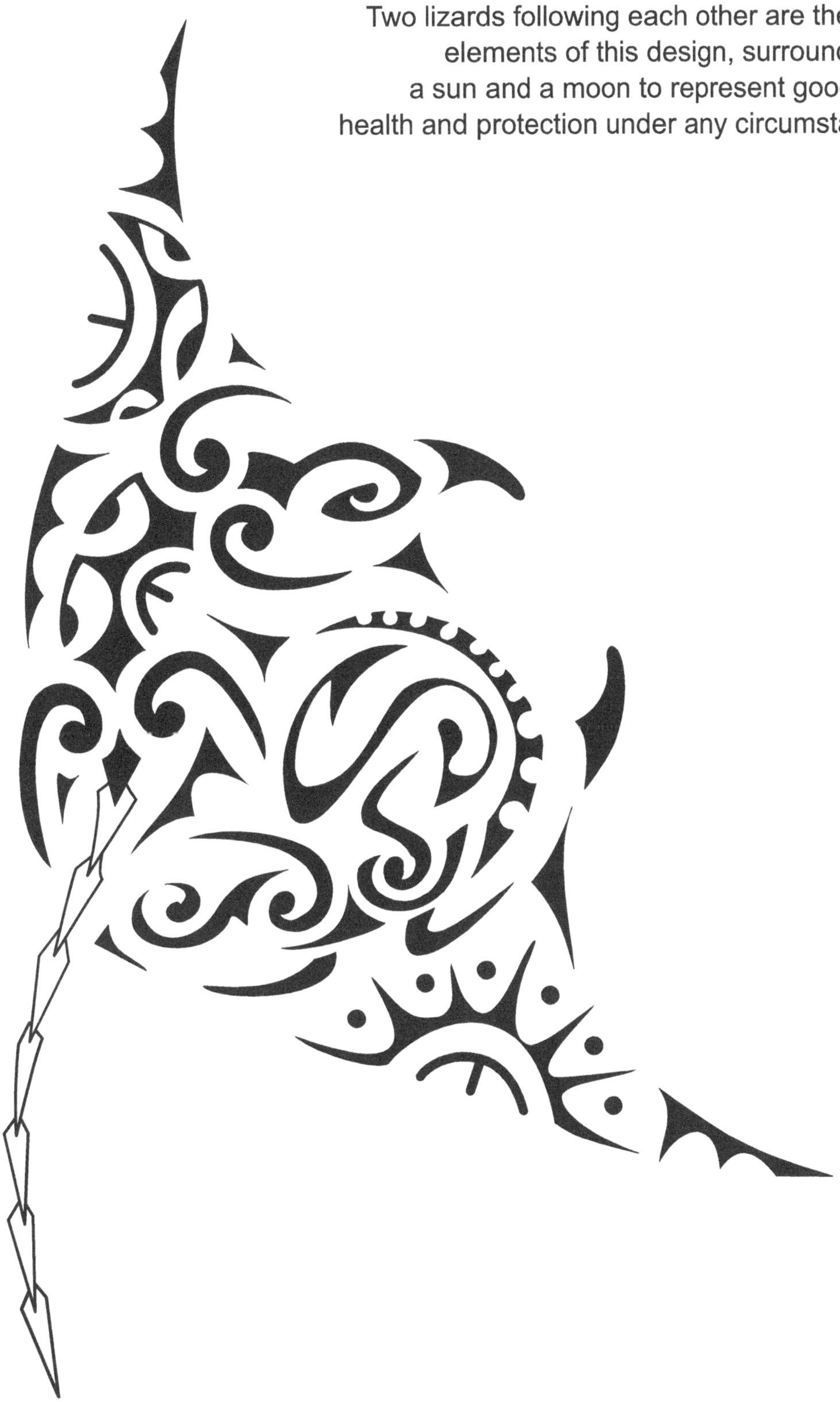

STENCIL: t014

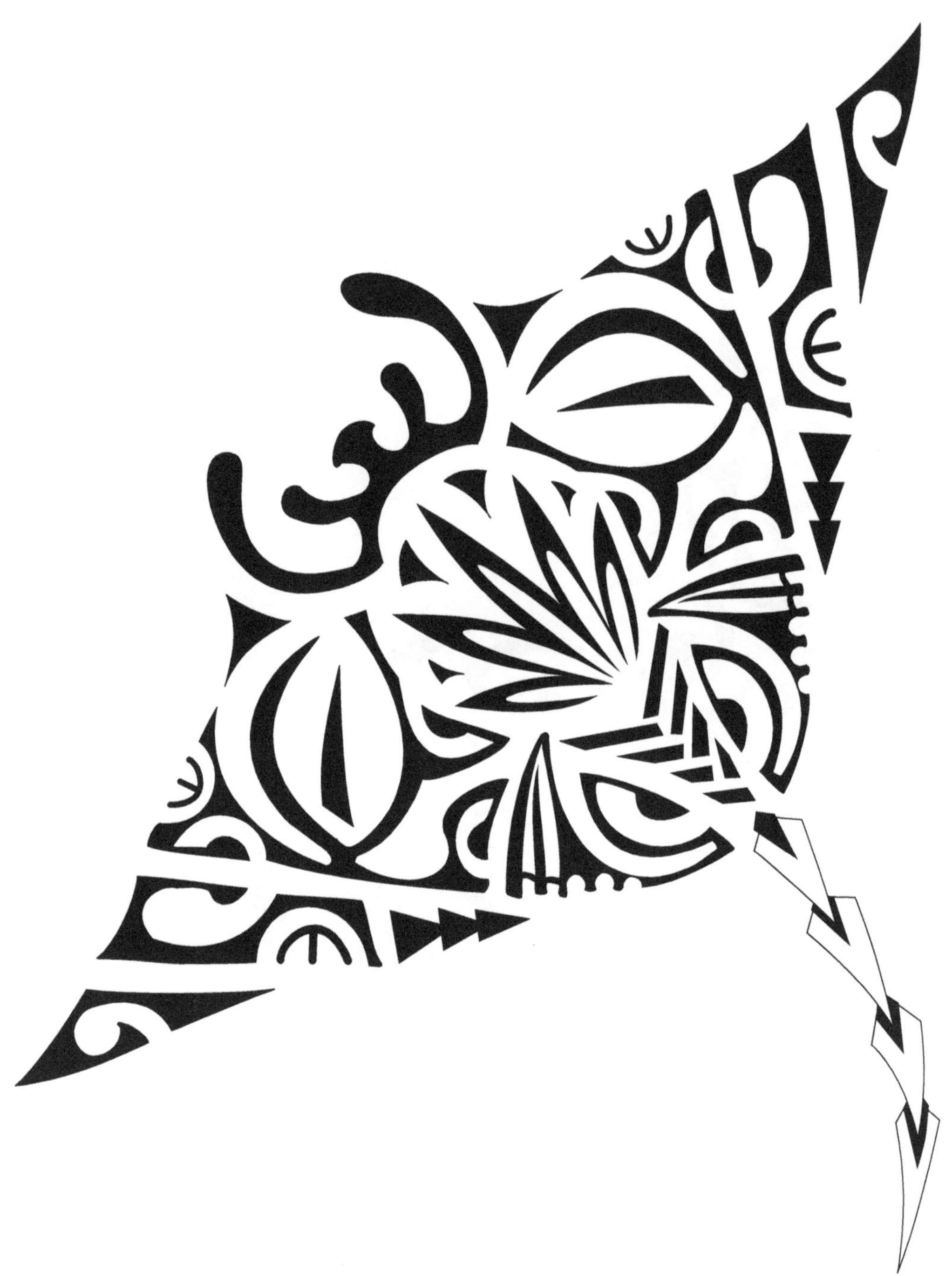

FAMILY PROTECTOR

The human figure on top represents an ancestor protecting the family represented by the flax leaves and braid, guarded by the *tiki* from all sides.

STENCIL: t015

ADAPTABILITY

Shark teeth and octopus tentacles are symbols for adaptability and tenacity. Spear heads represent the warrior and *koru* motifs are for new beginnings and life.

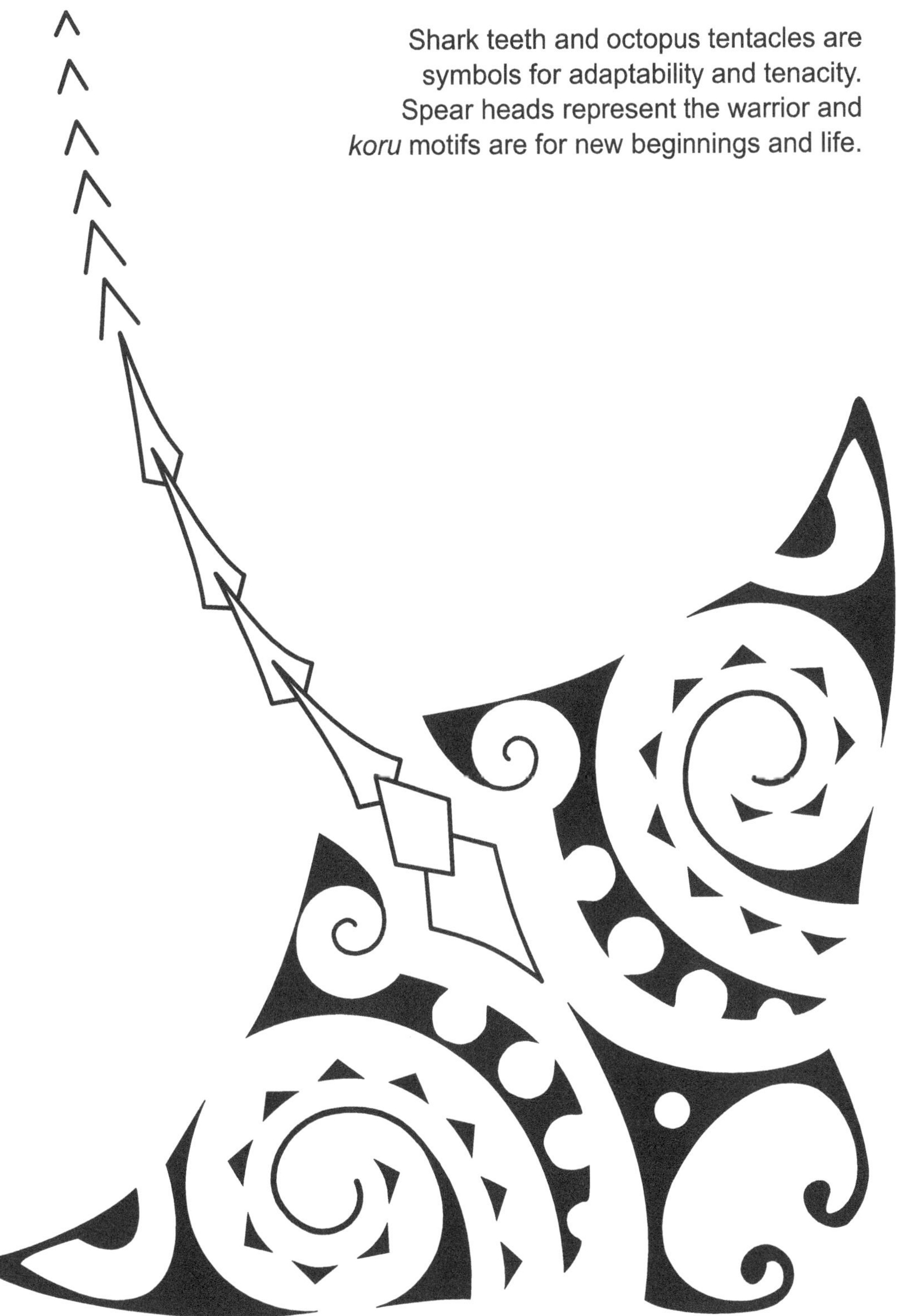

STENCIL: t016

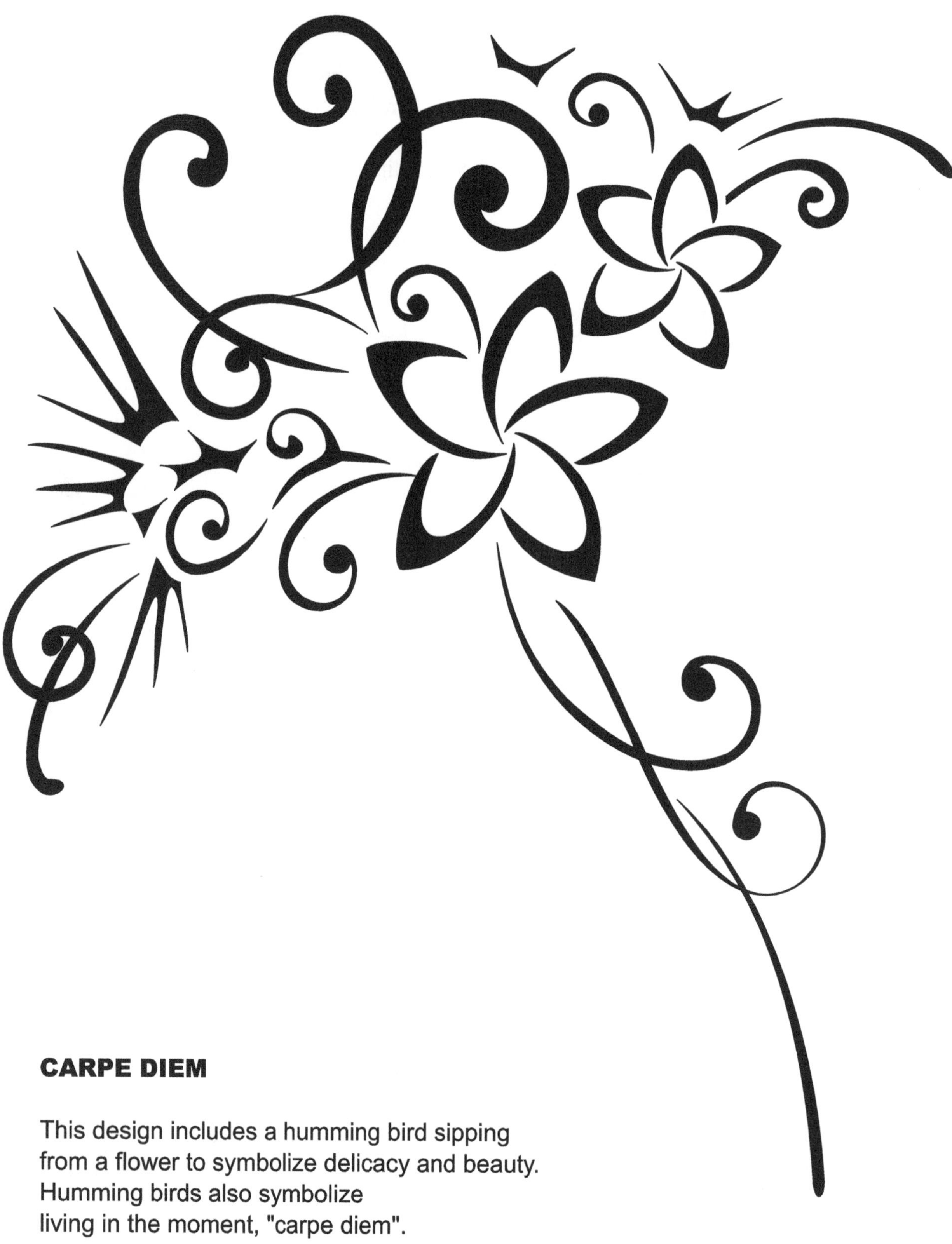

CARPE DIEM

This design includes a humming bird sipping from a flower to symbolize delicacy and beauty. Humming birds also symbolize living in the moment, "carpe diem".

STENCIL: t017

LIFE

This mixed design includes several motifs representing different aspect of life: tenacity, adaptability, prosperity, protection. *Koru* symbolize new beginnings and the twist in the middle represents eternal love.

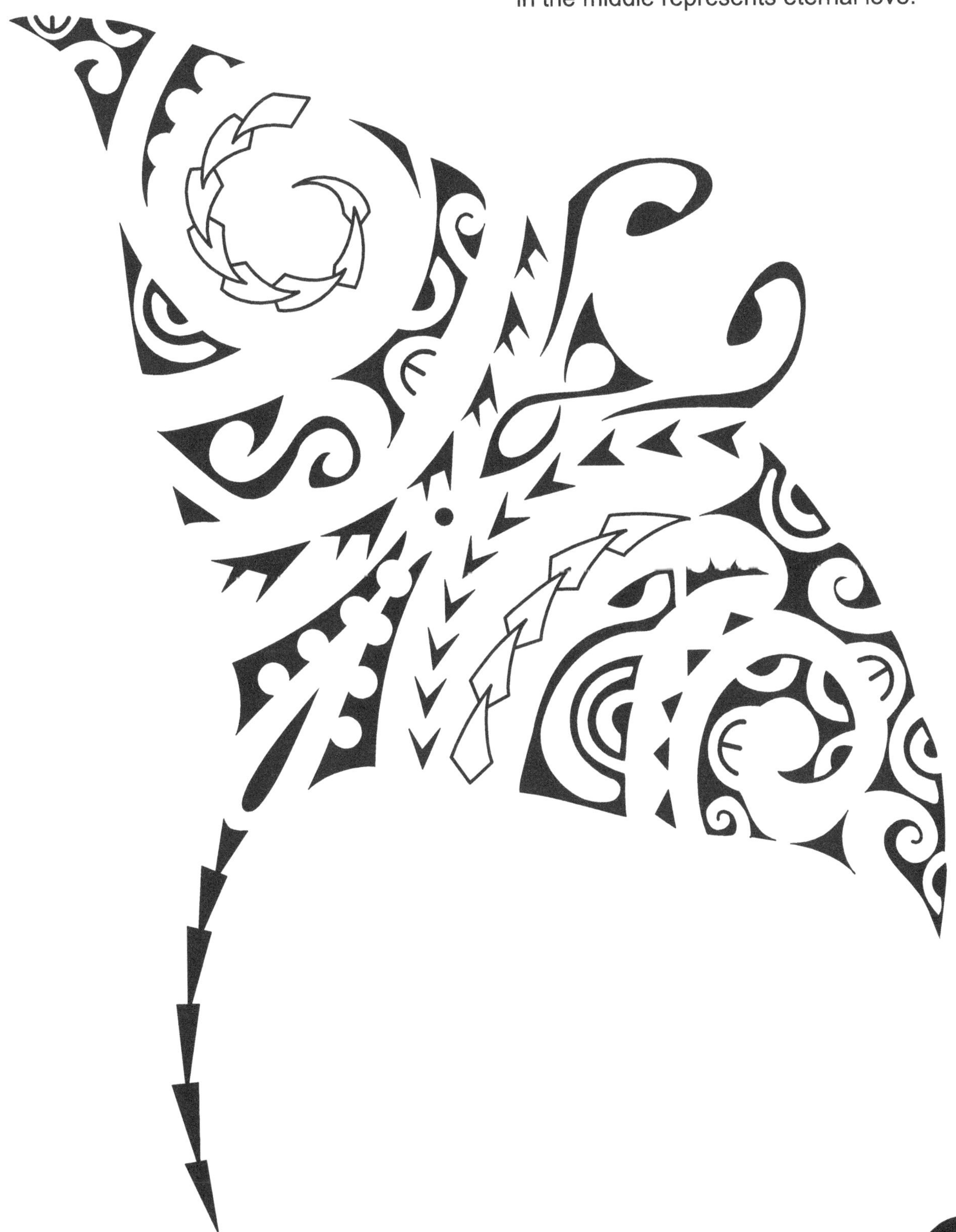

STENCIL: t018

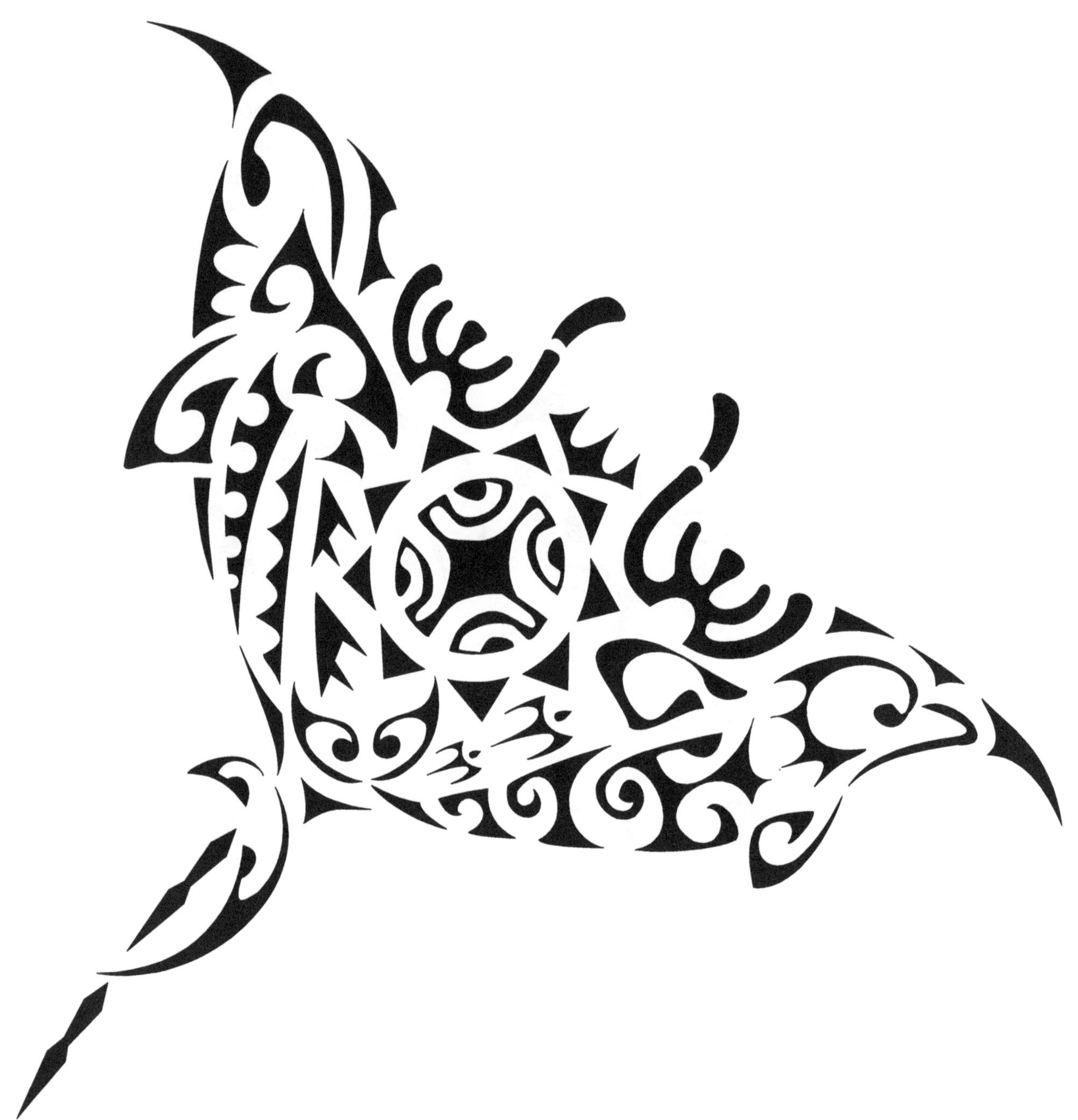

BALANCE

The central Marquesan cross symbolizing balance and harmony is surrounded by a shark and a dolphin to represent different aspects of life, strength and joy, as both necessary to reach a balance and prosperity.

STENCIL: t019

RIDE THE WAVES

This manta is made of waves and the warrior on top is meant to symbolize a wave rider. The smaller version shows a possible integration with motifs for sun and wind.

STENCIL: t020

TURTLES

The turtle, or honu, is an important creature throughout all Polynesian cultures and has been associated to several meanings.

Mostly, sea turtles symbolize health, fertility, long life, foundation, peace, rest, the navigator.

The word hono designating the turtle in Marquesan language has also other meanings, among which we'll report "to join, to stitch together", which may explain why the turtle also represents union, family.

The Ocean is the source of life for islanders; the Polynesian sea is rich in all kinds of fish and represents wealth, but it is often the place of rest too. Land and sea are the two halves of the world and the turtle can live in and on both and move from one to the other. On this account the turtle is believed to move between the world of the living and the world beyond and to join and shepherd the departed along their last voyage, taking them safe to their place of rest.

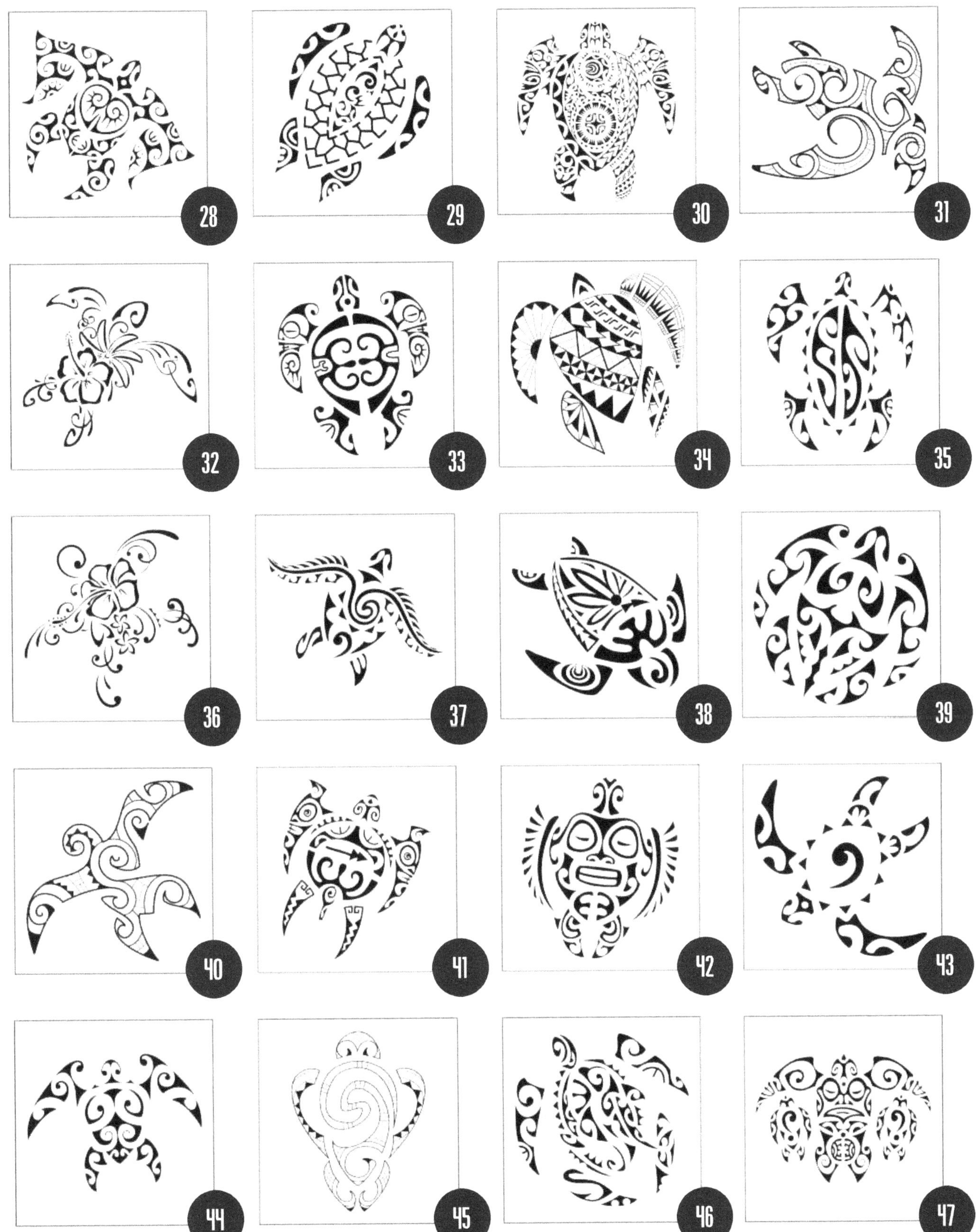
28
29
30
31
32
33
34
35
36
37
38
39
40
41
42
43
44
45
46
47

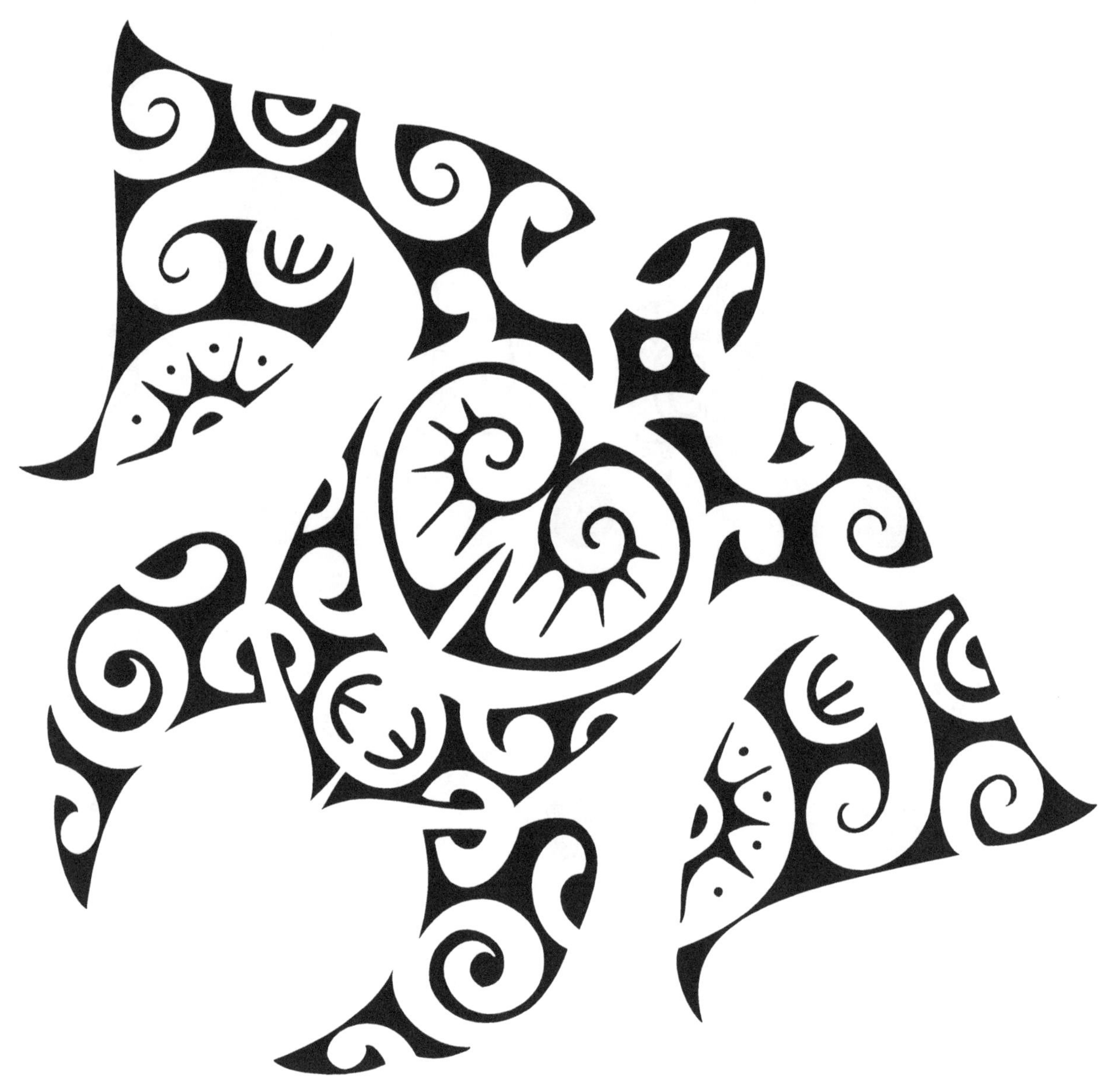

PROTECTION, INTIMACY

Sea shells represent love, intimacy and safe shelter.
Here they are surrounded by tiki eyes and hands
for protection through all changes (waves).
The sun represents positivity.

STENCIL: t021

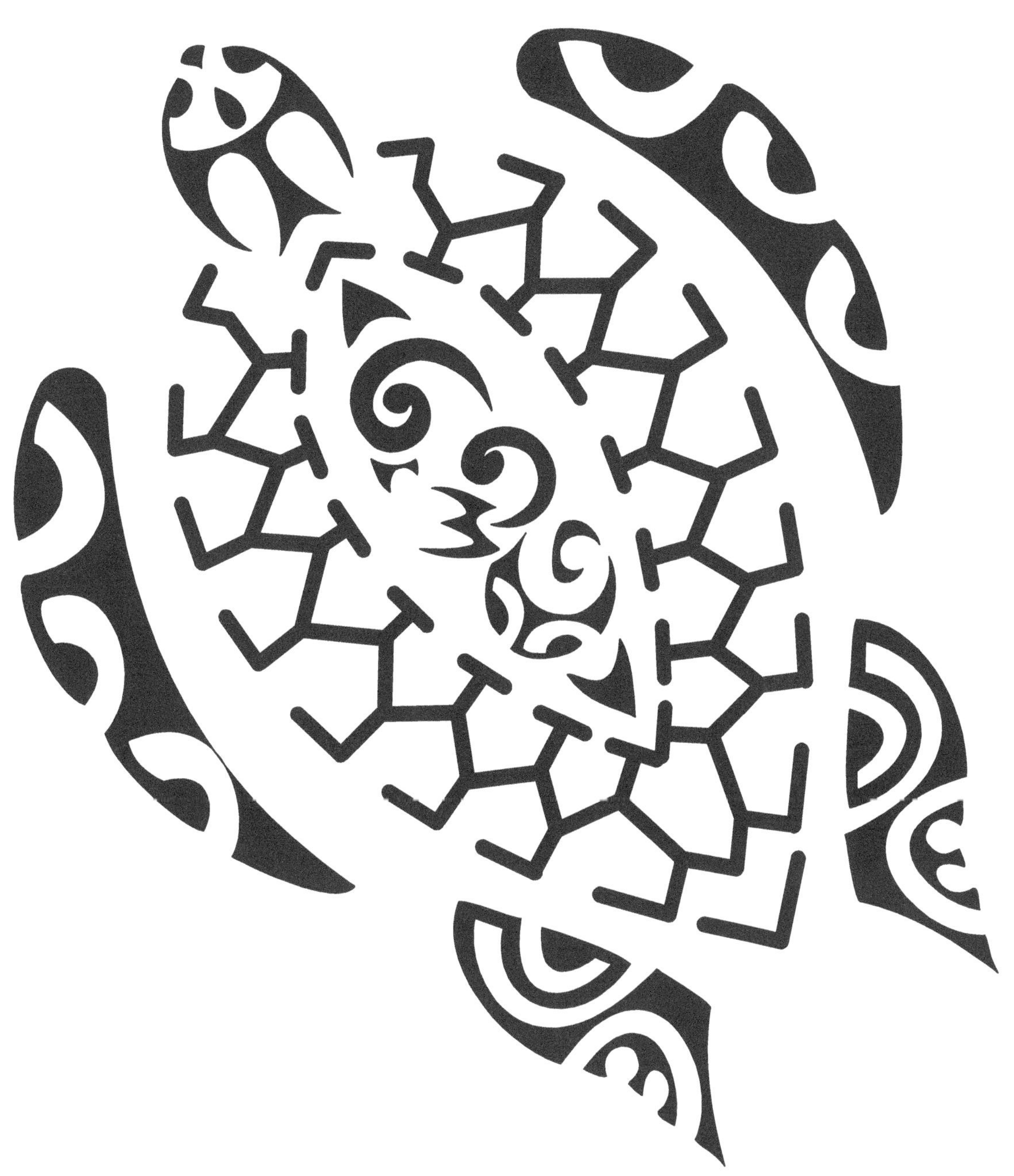

PROTECTION

The rows of ani ata surrounding the manaia in the center and the manaia itself are protectors guarding upon the family.

STENCIL: t022

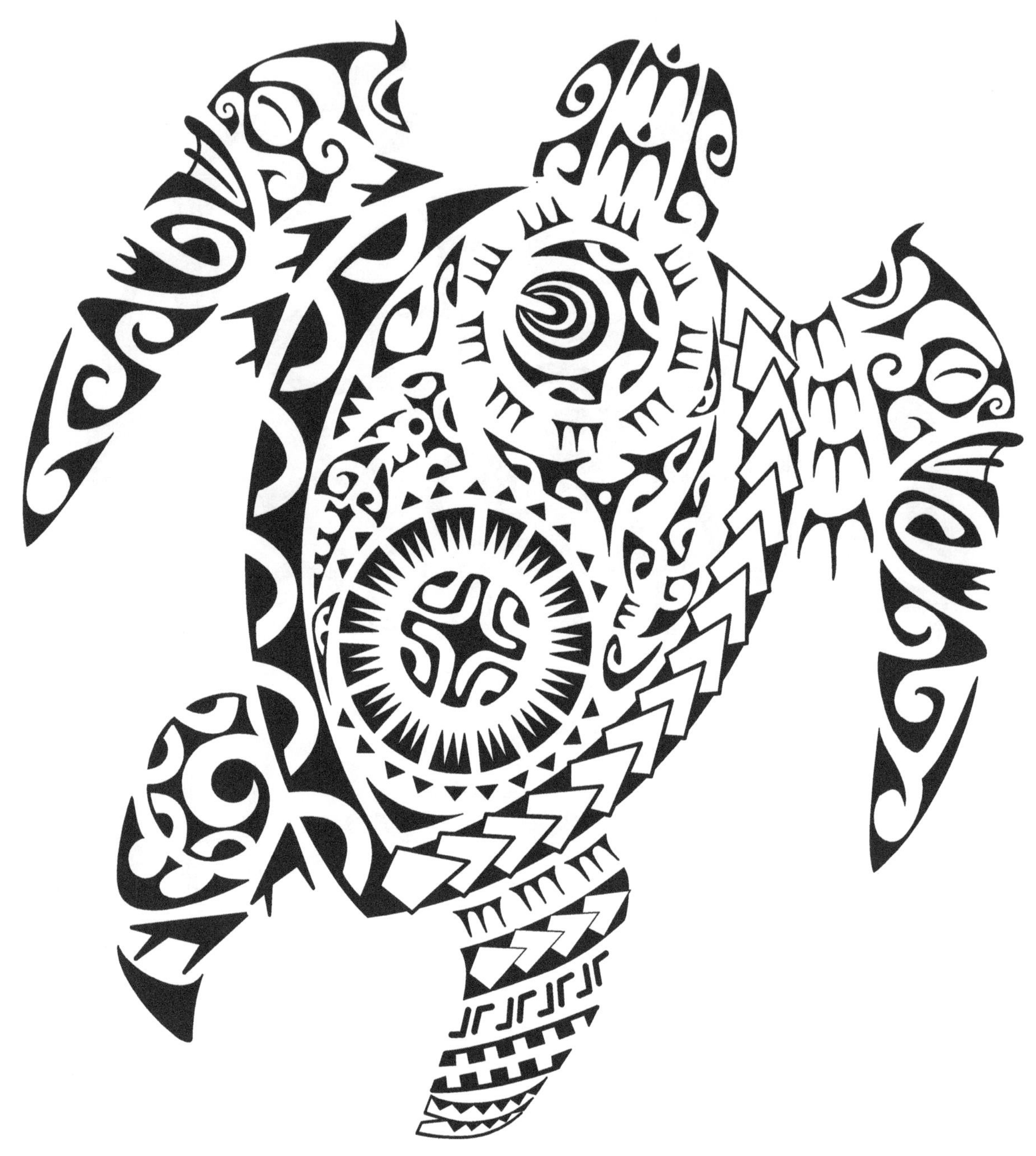

BALANCE, YING AND YANG

The designs inside the shell of this turtle recall a ying yang to symbolize balance and union of the opposites. This meaning is enforced by elements like the sun-moon and the Marquesan cross, representing prosperity and adversities. Also, waves are for woman and spear heads for man.

STENCIL: t023

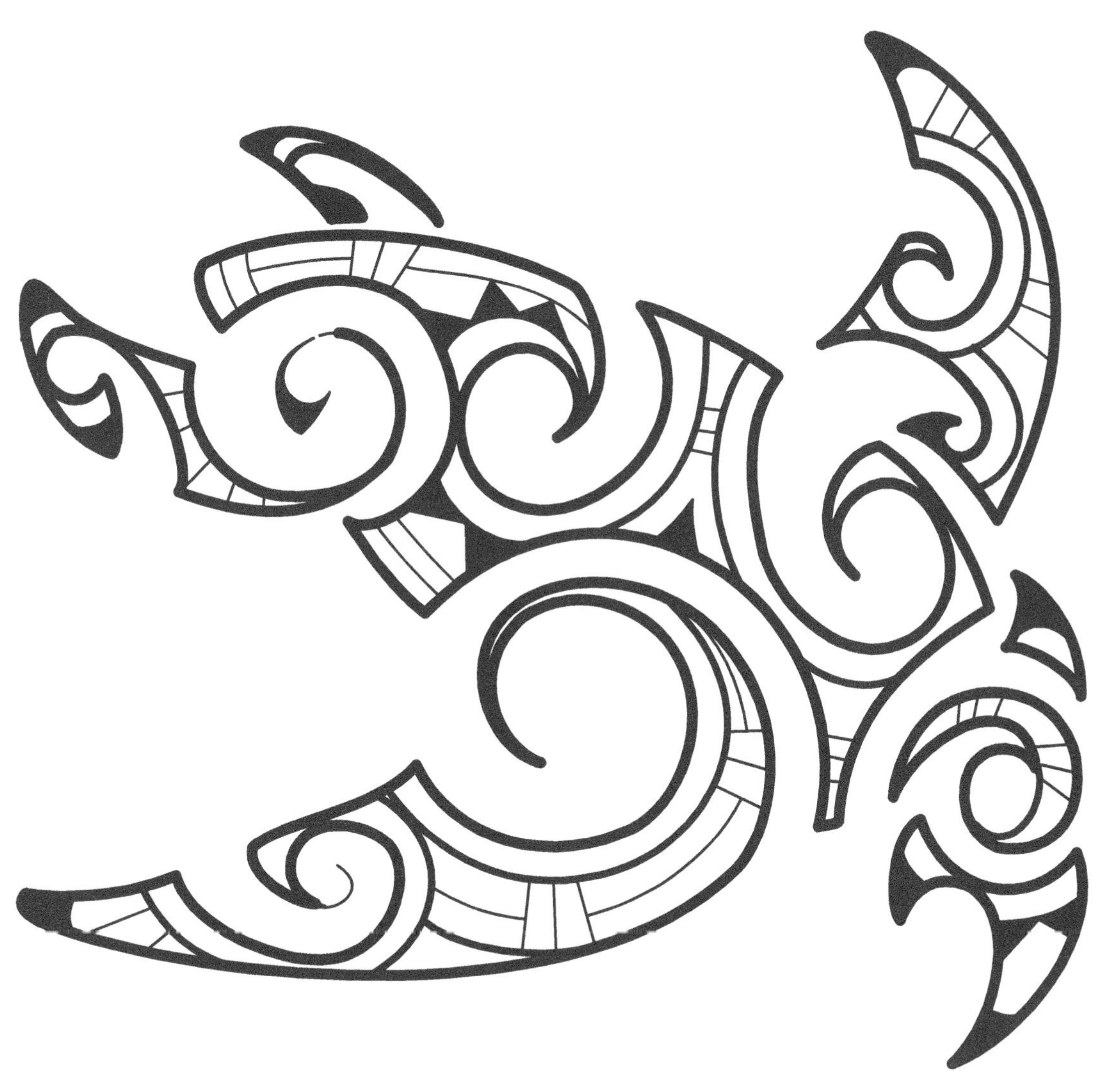

UNITY

In this Maori styled turtle we emphasize the concept of unity through the use of braids to fill the elements.
The head recalls a manaia for protection.

STENCIL: t024

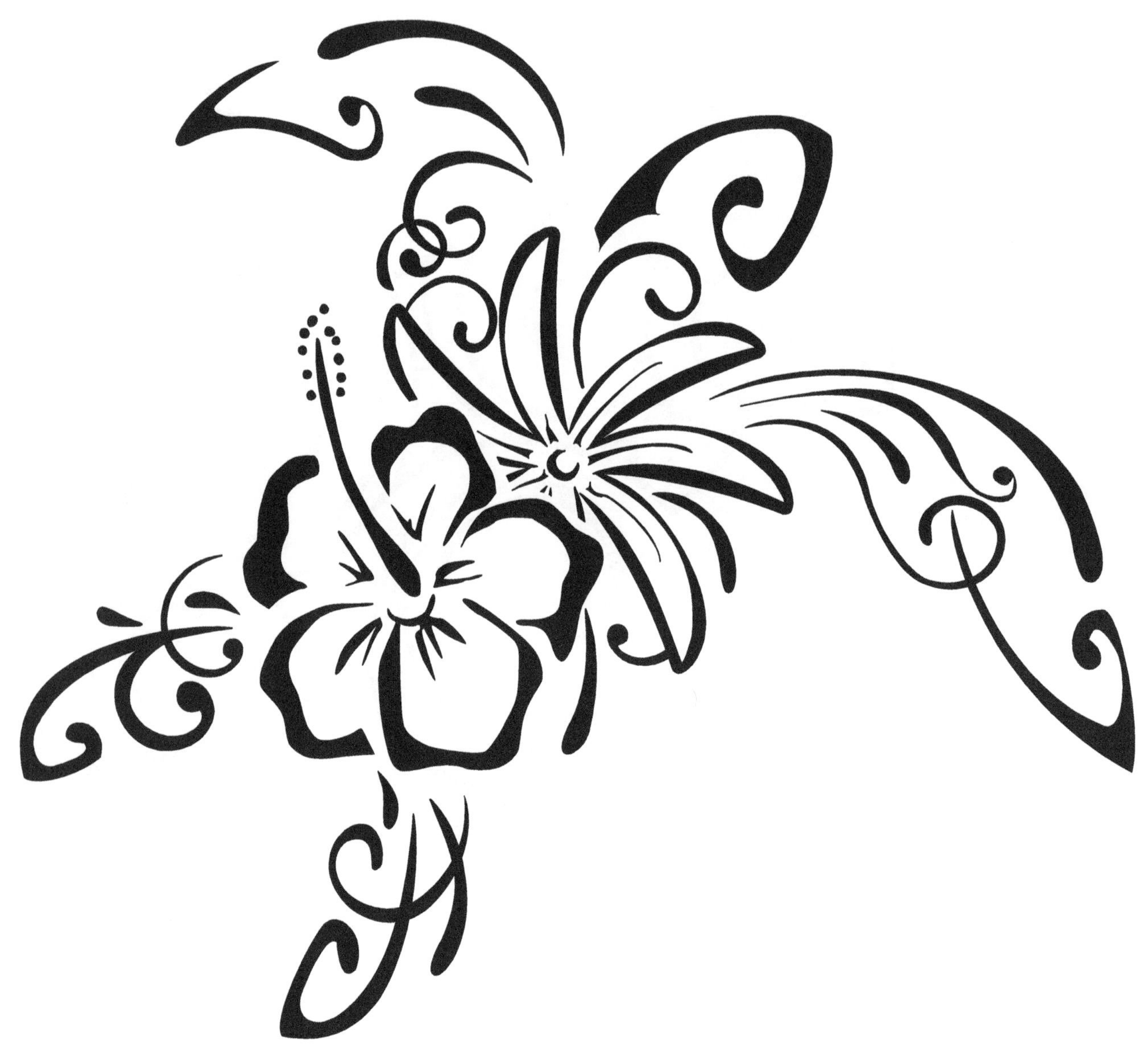

BEAUTY, GRACE

This turtle features two prominent elements: a flower of hibiscus and a tiare flower. They represent the beauty of life, grace and living each day with joy as a gift.

STENCIL: t025

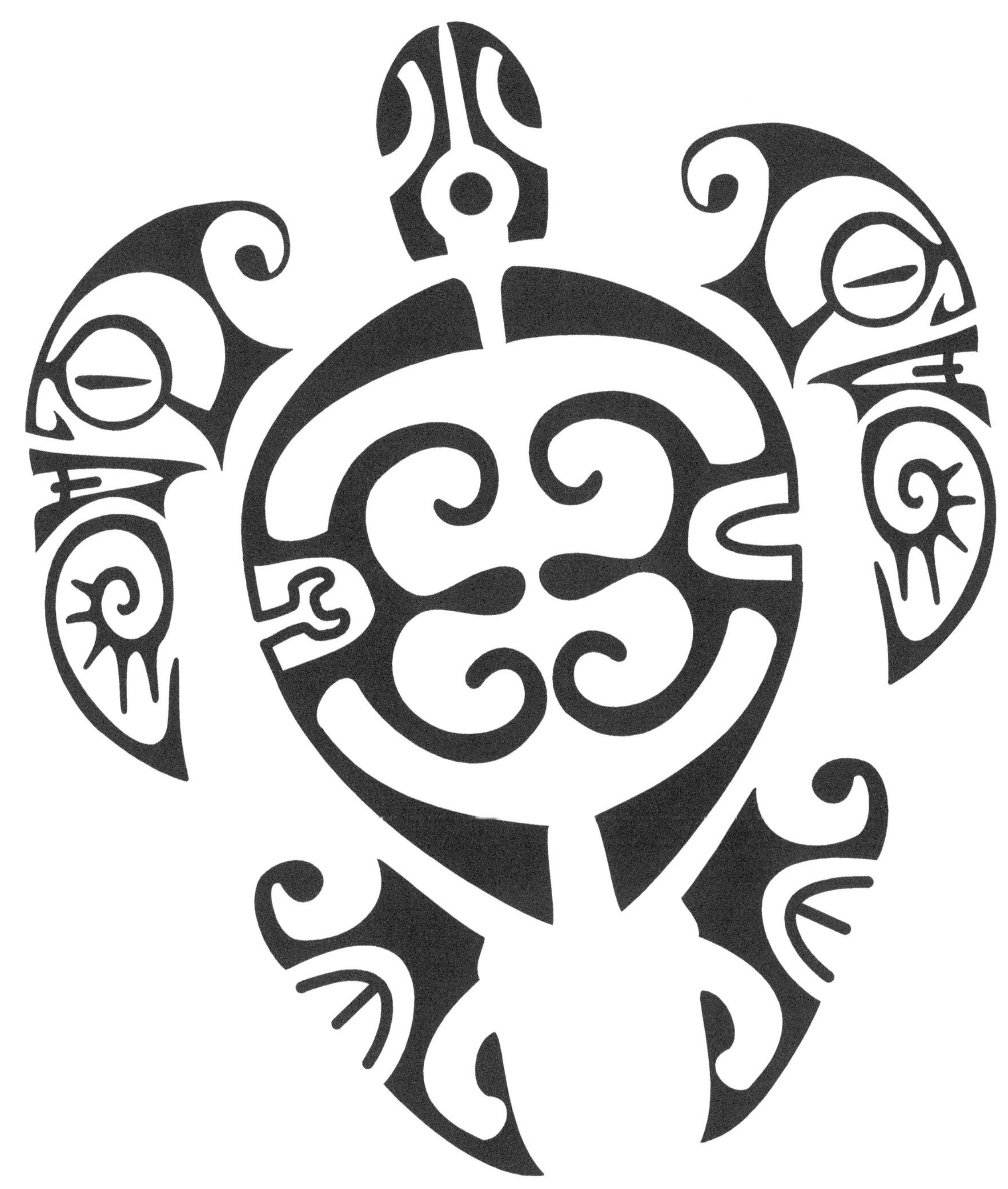

HUSBAND AND WIFE

This turtle represents protection upon marriage,
with two tikis guarding the union of a man and a woman.

STENCIL: t026

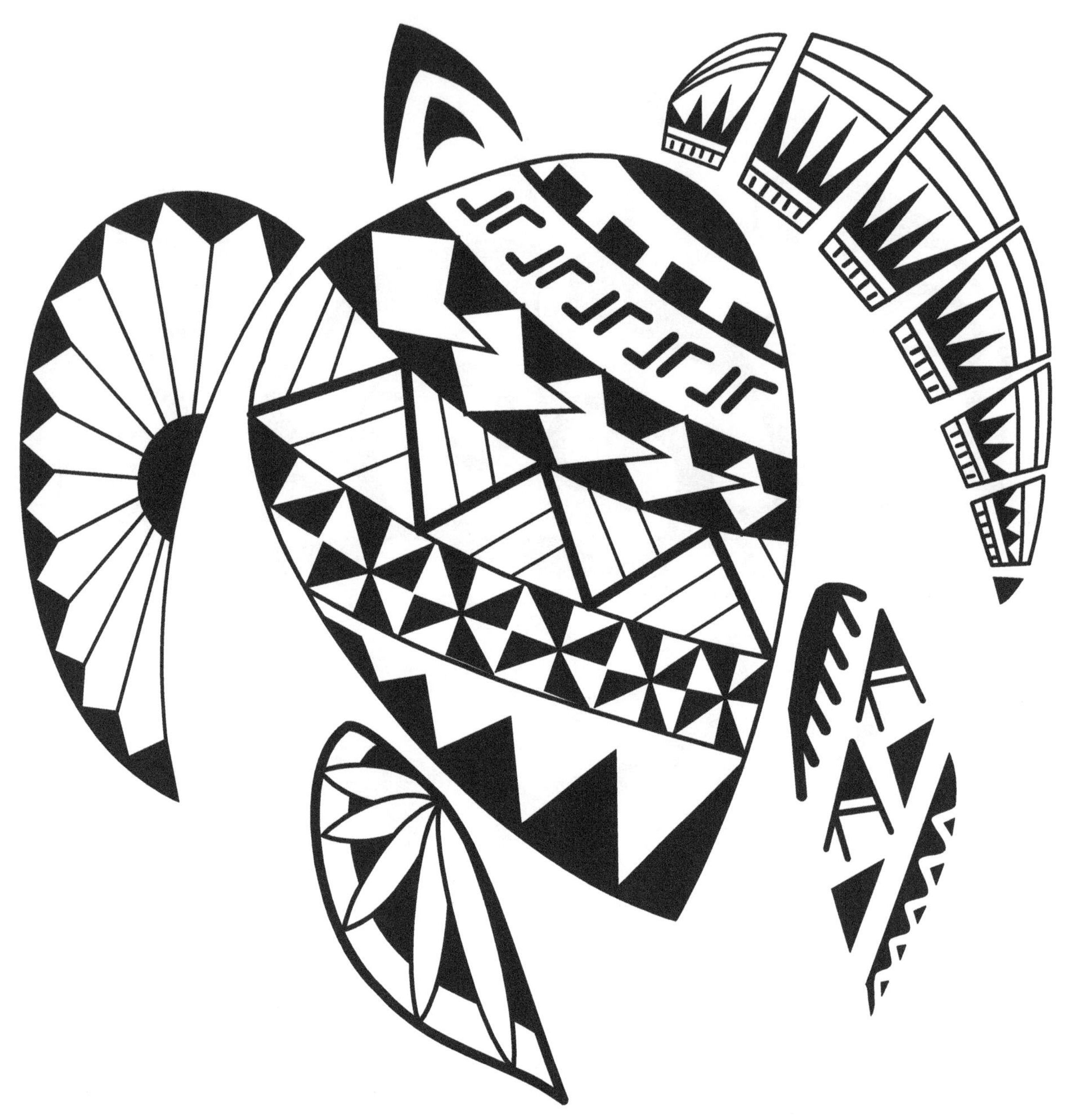

PROSPERITY

This turtle features various elements,
mostly from Samoa and Fiji,
symbolizing status, community and prosperity.

STENCIL: t027

NURTURING

The whale inside the shell is a symbol for nurturing and care and the sun represents positivity and protection. Chasing birds symbolize the help that is always granted to our dear ones.

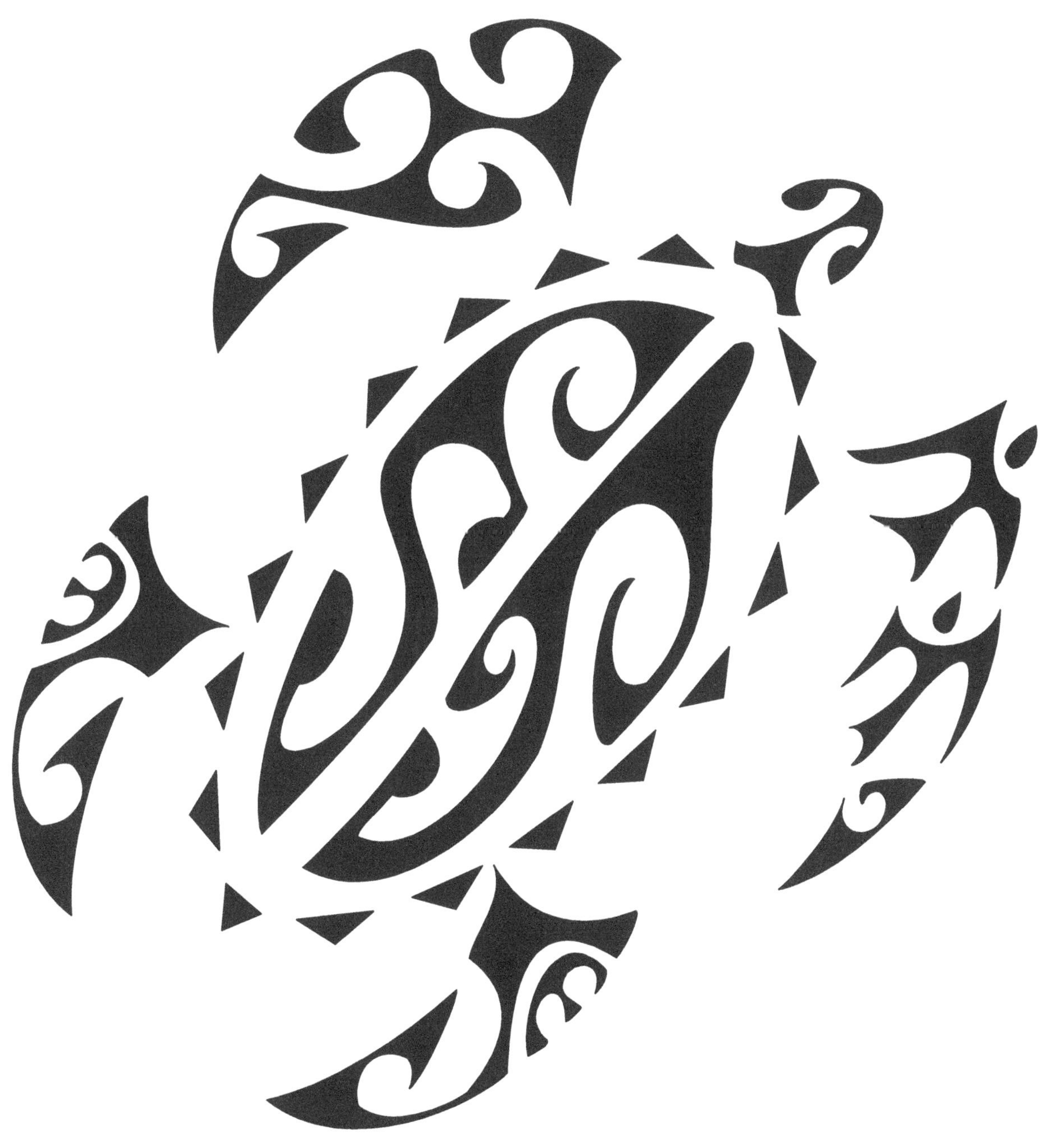

STENCIL: t028

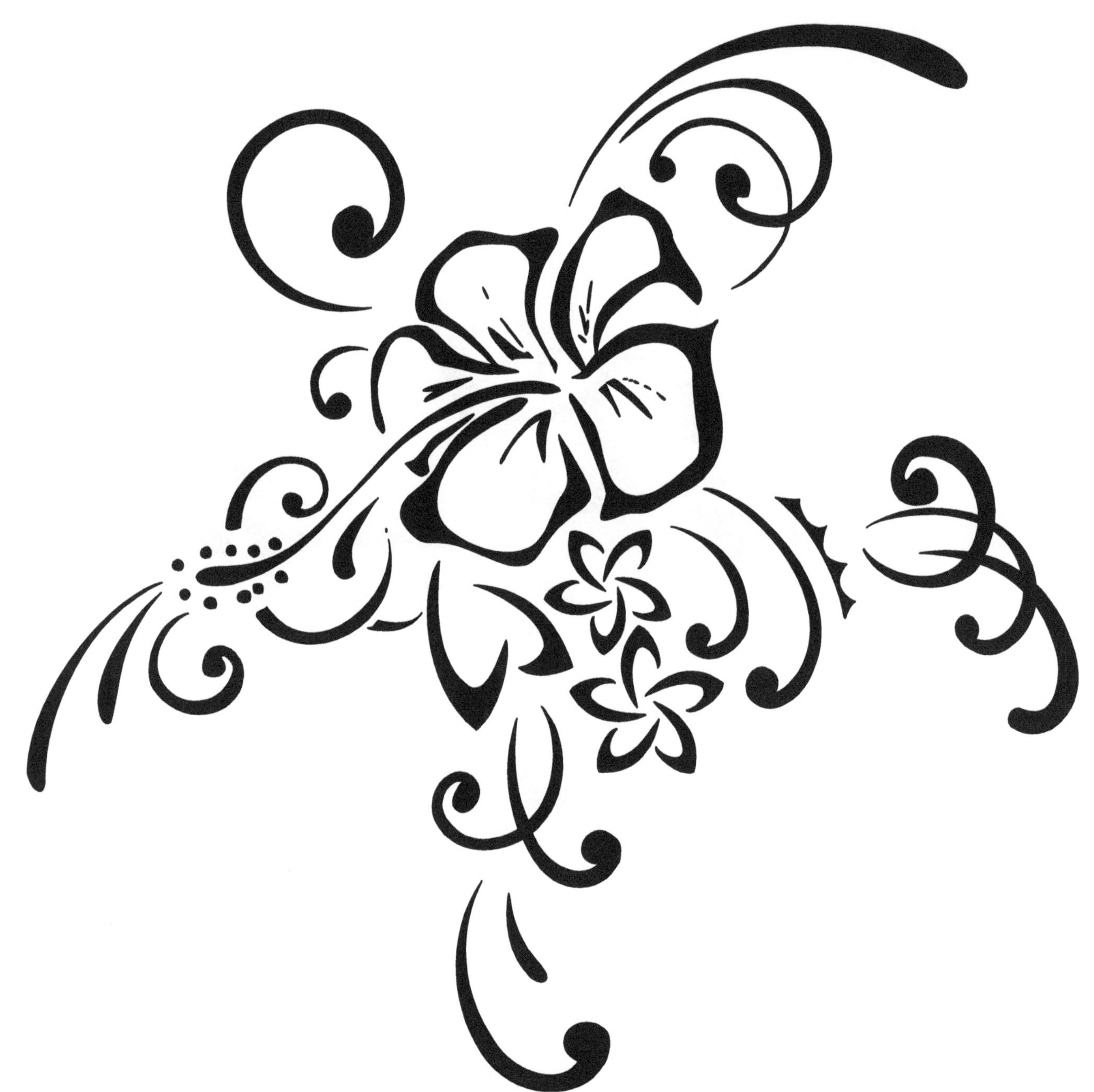

FEMININITY

This turtle is fully made of flowers,
hibiscus and frangipani,
to symbolize femininity and beauty,
delicacy and joy.

STENCIL: t029

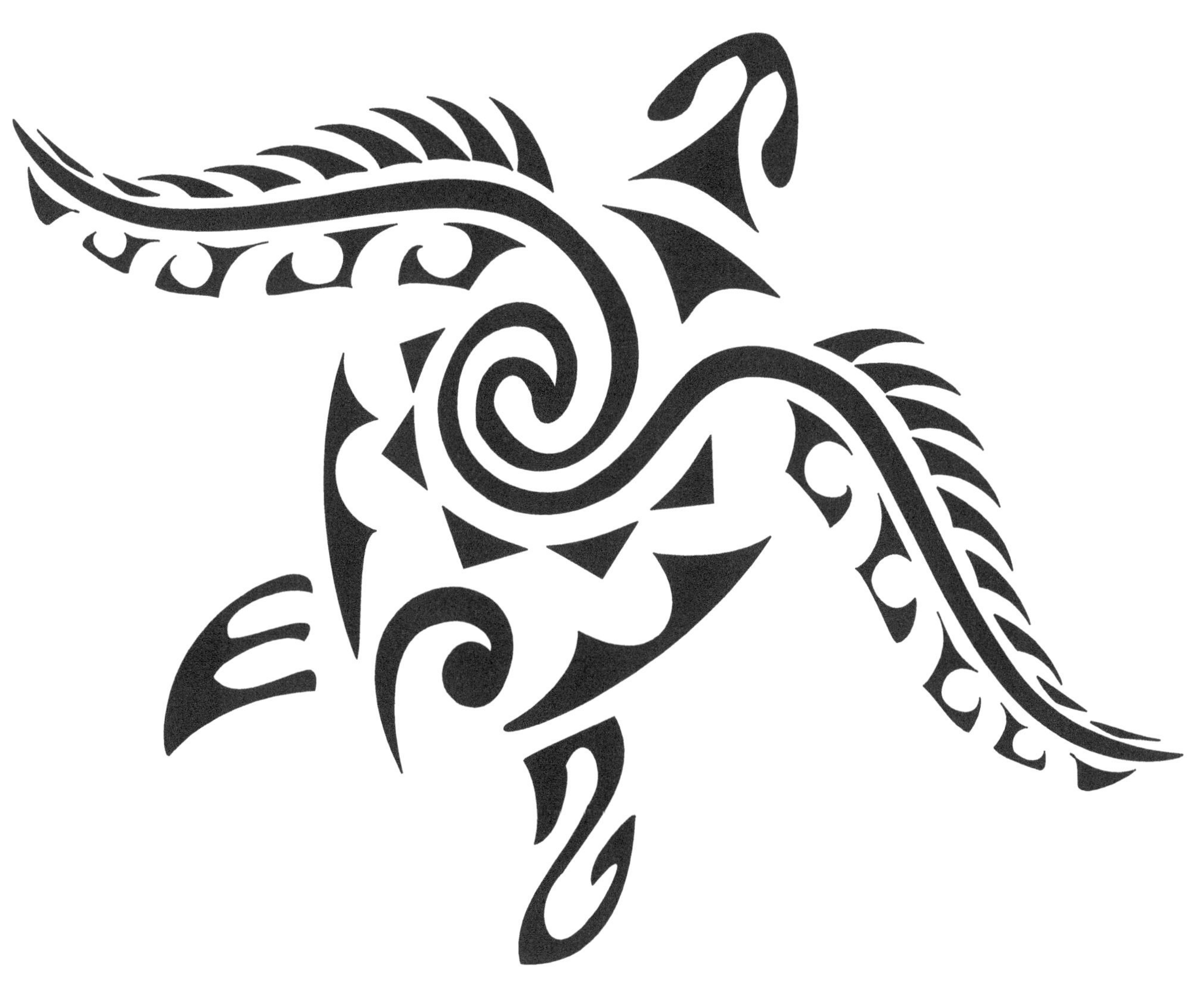

CHILD

Two fern fronds are joined into a double spiral symbolizing their eternal union, blessed by the sun, which gave birth to a new life represented by the koru below.

STENCIL: t030

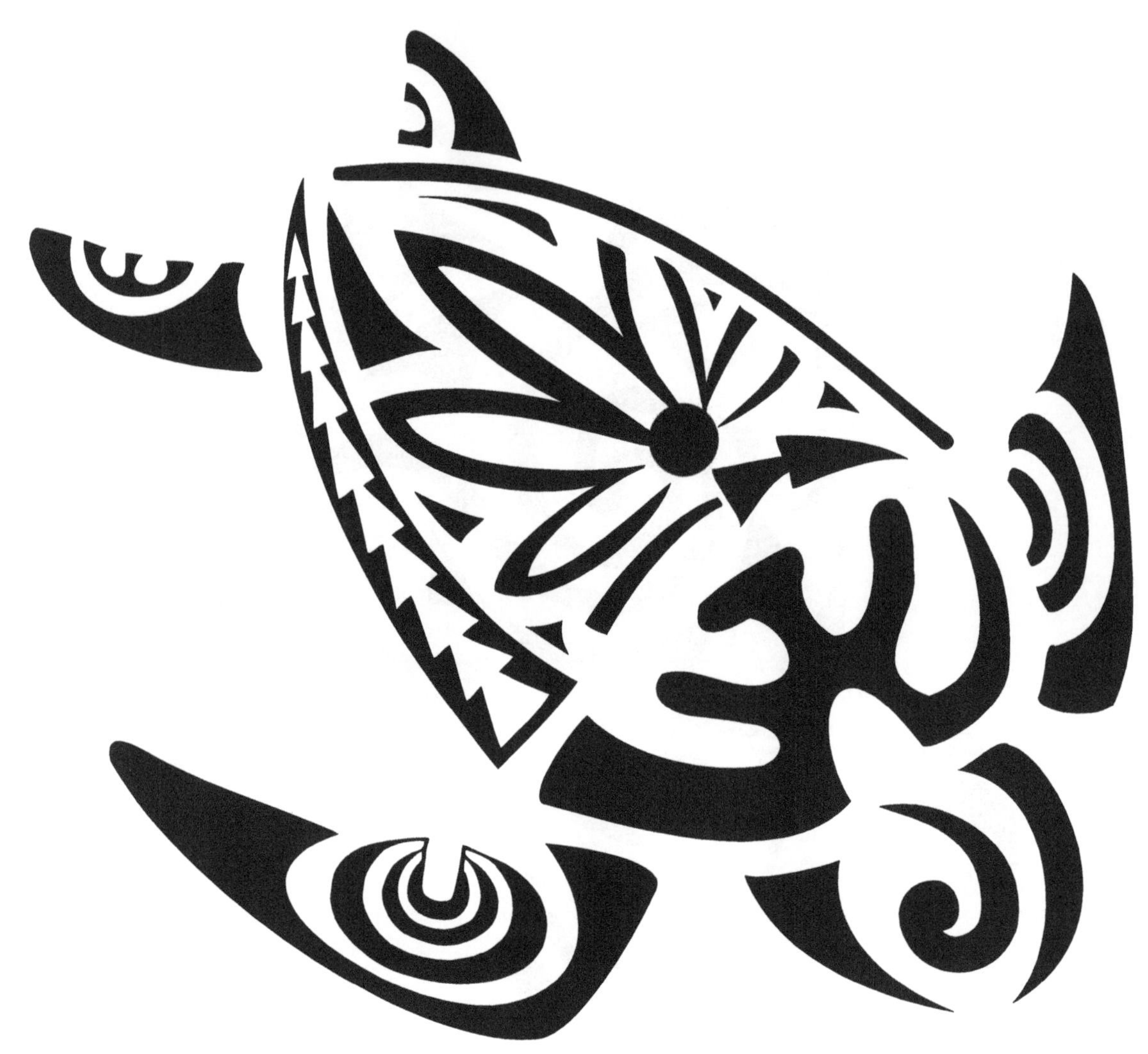

FAMILY PROTECTOR

The flax leaves represent family
and the warrior on the shell supports and protects it.

STENCIL: t031

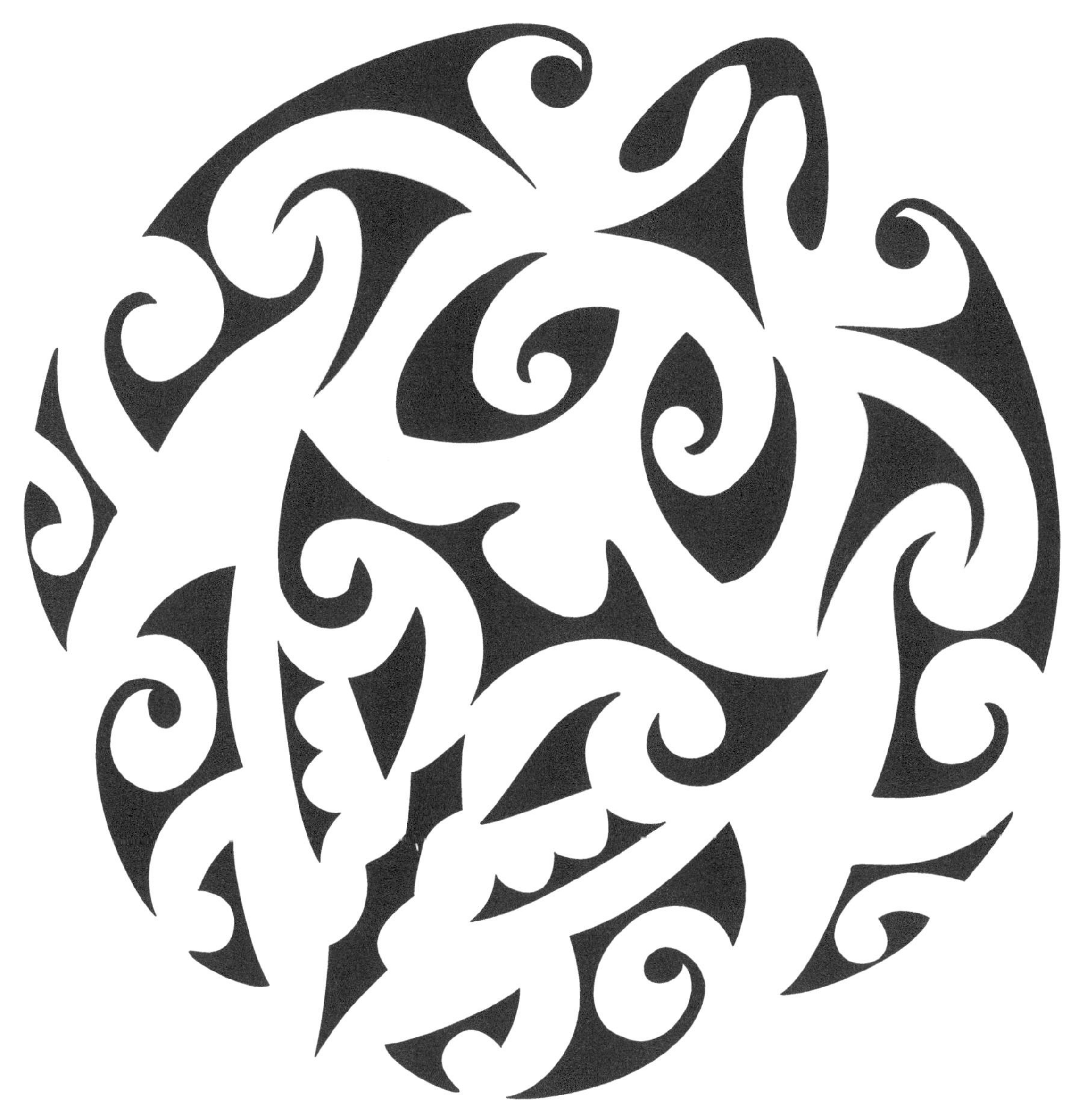

TRAVELLER

This turtle includes symbols representing change and freedom, such as the manta and waves. The turtle itself is a symbol for the navigator while the hammerhead shark symbolizes tenacity and sociality.

STENCIL: t032

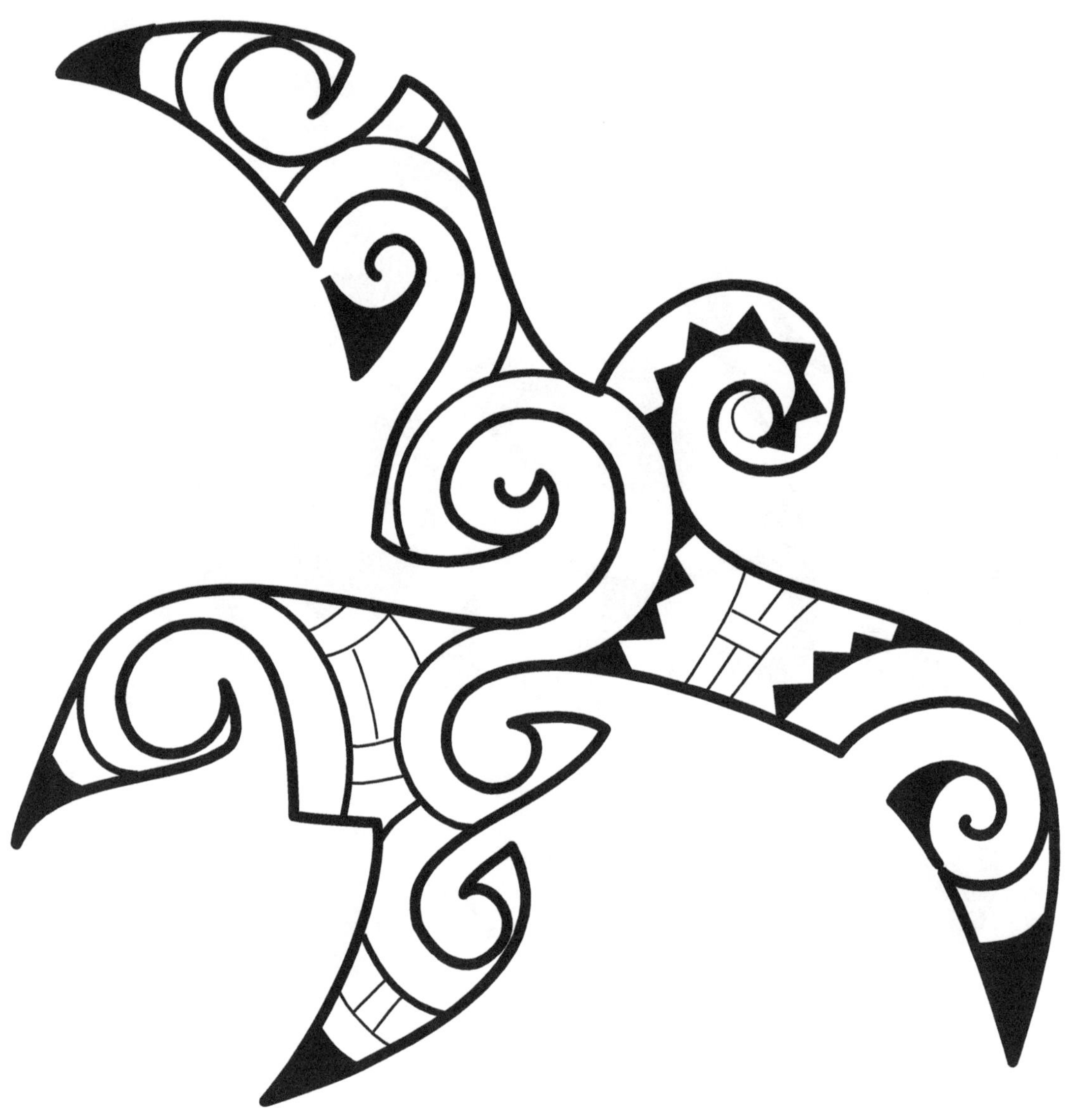

VOYAGE

This turtle is combined with a frigate shape to symbolize voyage.
Koru represent new beginnings.

STENCIL: t033

FAMILY PROTECTOR

The moray eels being the back flippers of the turtle
are kept at bay and far from the family
by the warrior on the shell
with the help of the two tiki.

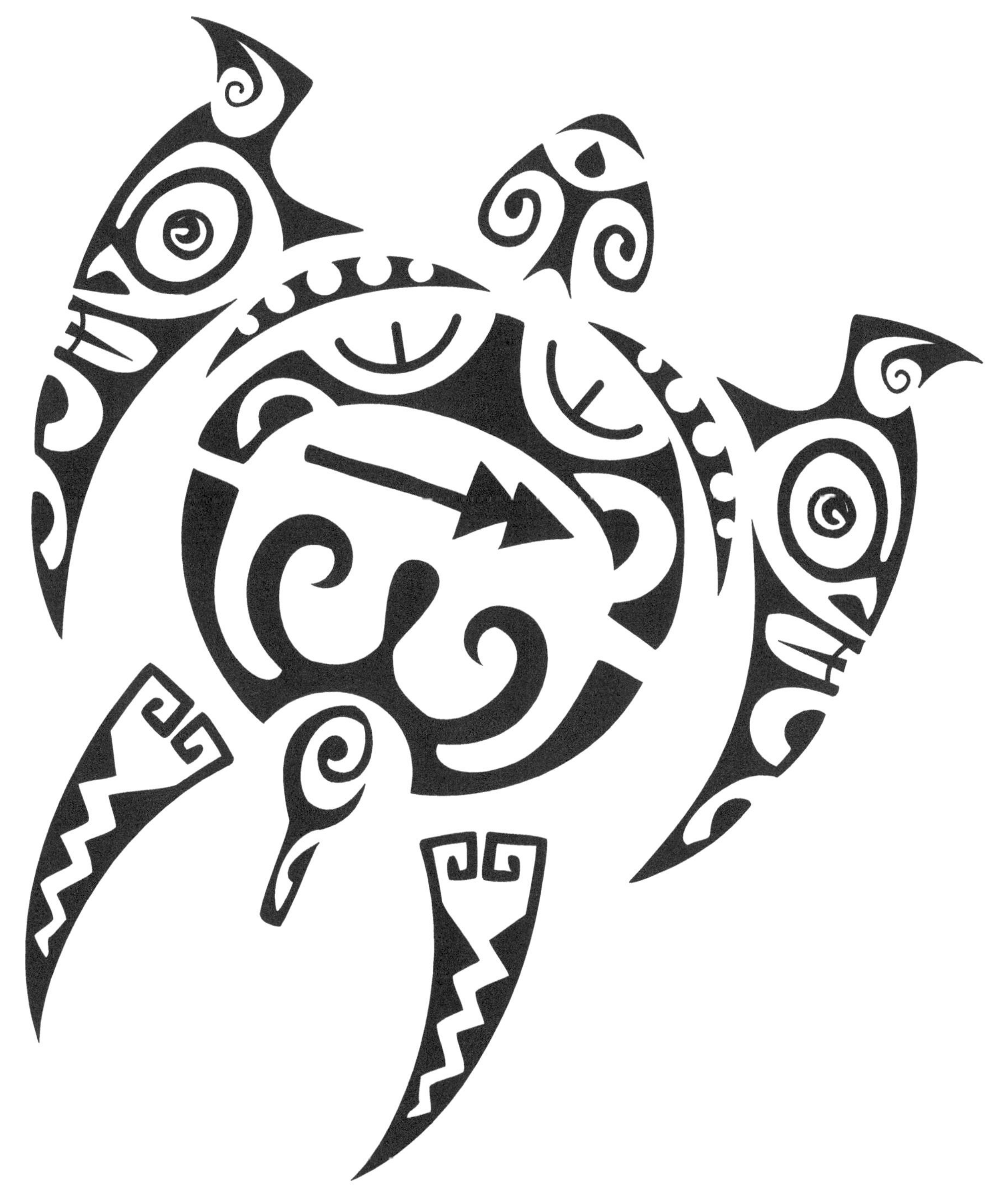

STENCIL: t034

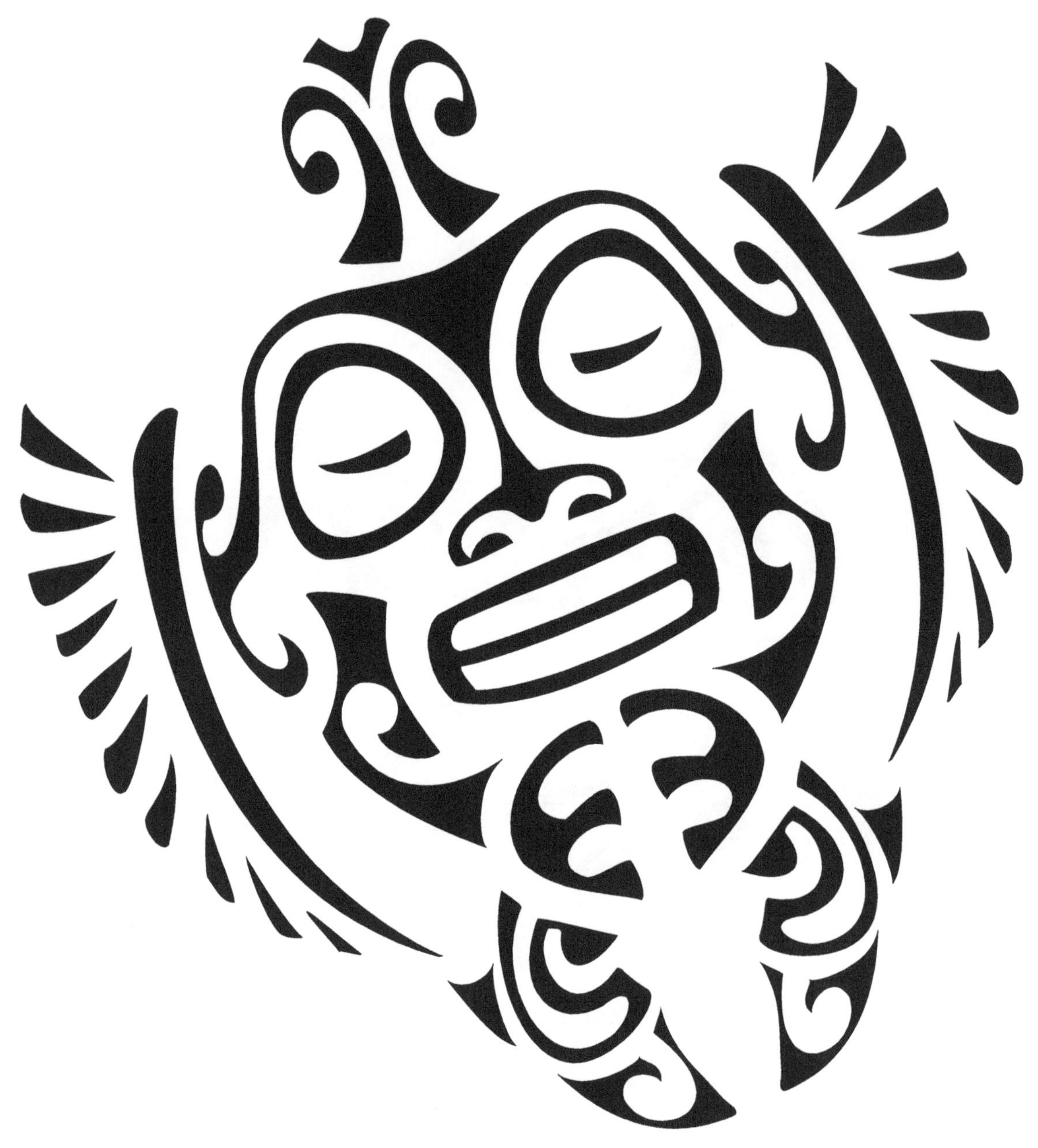

ANCESTOR

The tiki that shapes the turtle shell represents here an ancestor, a guide and a chief who protects the family.

STENCIL: t035

NEW LIFE

The koru inside the sun represents a newborn baby who brings joy to the family.

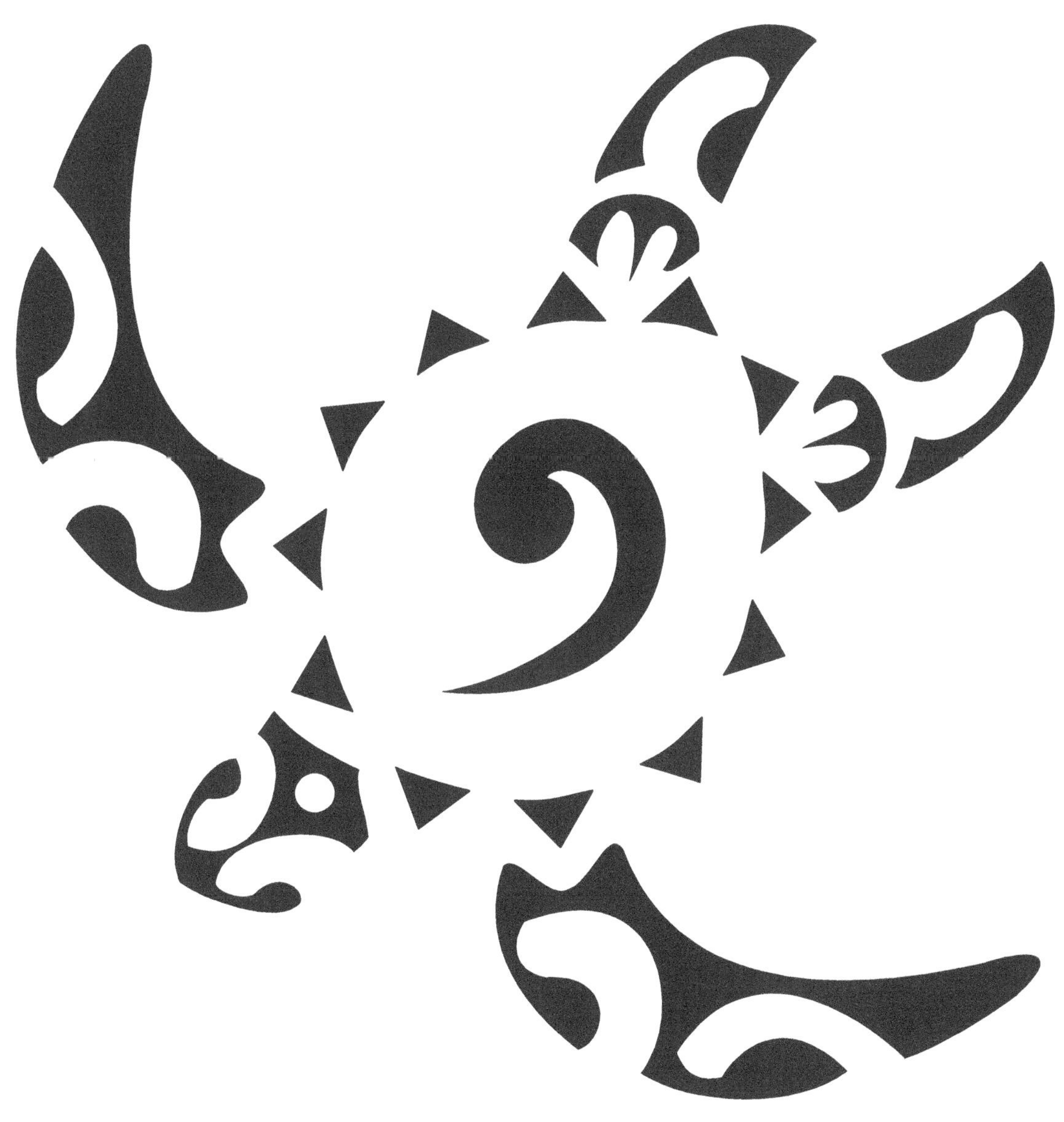

STENCIL: t036

TENACITY

The hammerhead shark motifs represent the tenacity needed to achieve the prosperity which is represented here by the fish hooks.

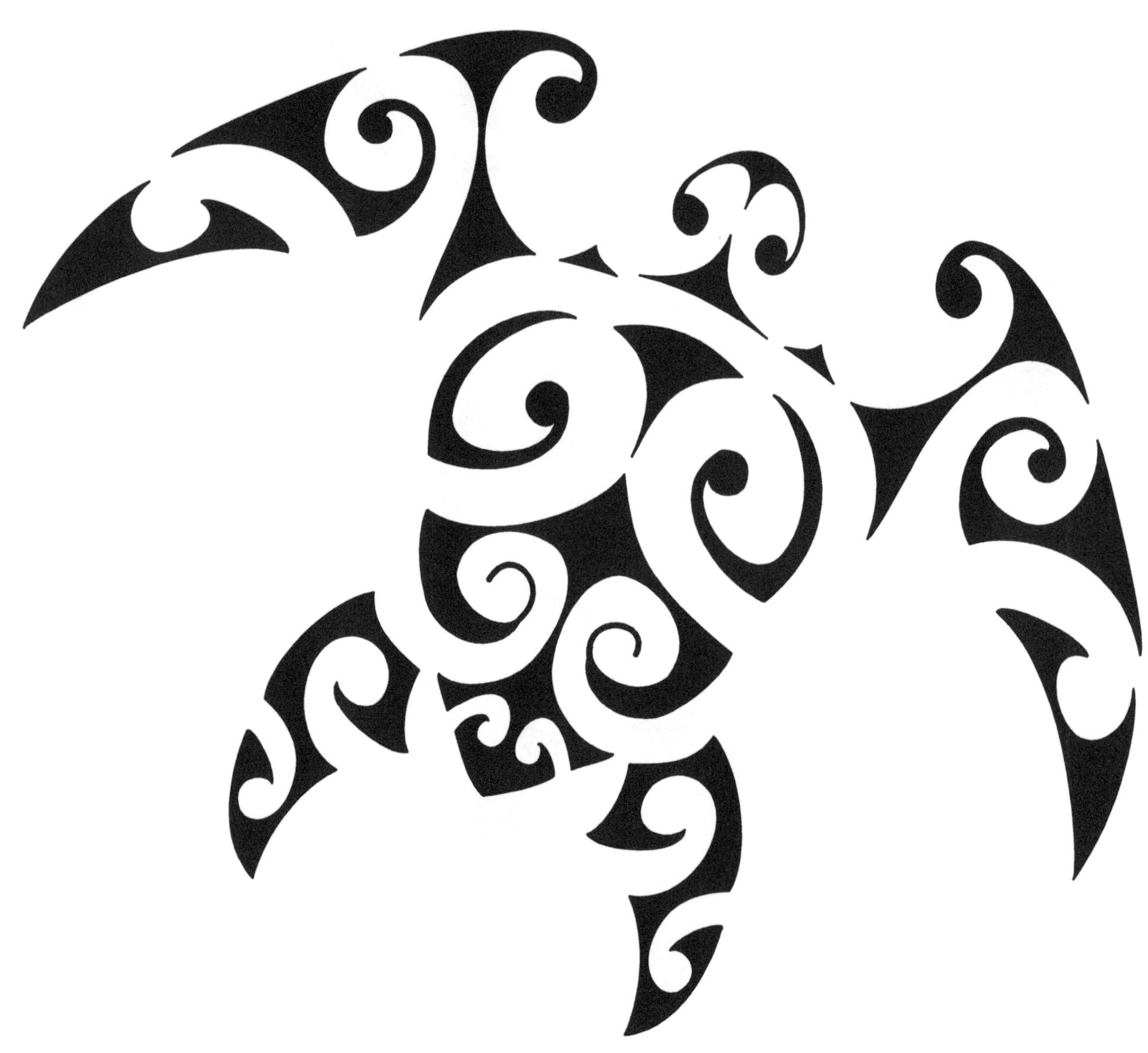

STENCIL: t037

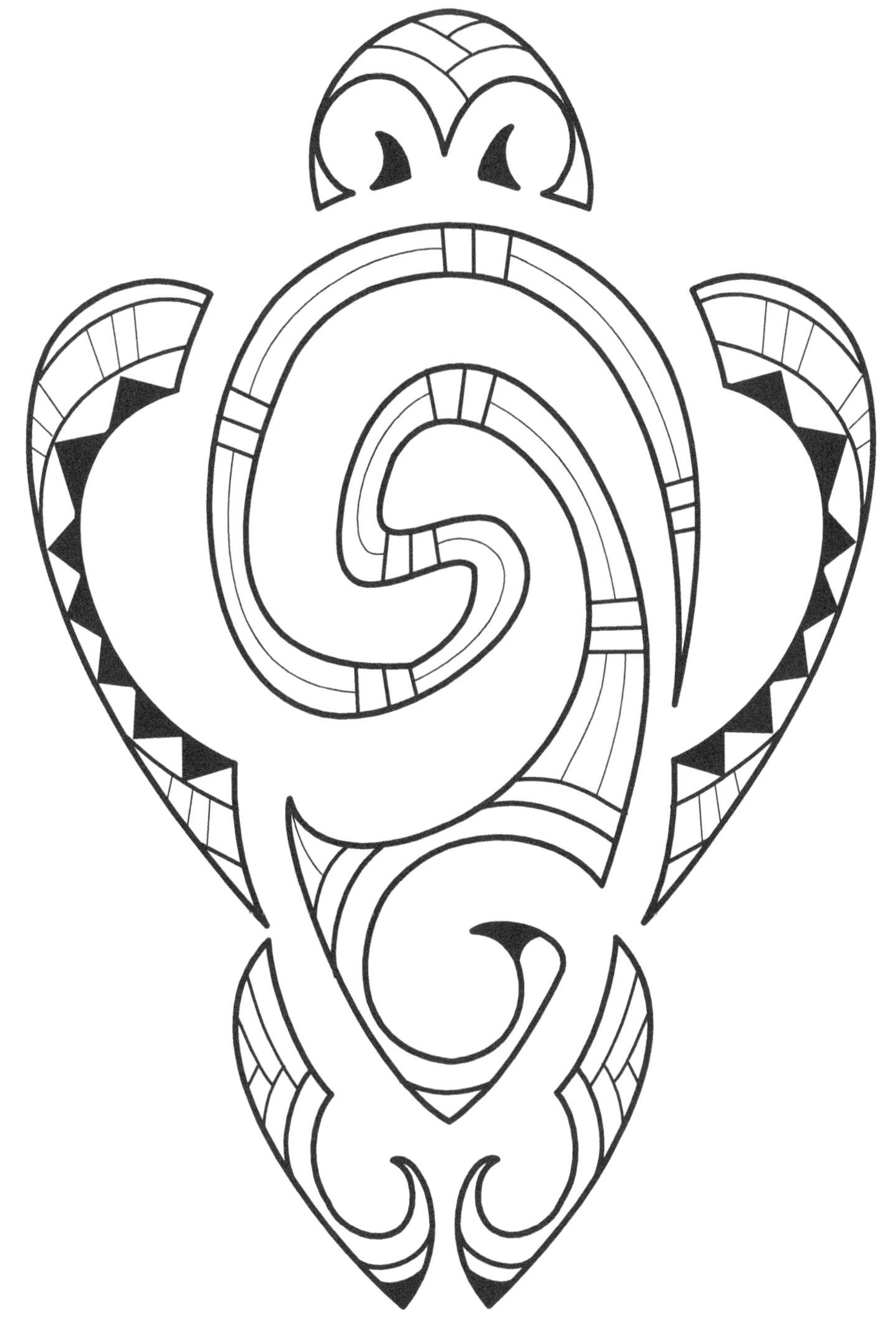

FAMILY UNION

The double spiral and braid motifs included in this design symbolize the strong union of this family, while shark teeth are for protection.

STENCIL: t038

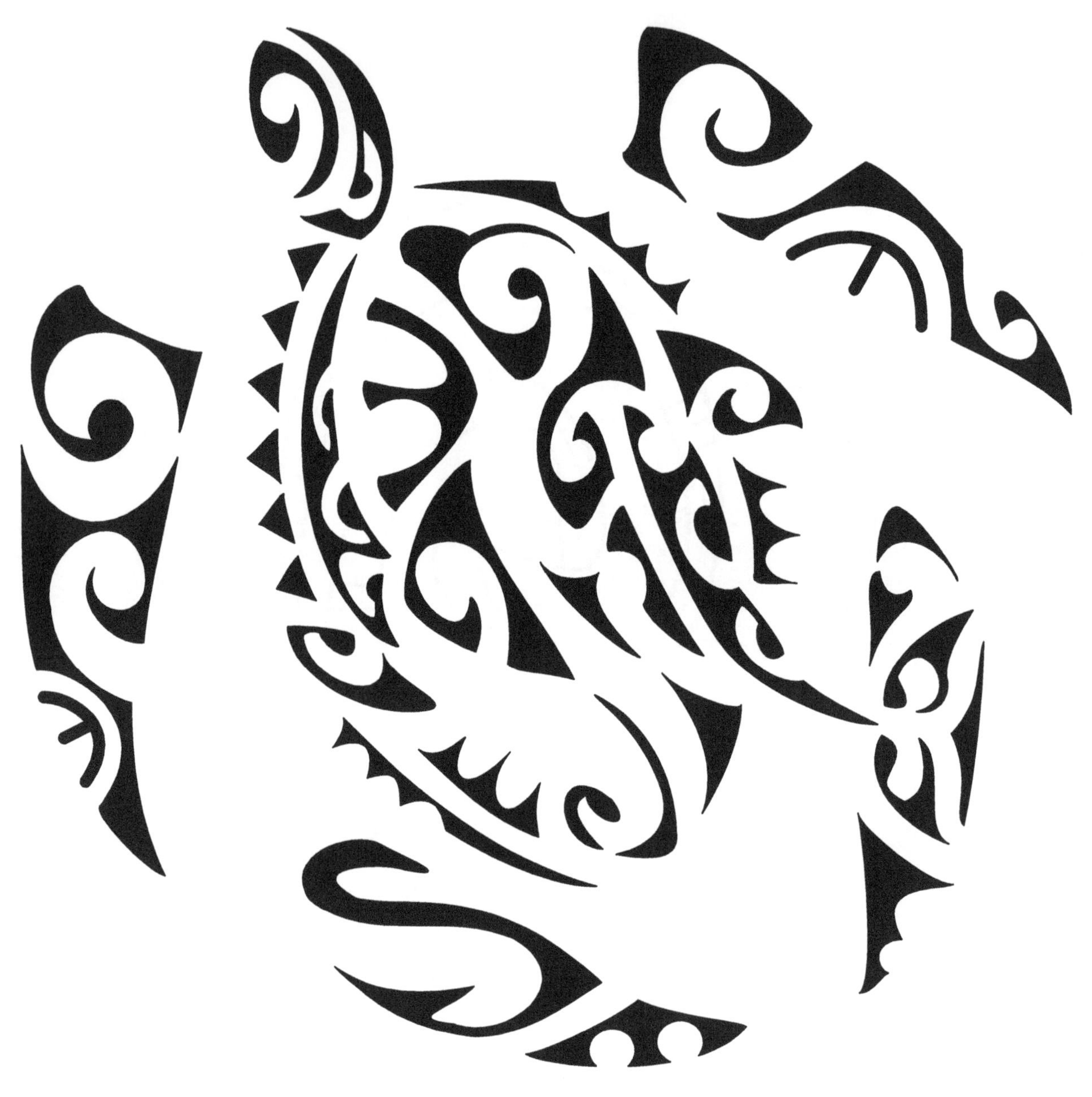

STRONG & JOYFUL

A shark and a dolphin are incorporated into the shell of this turtle representing the navigator who faces life with strength and joy on their path to prosperity.

STENCIL: t039

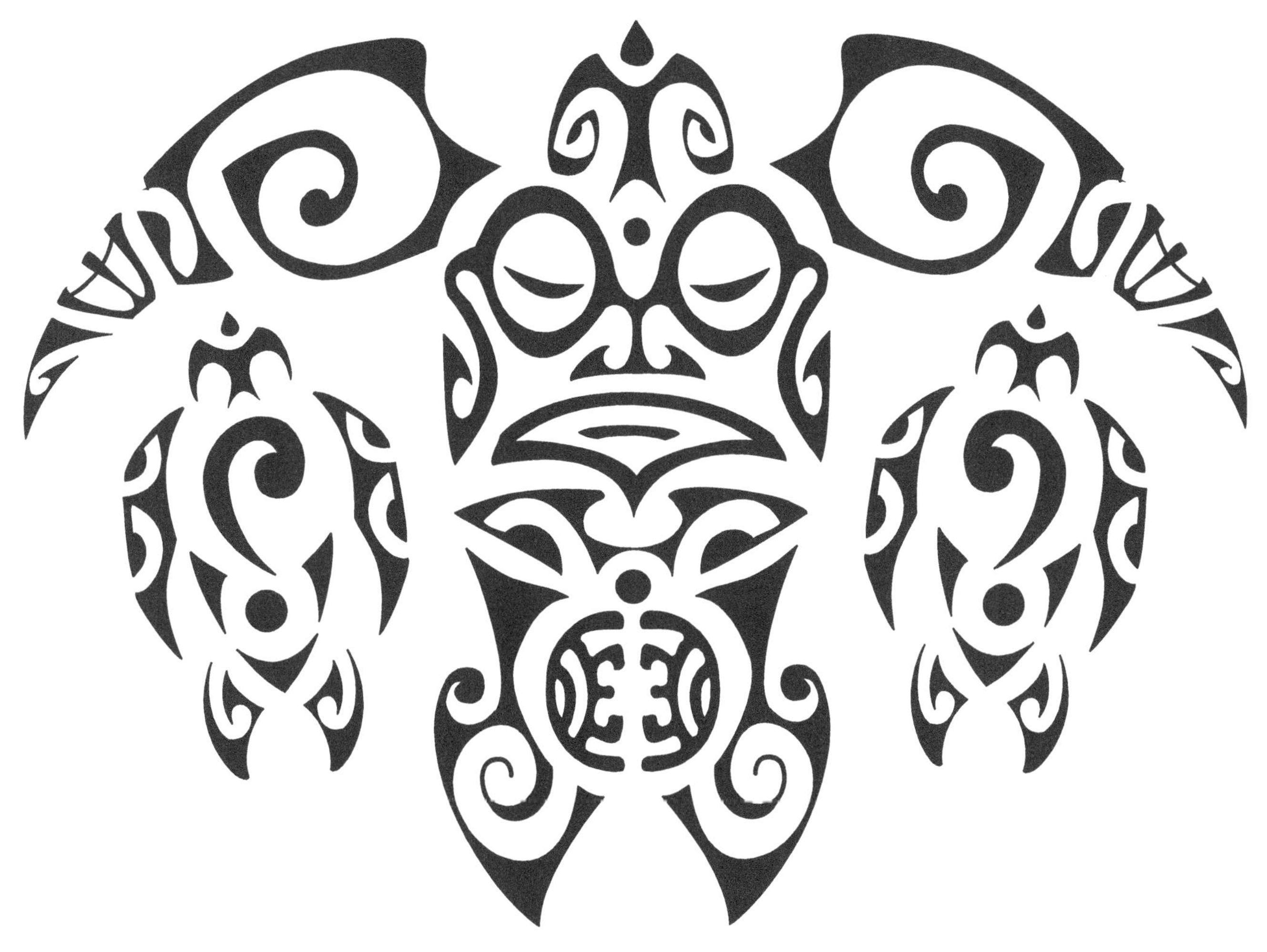

ALWAYS PROTECTED

The small turtles under the wings of the bigger one
represent two children who will always be protected by their parents
(the marriage symbol held by the central tiki)
even after they depart to join the gods.

STENCIL: t040

SHARKS

Shark teeth, or niho mano, deserve a space of their own: sharks are indeed one of the favourite shapes that aumakua (guiding spirits) choose to appear to men.
They represent protection, guidance and strength, fierceness, the warrior, but they are also symbols of adaptability in many cultures.
Hammerhead sharks represent tenacity, strength and determination and they also stand for sociality since they always move in large groups of many individuals

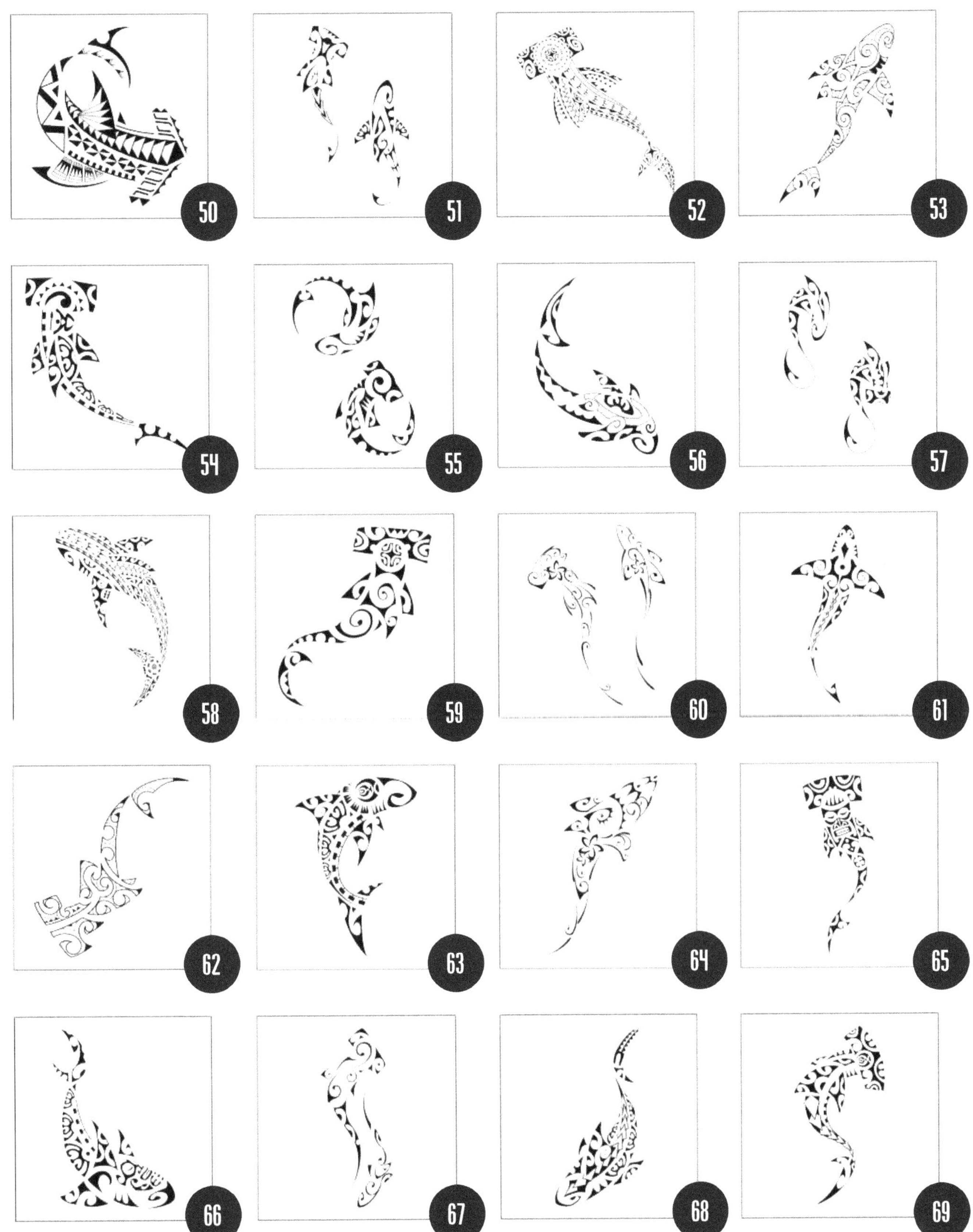
50
51
52
53
54
55
56
57
58
59
60
61
62
63
64
65
66
67
68
69

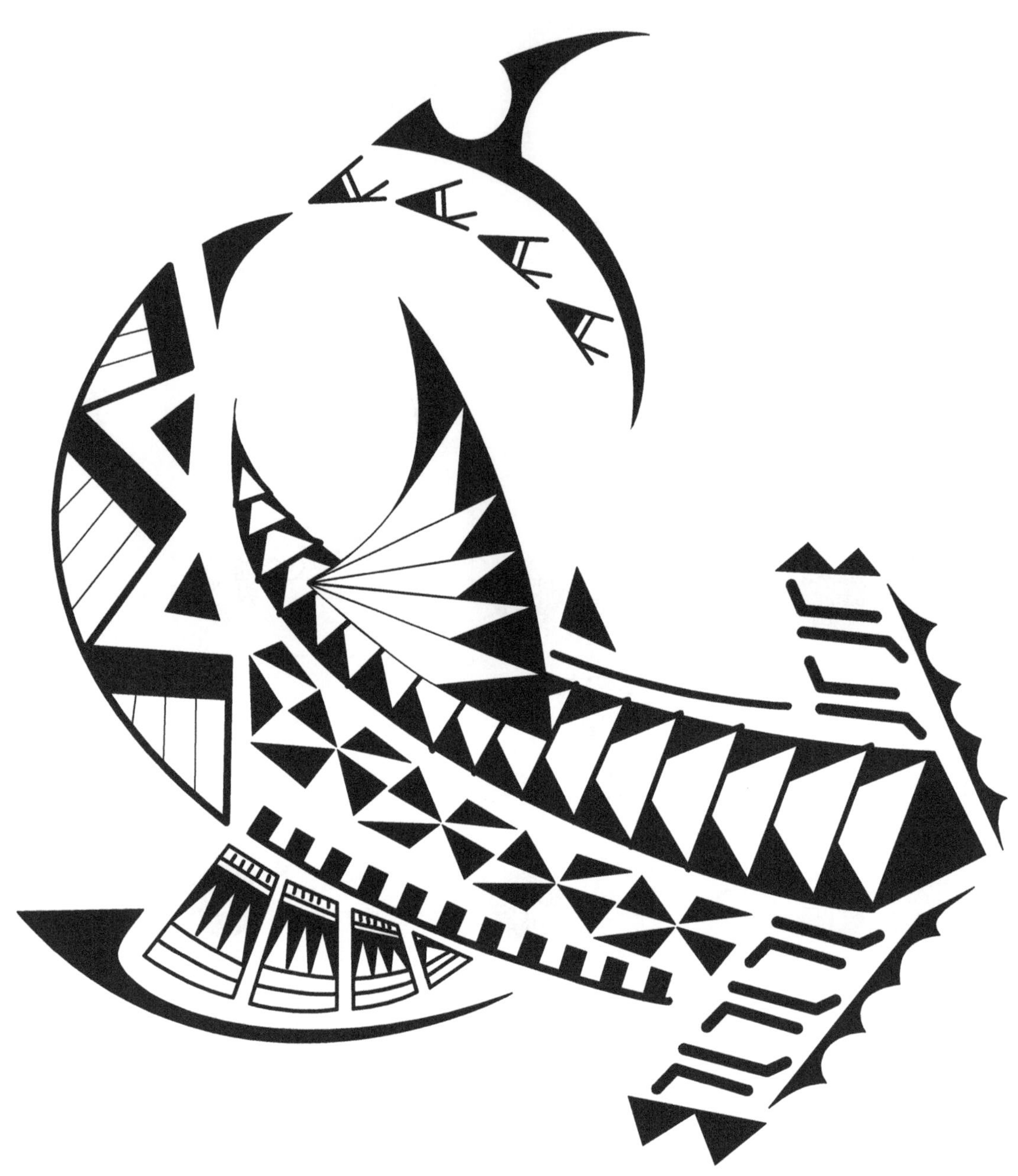

PROSPERITY

This hammerhead shark inspired by Samoan and Fijian motifs features tenacity, determination and courage as the means to reach prosperity.

STENCIL: t041

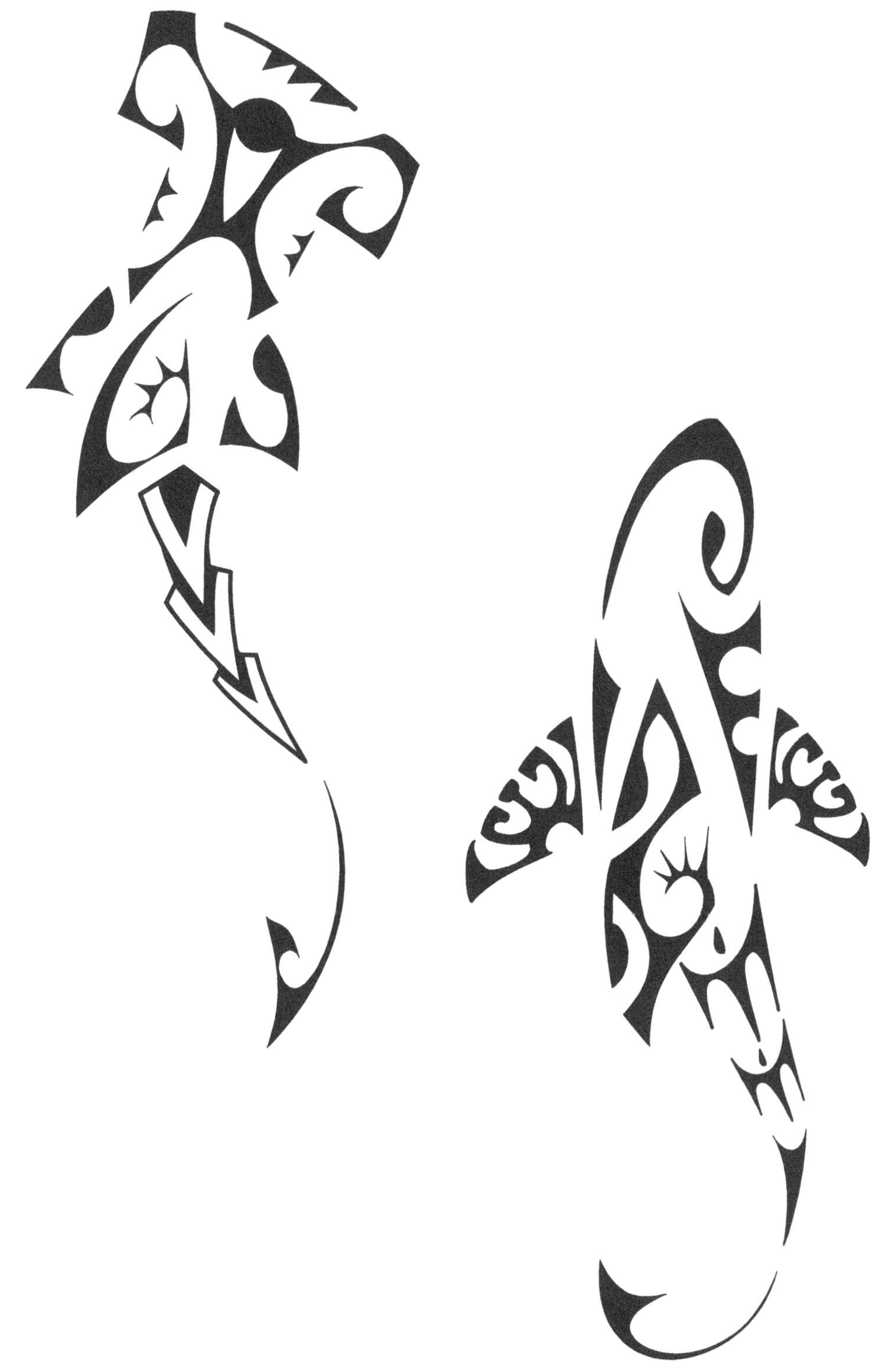

PROTECTING LOVE

The sea shell on the back fin represents faithful love,
protected by the warrior in the hammerhead shark
and nurtured by two people helping each other in the shark.

STENCIL: t042 - t043

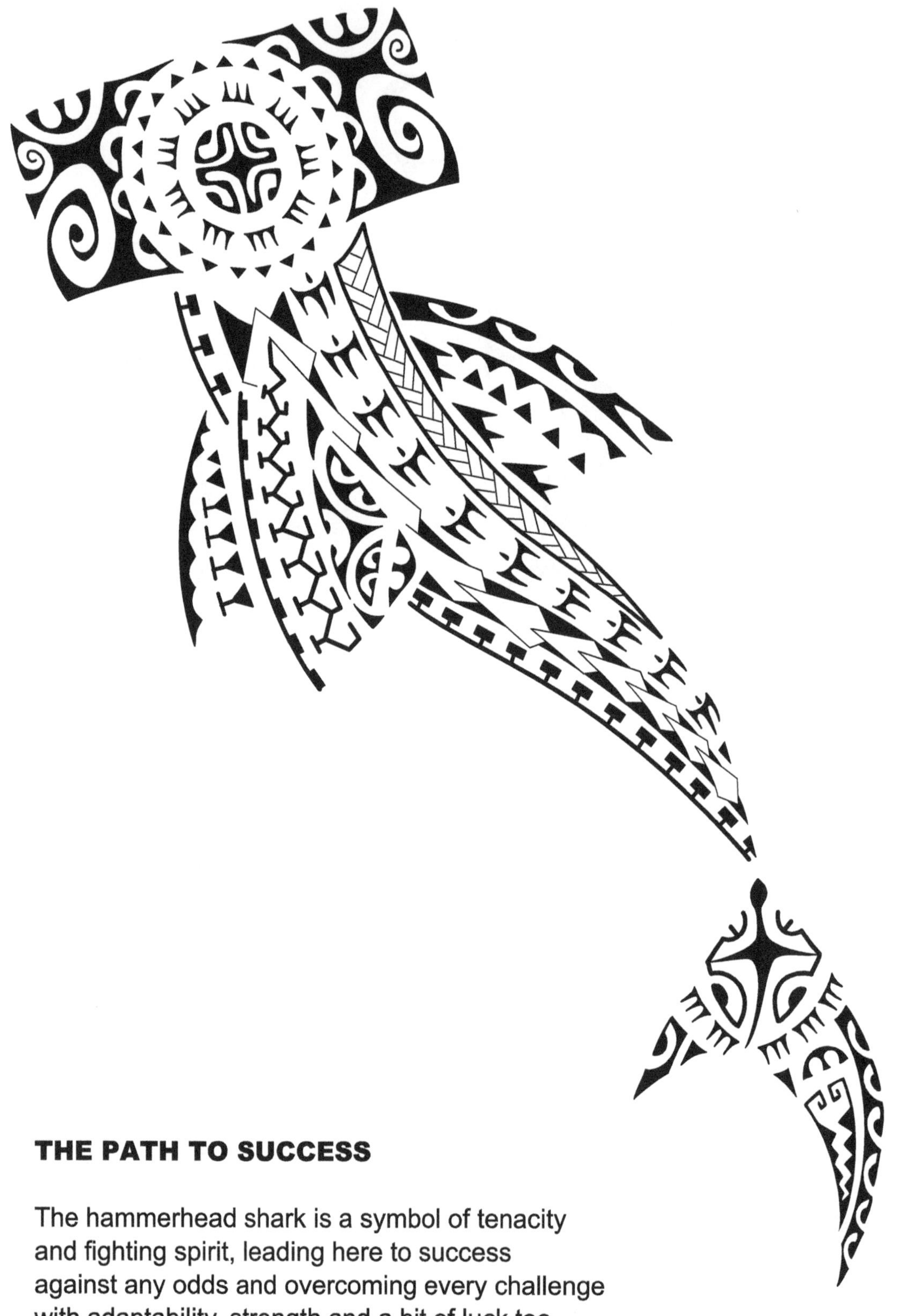

THE PATH TO SUCCESS

The hammerhead shark is a symbol of tenacity and fighting spirit, leading here to success against any odds and overcoming every challenge with adaptability, strength and a bit of luck too.

STENCIL: t044

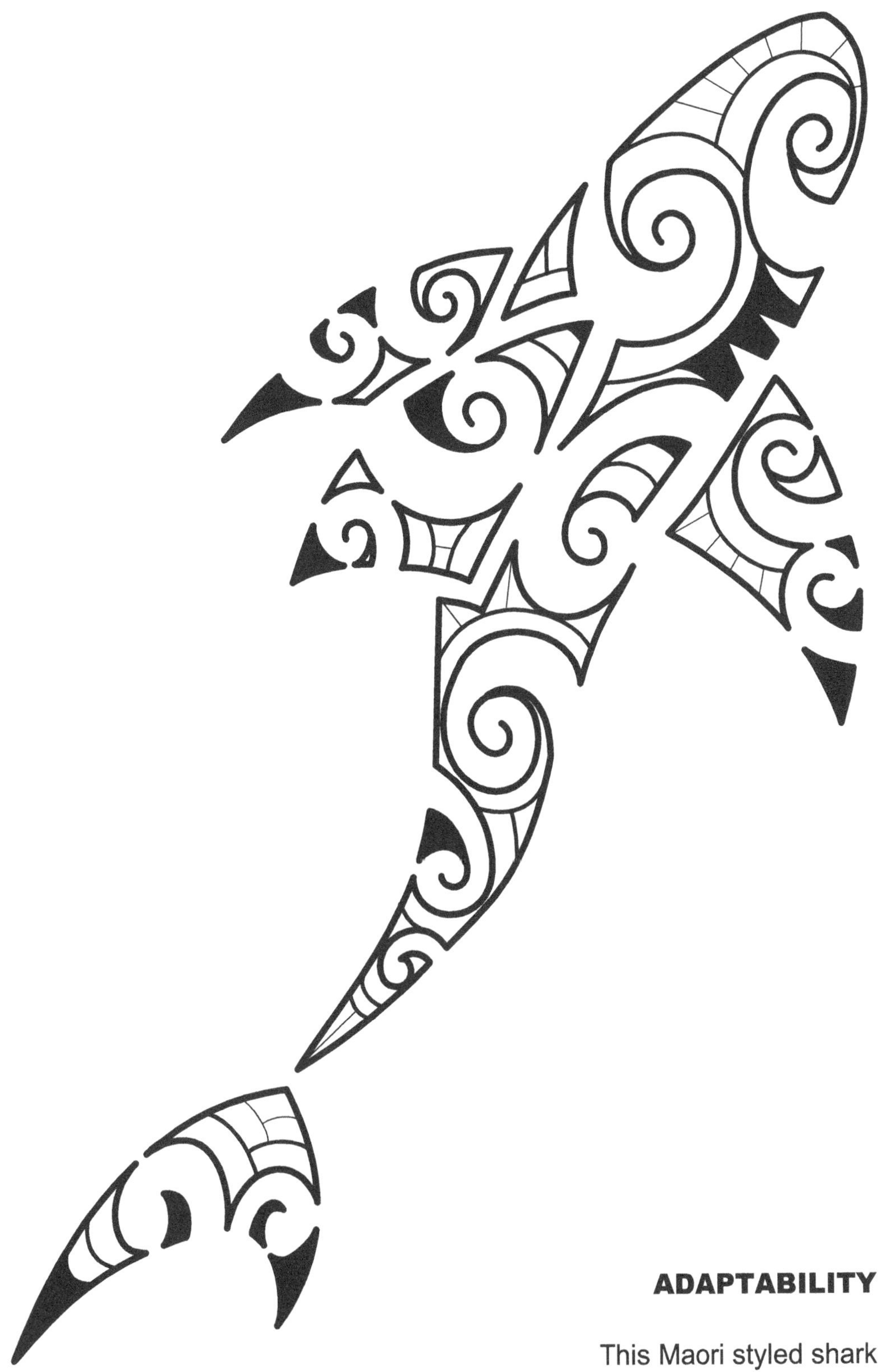

ADAPTABILITY

This Maori styled shark
recalls the flow of water to represent
adaptability and life through the use of koru motifs.

STENCIL: t045

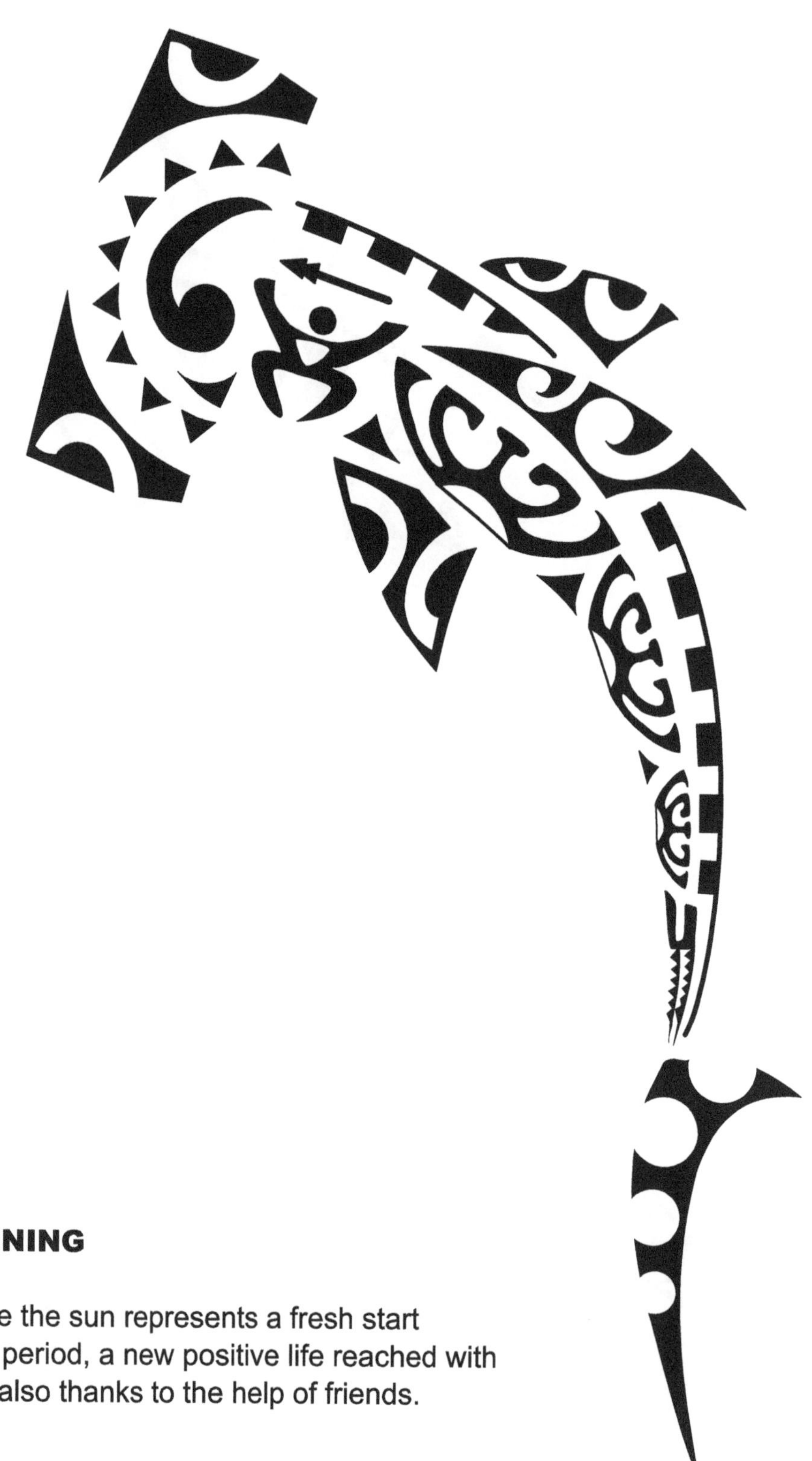

NEW BEGINNING

The koru inside the sun represents a fresh start after a difficult period, a new positive life reached with determination also thanks to the help of friends.

STENCIL: t046

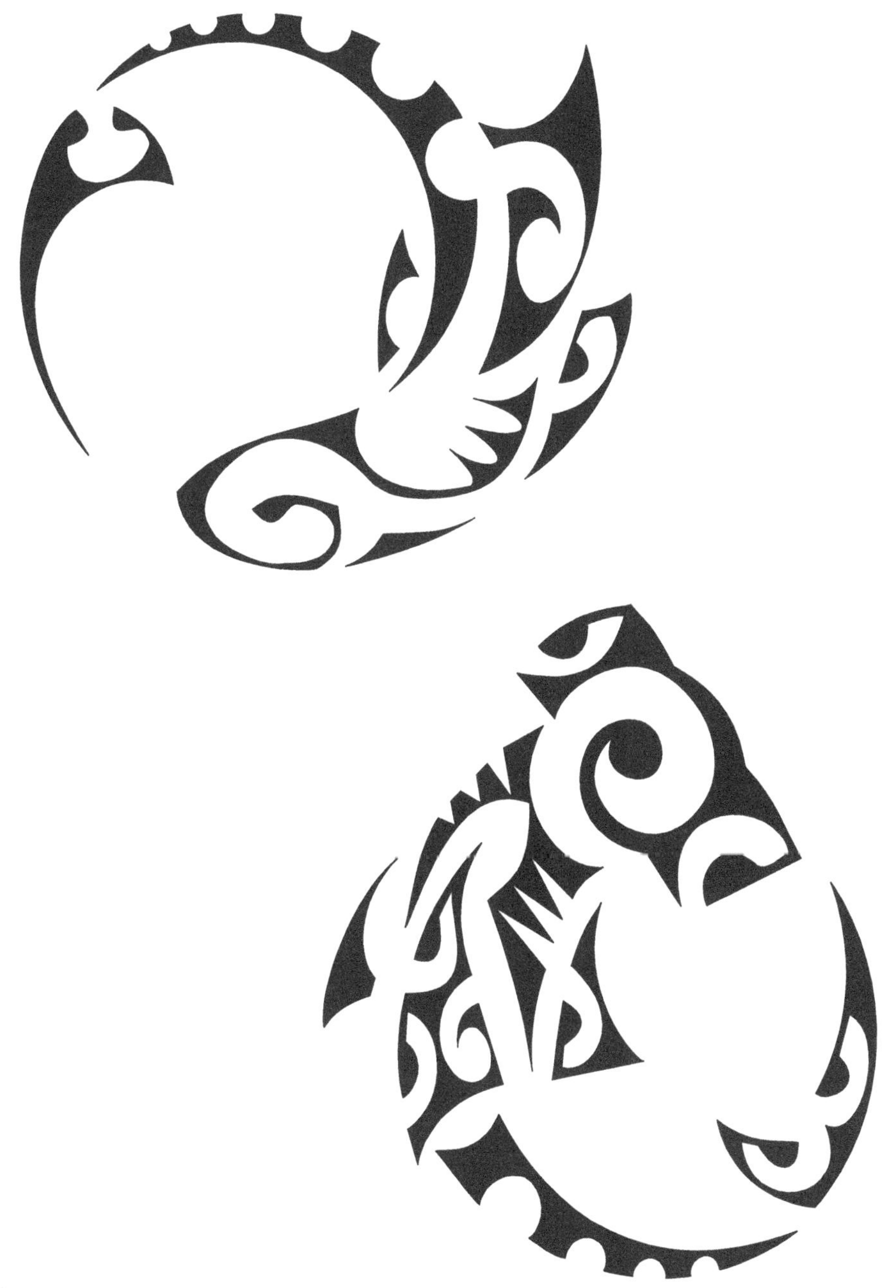

ETERNITY

The circle is a popular symbol for eternity, associated here with a shark for adaptability and a hammerhead shark for tenacity.

STENCIL: t047 - t048

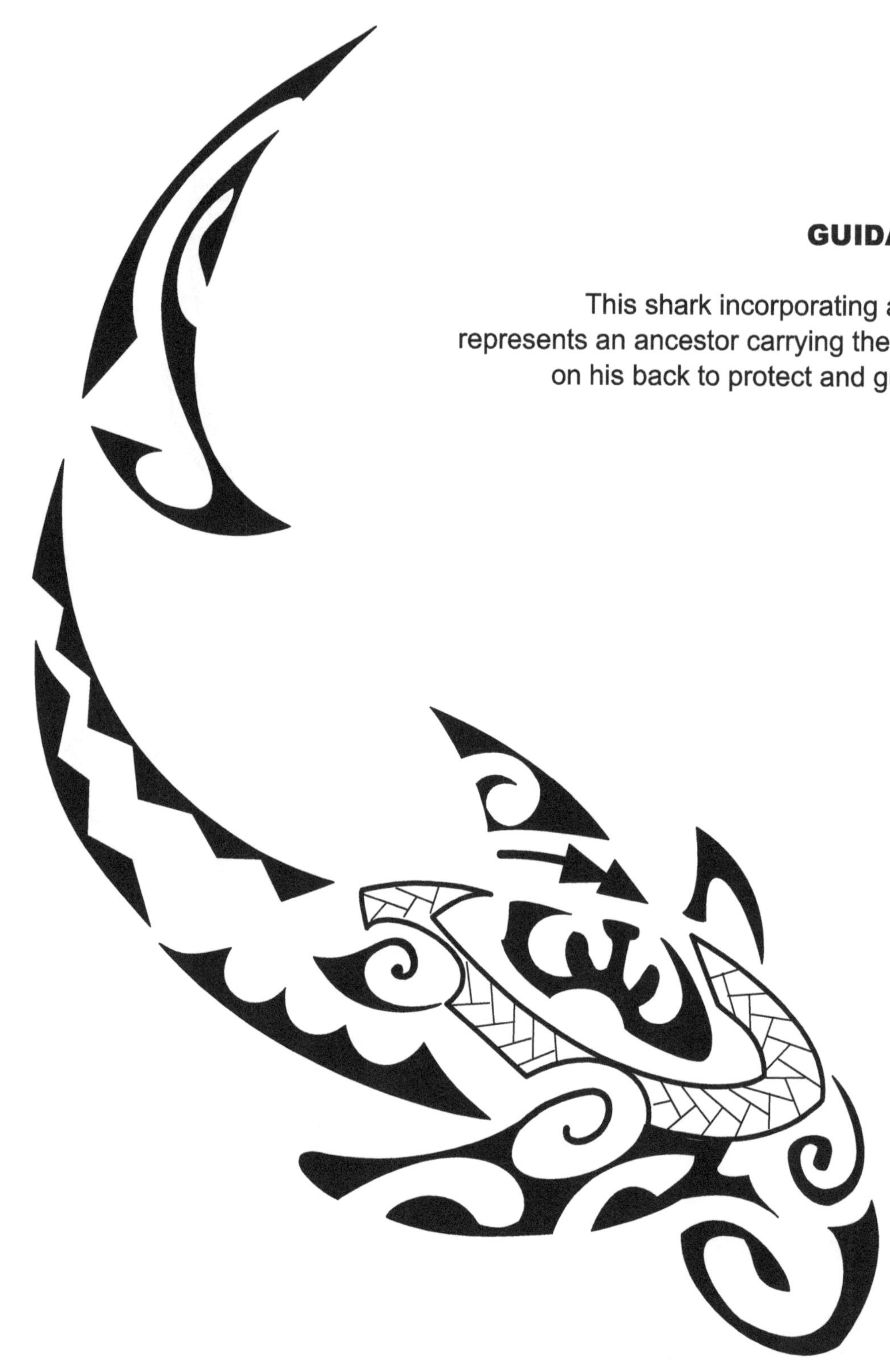

GUIDANCE

This shark incorporating a turtle represents an ancestor carrying the family on his back to protect and guide it.

STENCIL: t049

INFINITY

These sharks are shaped like twists to symbolize two persons always getting back together after every challenge and difficulty, with adaptability and tenacity.

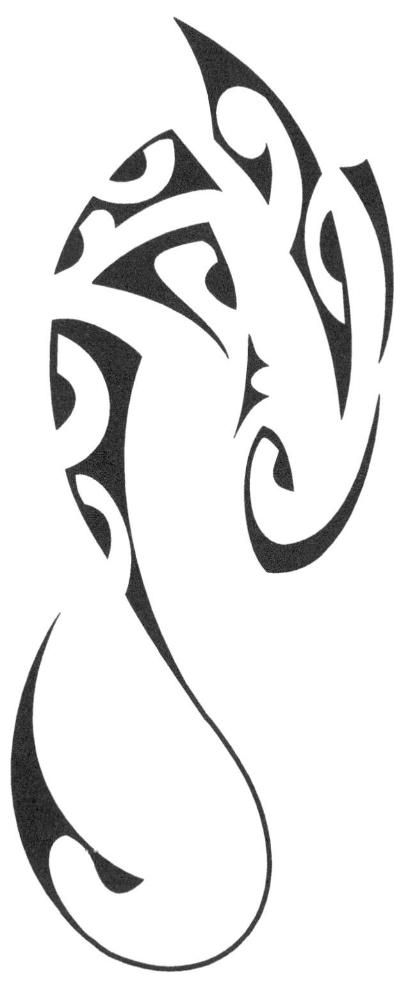

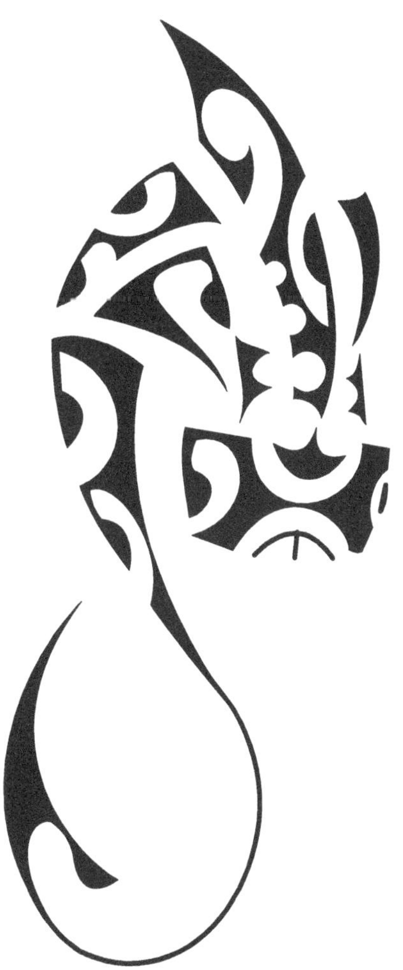

STENCIL: t050 - t051

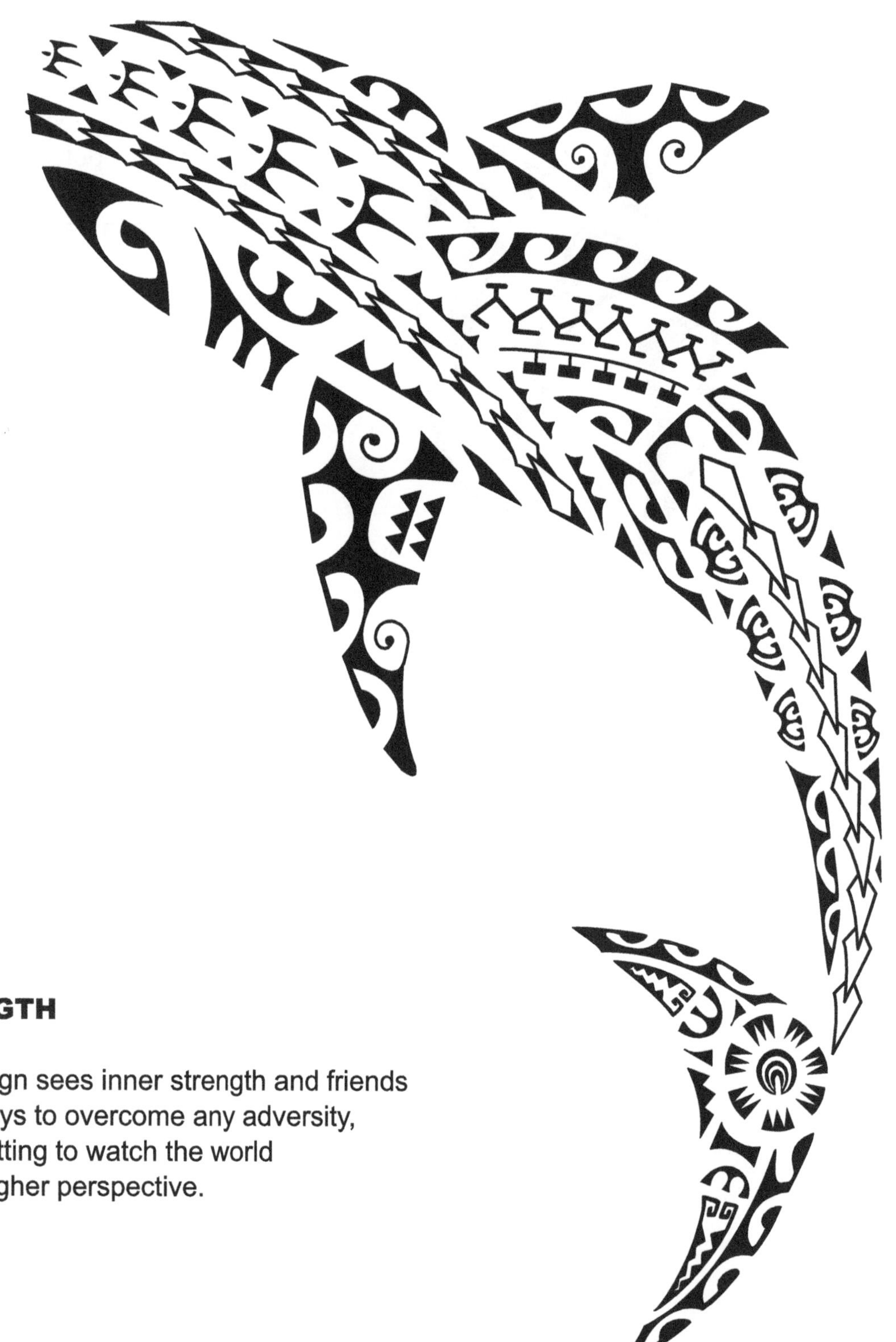

STRENGTH

This design sees inner strength and friends as the keys to overcome any adversity, finally getting to watch the world from a higher perspective.

STENCIL: t052

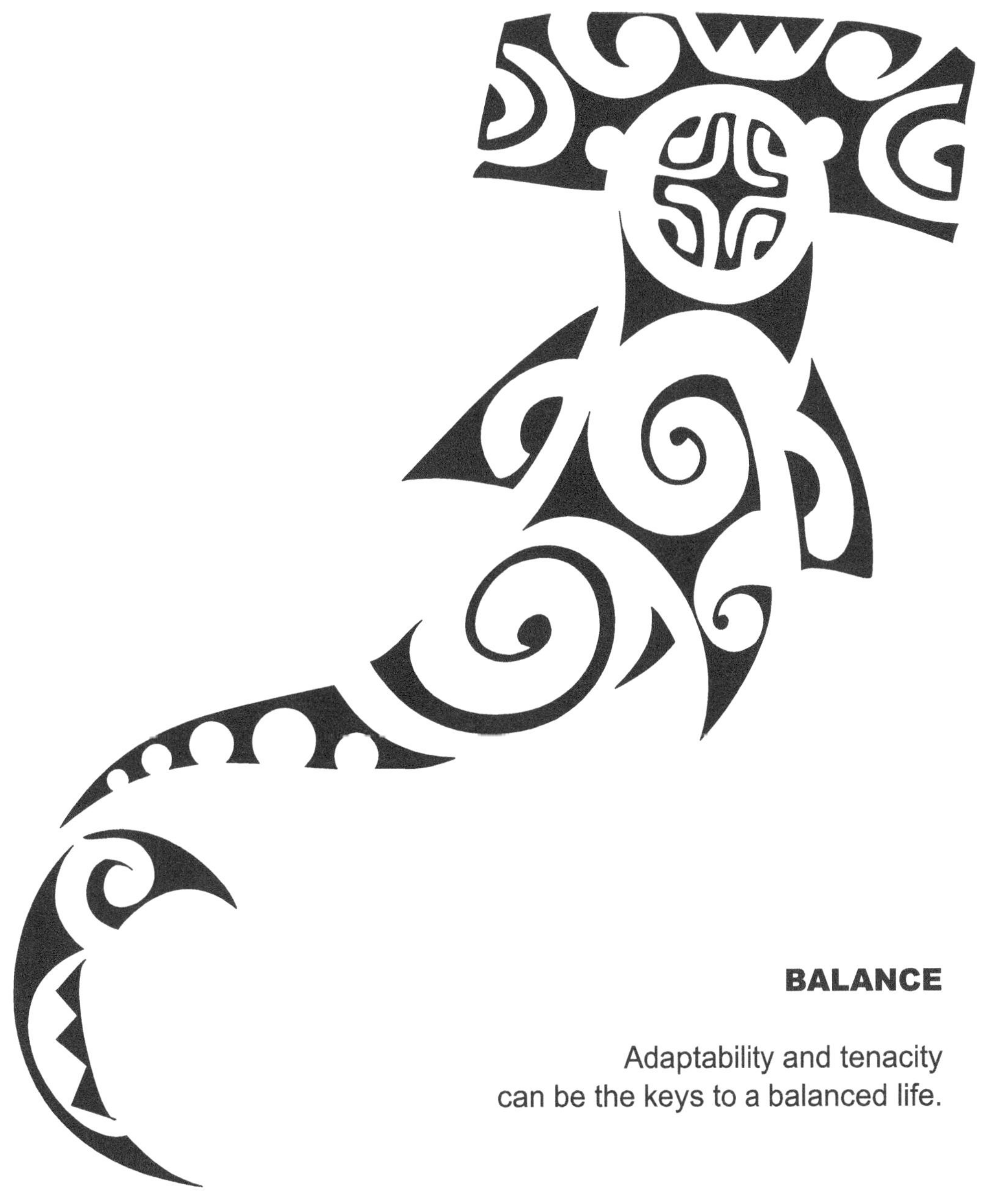

BALANCE

Adaptability and tenacity
can be the keys to a balanced life.

STENCIL: t053

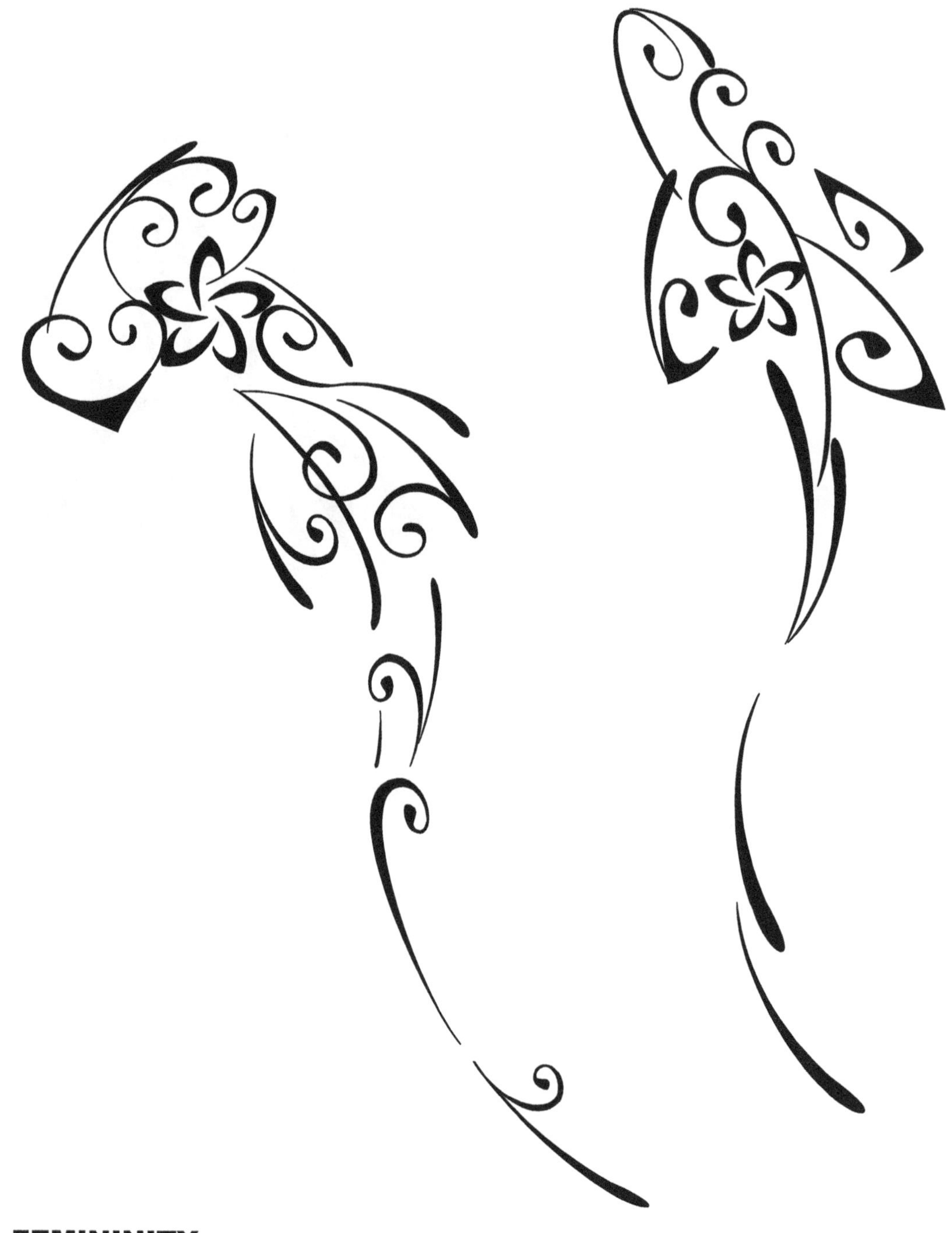

FEMININITY

There can be femininity in strength too.

STENCIL: t054 - t055

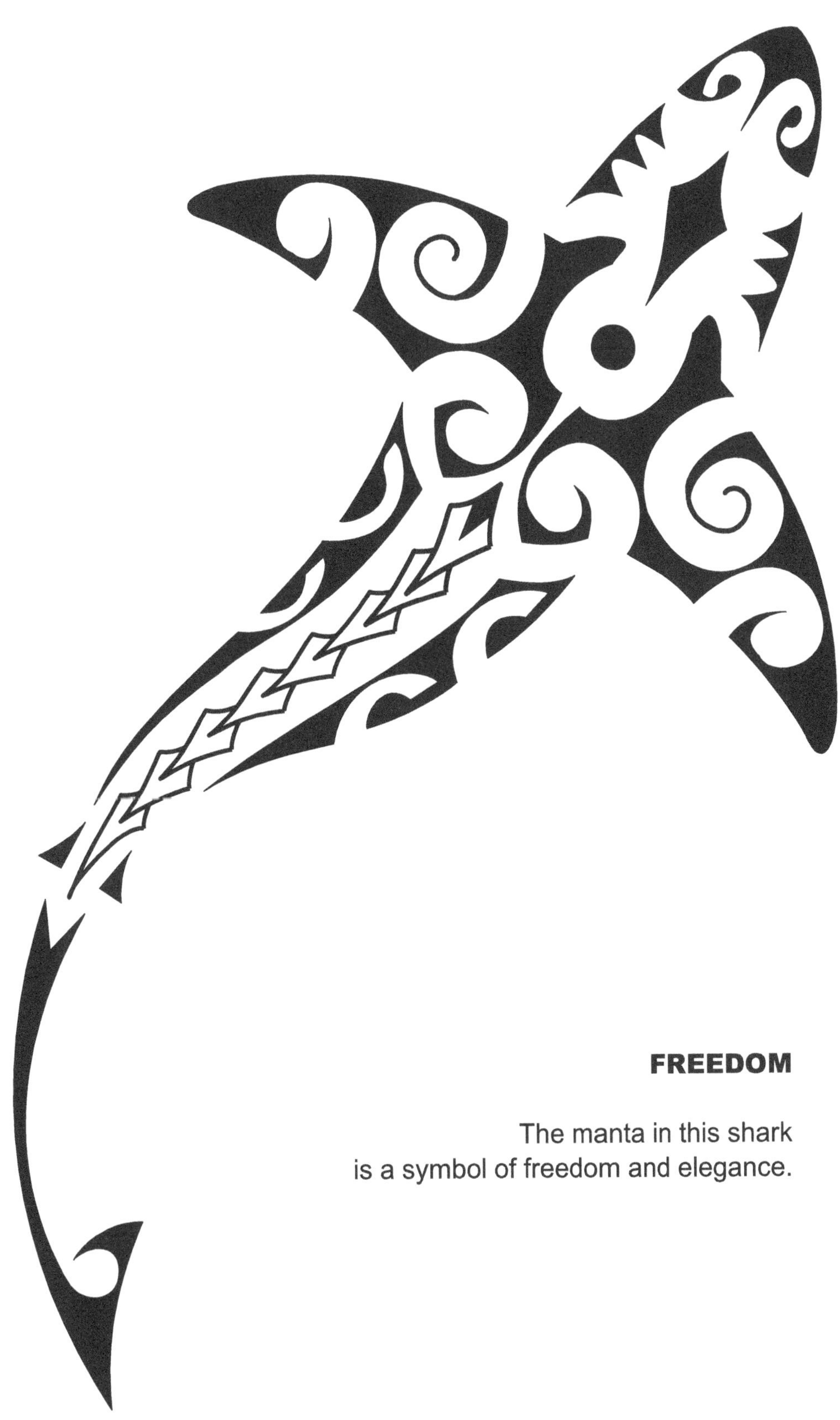

FREEDOM

The manta in this shark
is a symbol of freedom and elegance.

STENCIL: t056

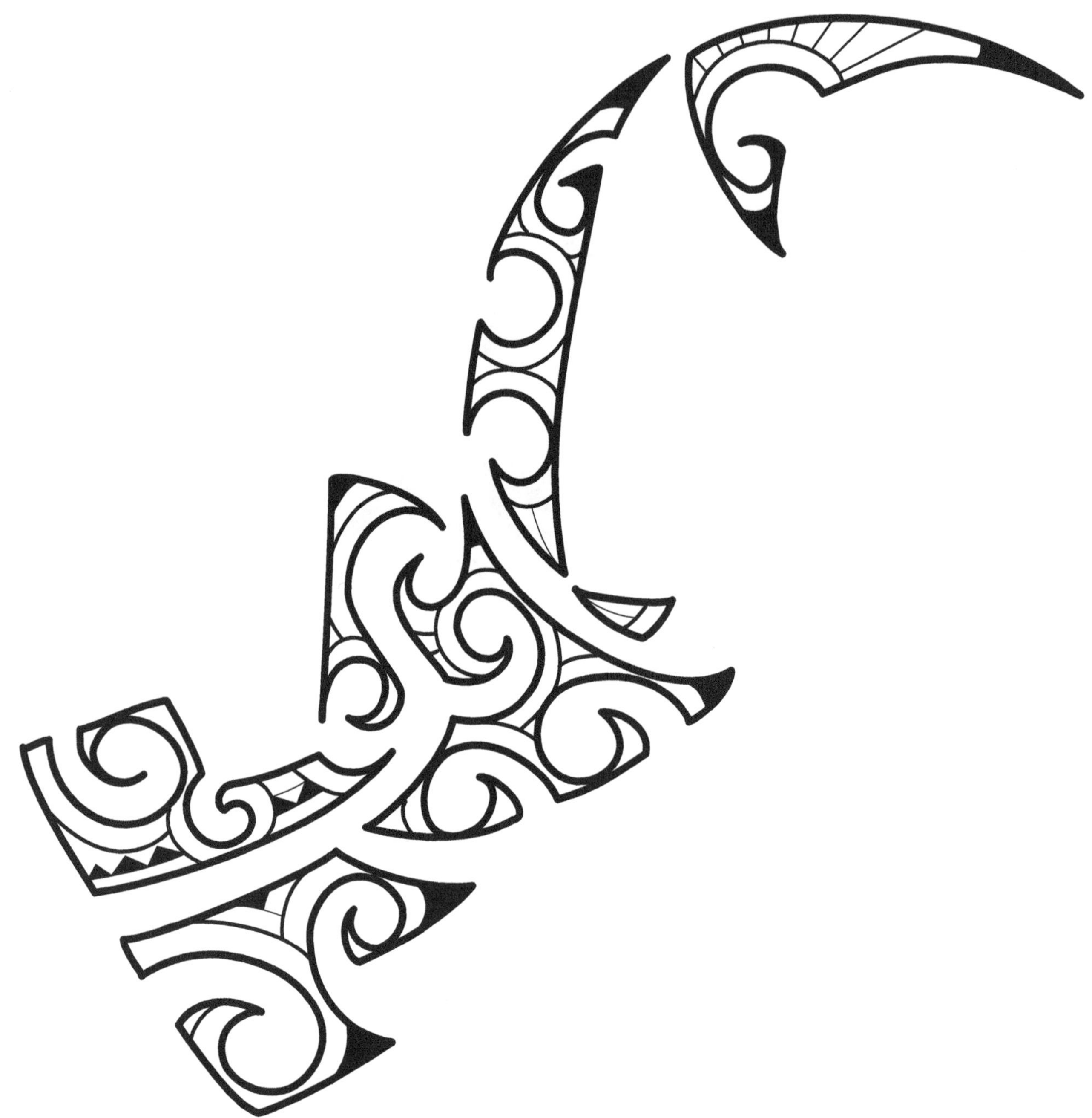

TENACITY

This Maori styled hammerhead shark symbolizes tenacity and strength.

STENCIL: t057

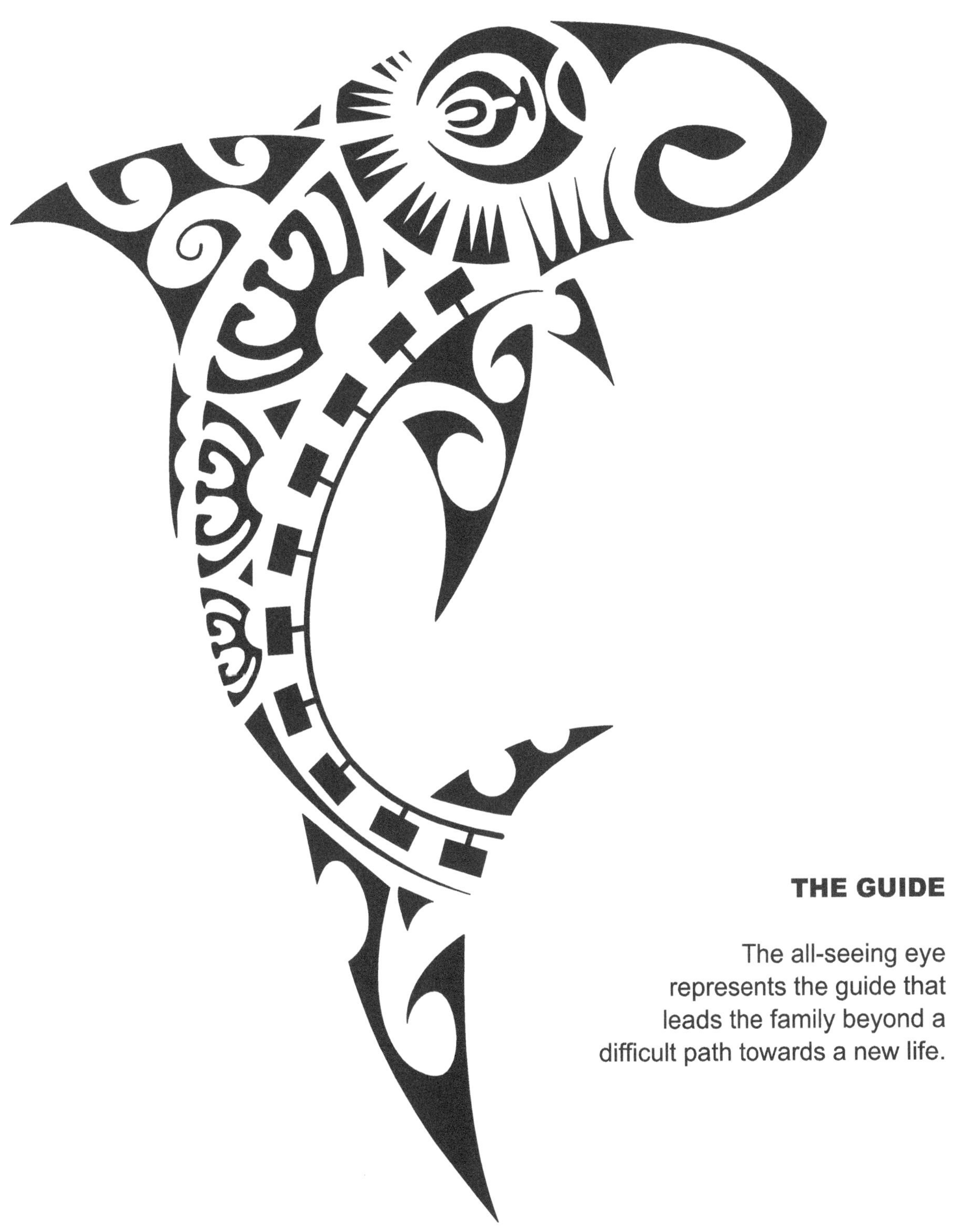

THE GUIDE

The all-seeing eye represents the guide that leads the family beyond a difficult path towards a new life.

STENCIL: t058

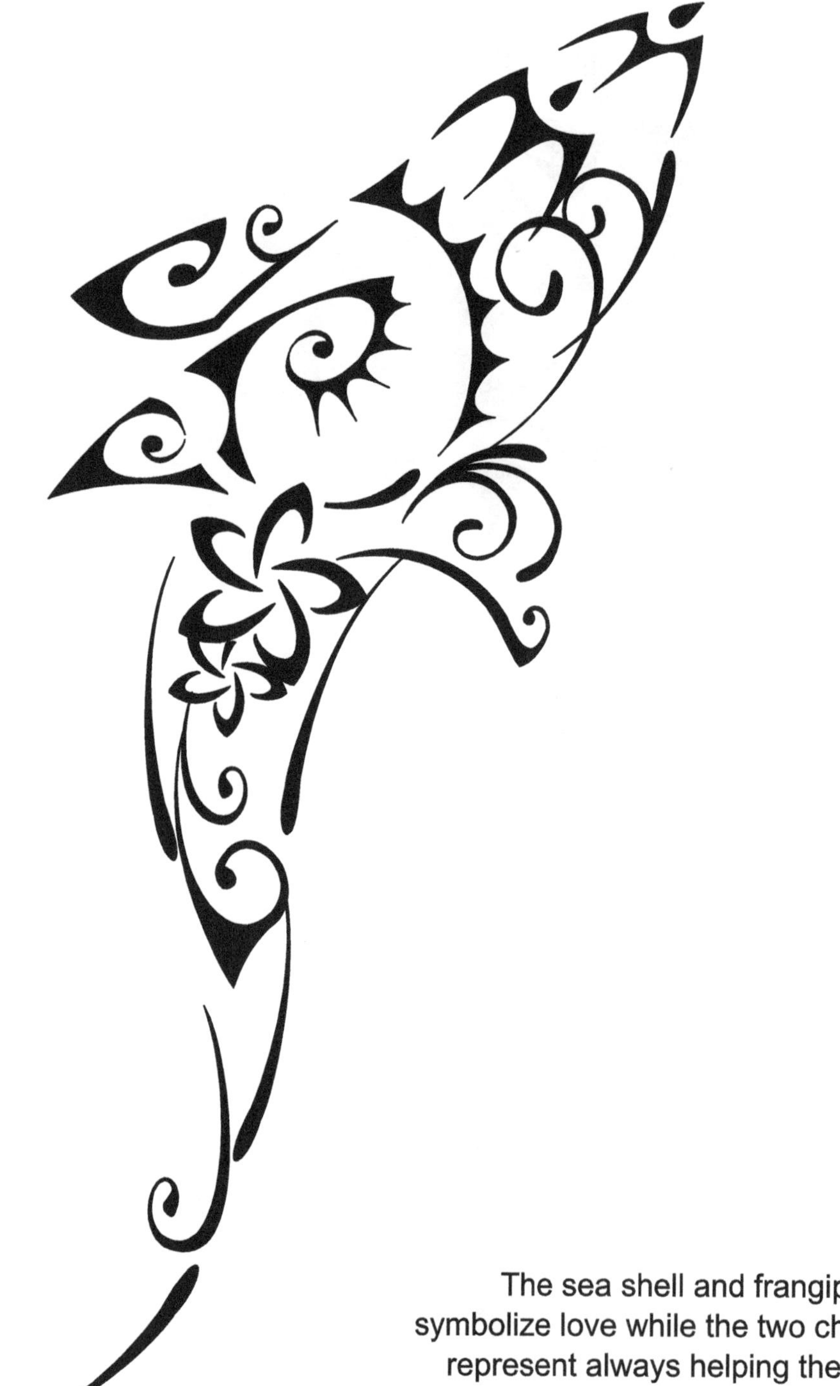

LOVE

The sea shell and frangipani flowers symbolize love while the two chasing birds represent always helping the dear ones.

STENCIL: t059

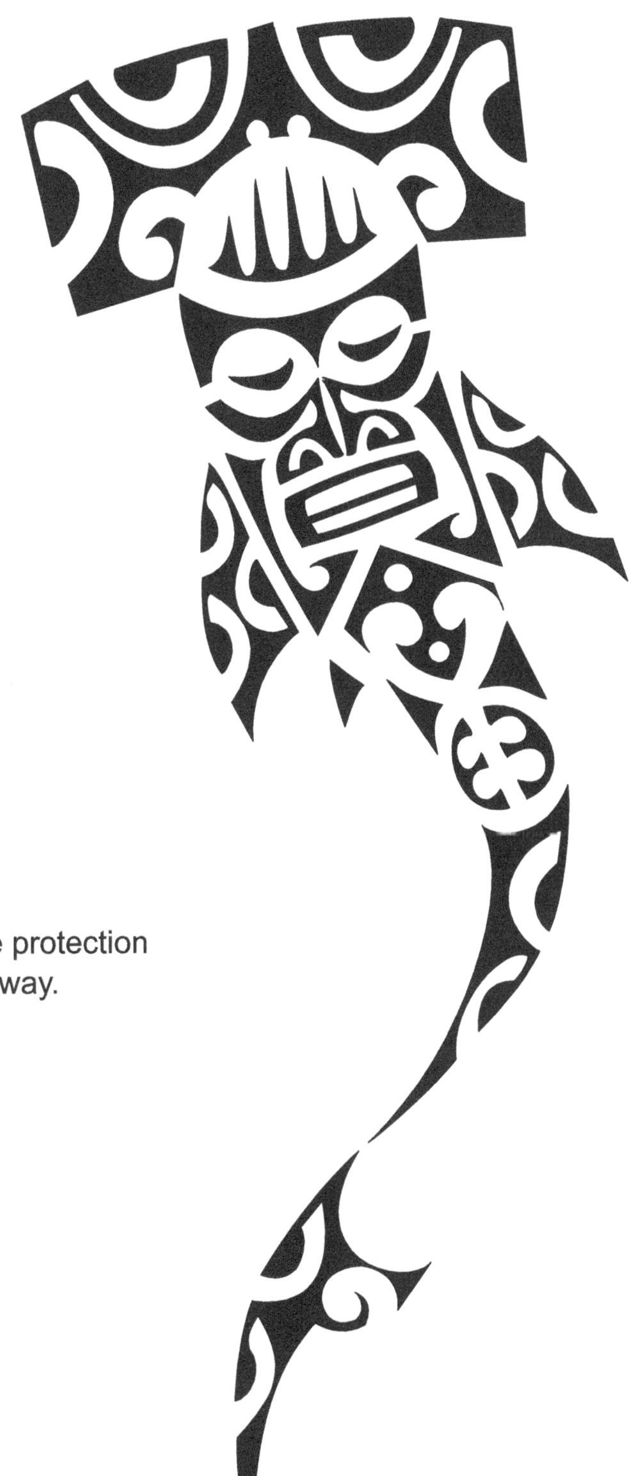

PROTECTOR

Two tikis symbolize here protection while scaring enemies away.

STENCIL: t060

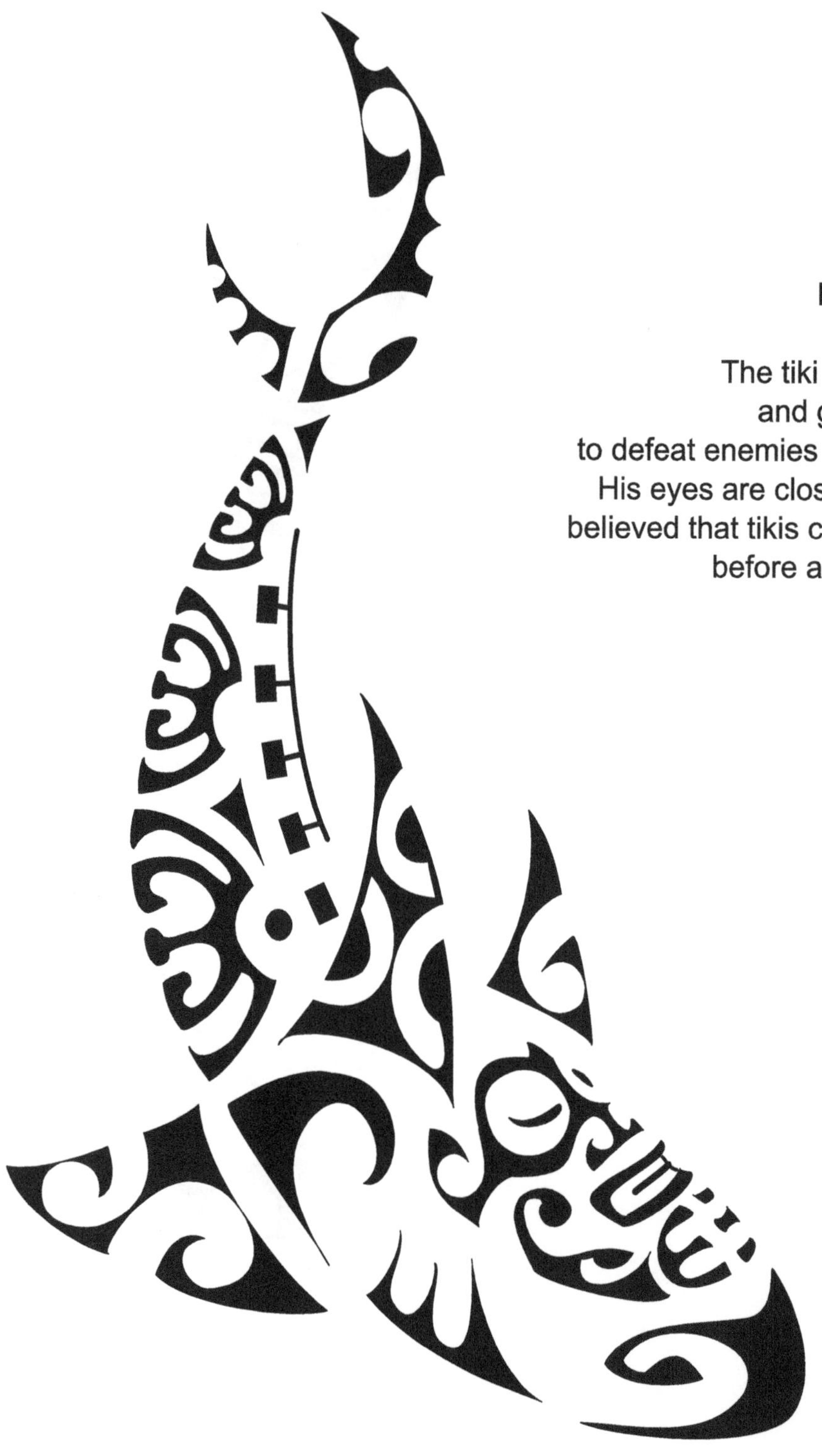

PROTECTION

The tiki gives protection
and guides the shark
to defeat enemies and adversities.
His eyes are closed because it is
believed that tikis can smell danger
before actually seeing it.

STENCIL: t061

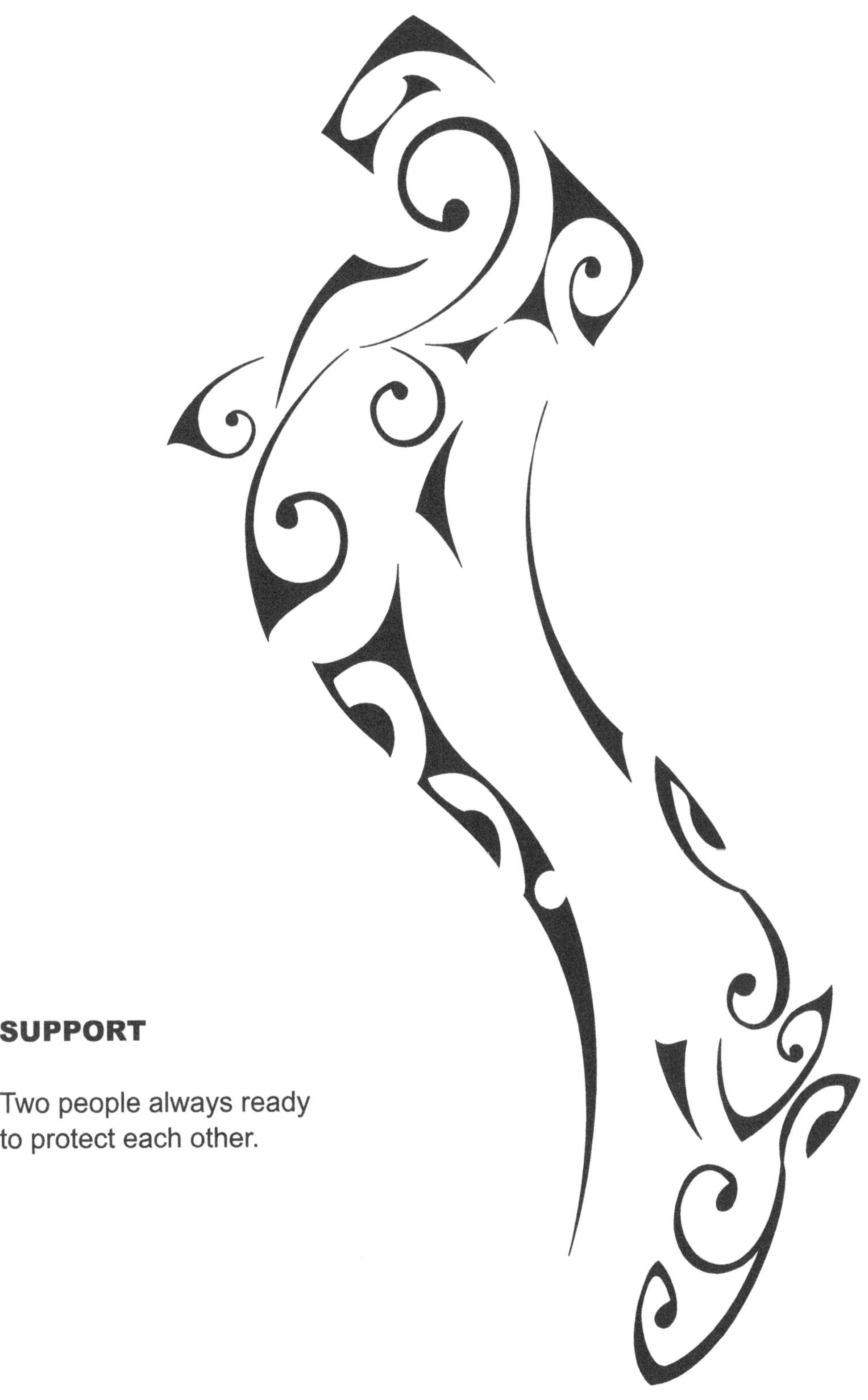

SUPPORT

Two people always ready to protect each other.

FIGHTER

The warrior who fights his way among enemies to leave defeat behind.

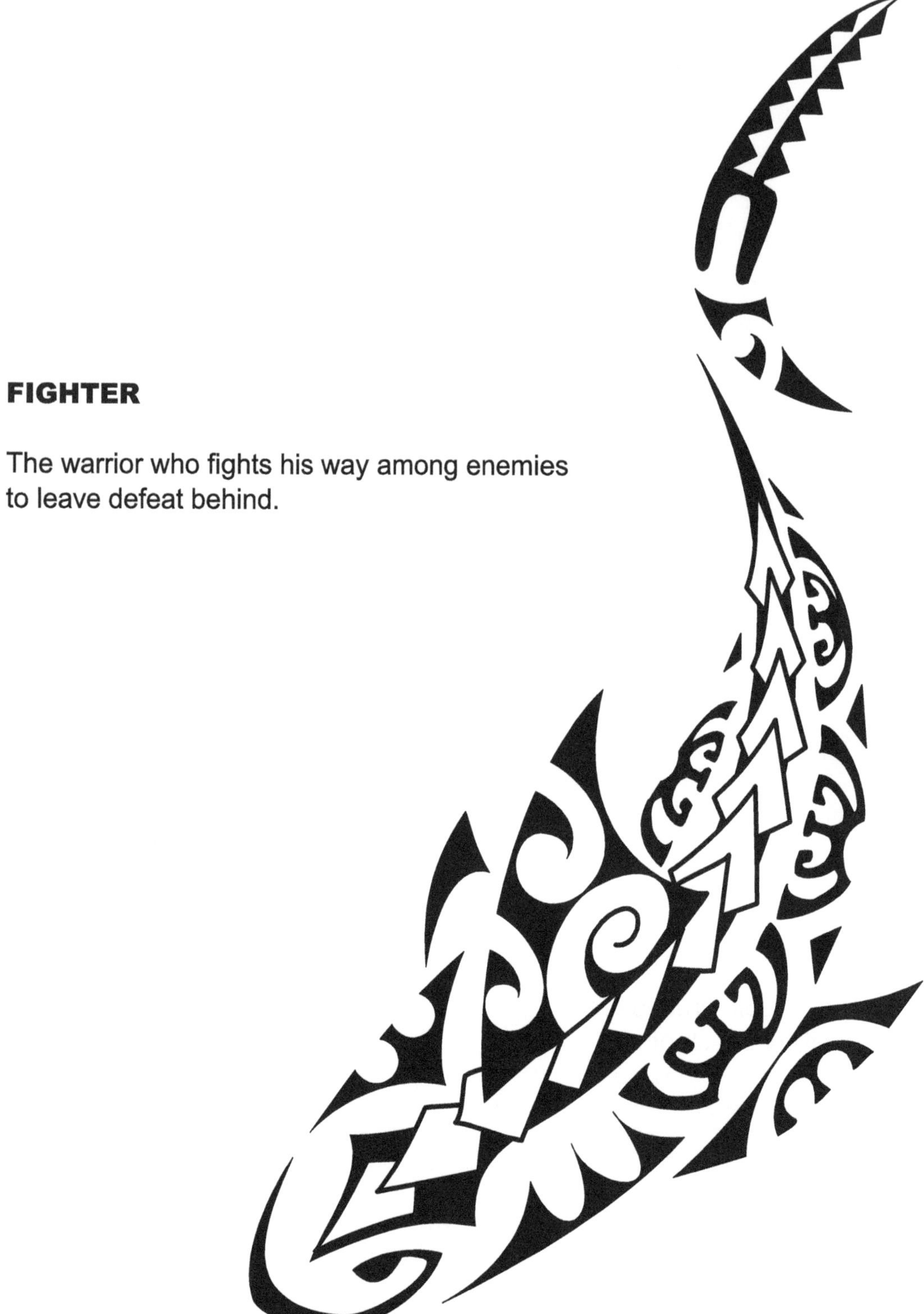

STENCIL: t063

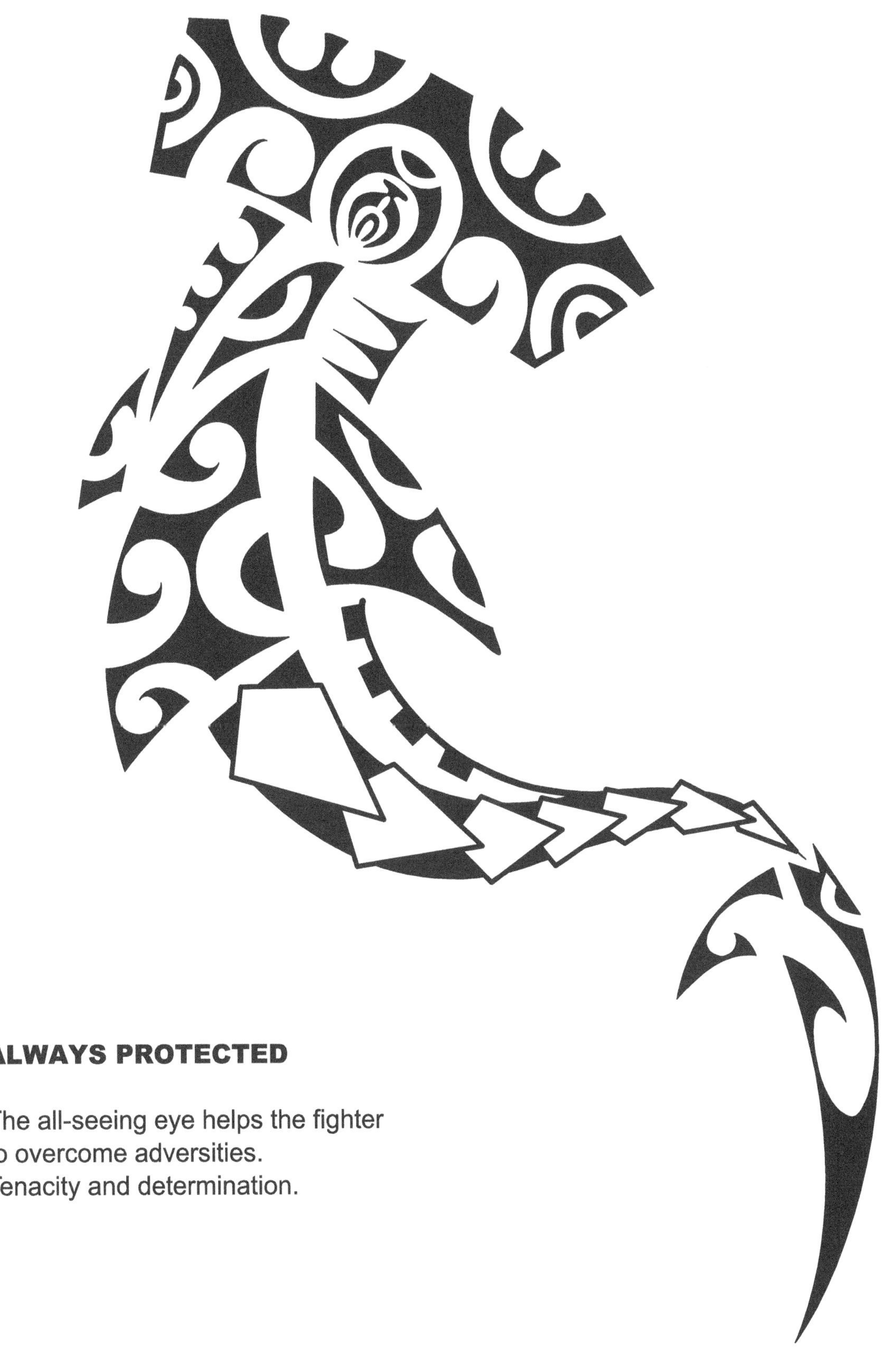

ALWAYS PROTECTED

The all-seeing eye helps the fighter
to overcome adversities.
Tenacity and determination.

An Aumakua is an entity having supernatural powers (usually a deified ancestor or a spirit), which appears to men usually in the form of an animal, to give them advice, omens and sometimes punishments.
In the case of deified ancestors, families will maintain in time a special relation to their specific animals, which can often be sea creatures or birds.

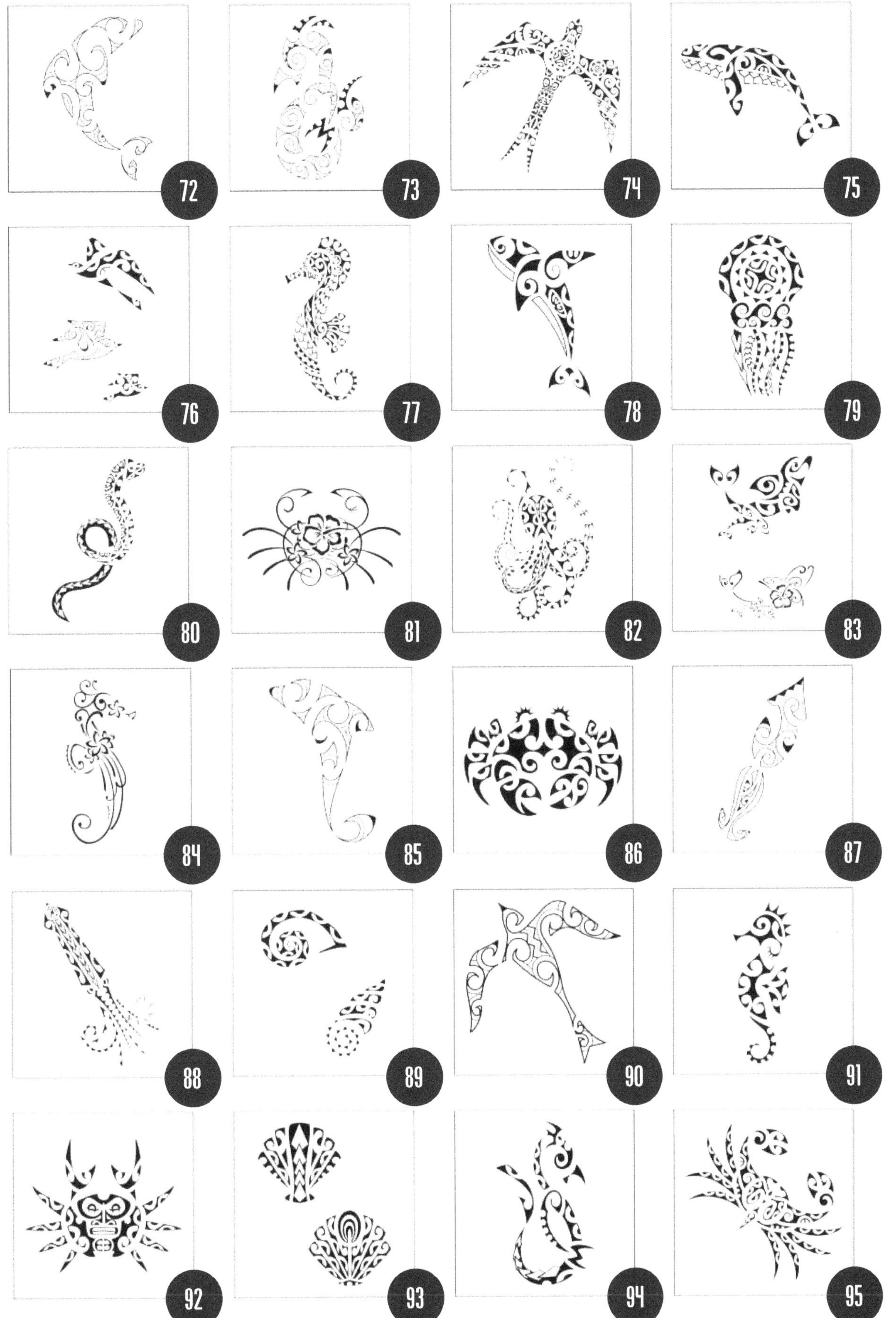
72
73
74
75
76
77
78
79
80
81
82
83
84
85
86
87
88
89
90
91
92
93
94
95

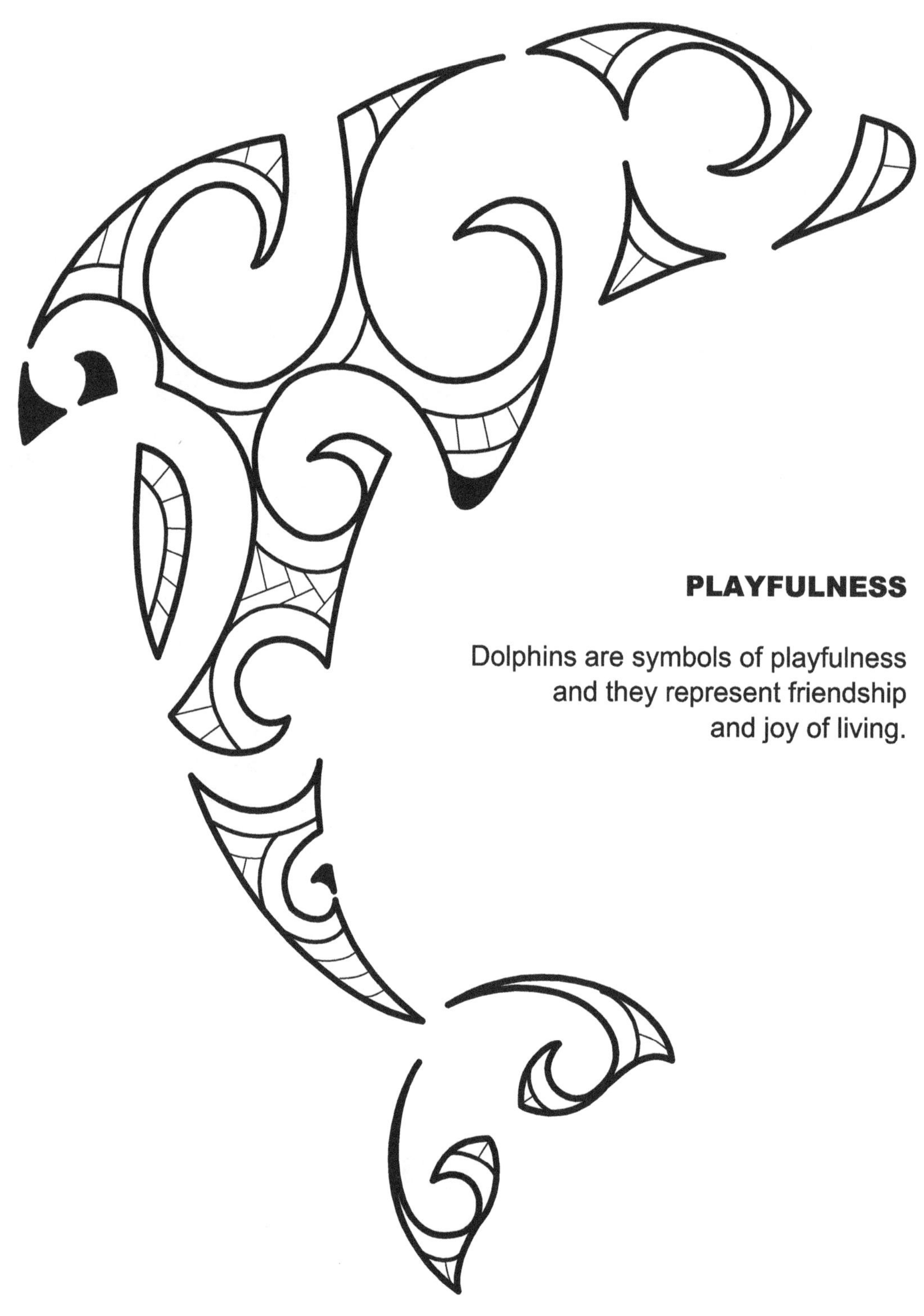

PLAYFULNESS

Dolphins are symbols of playfulness and they represent friendship and joy of living.

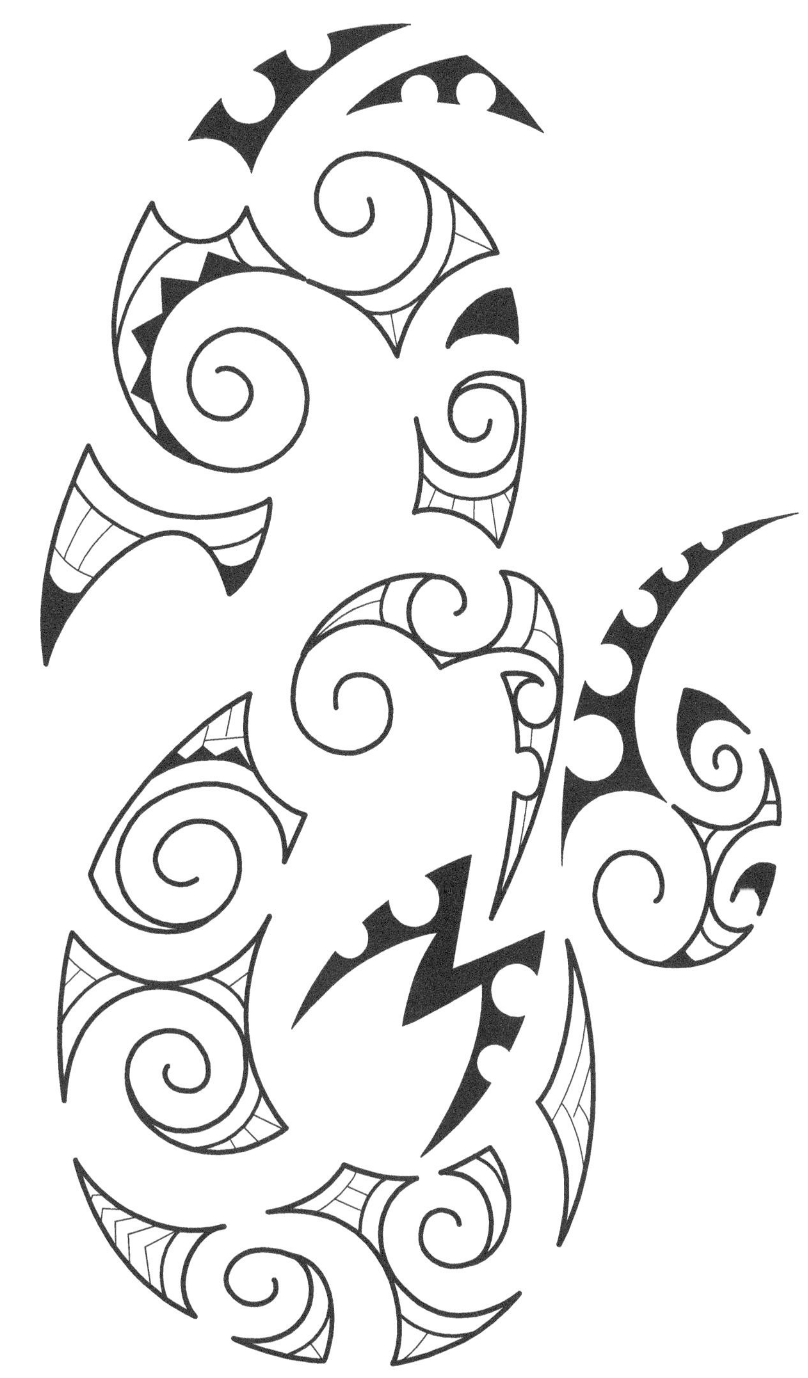

PROTECTION

The manaia is a guardian spirit
from Maori traditions,
often an ancestor guarding on family.

STENCIL: t066

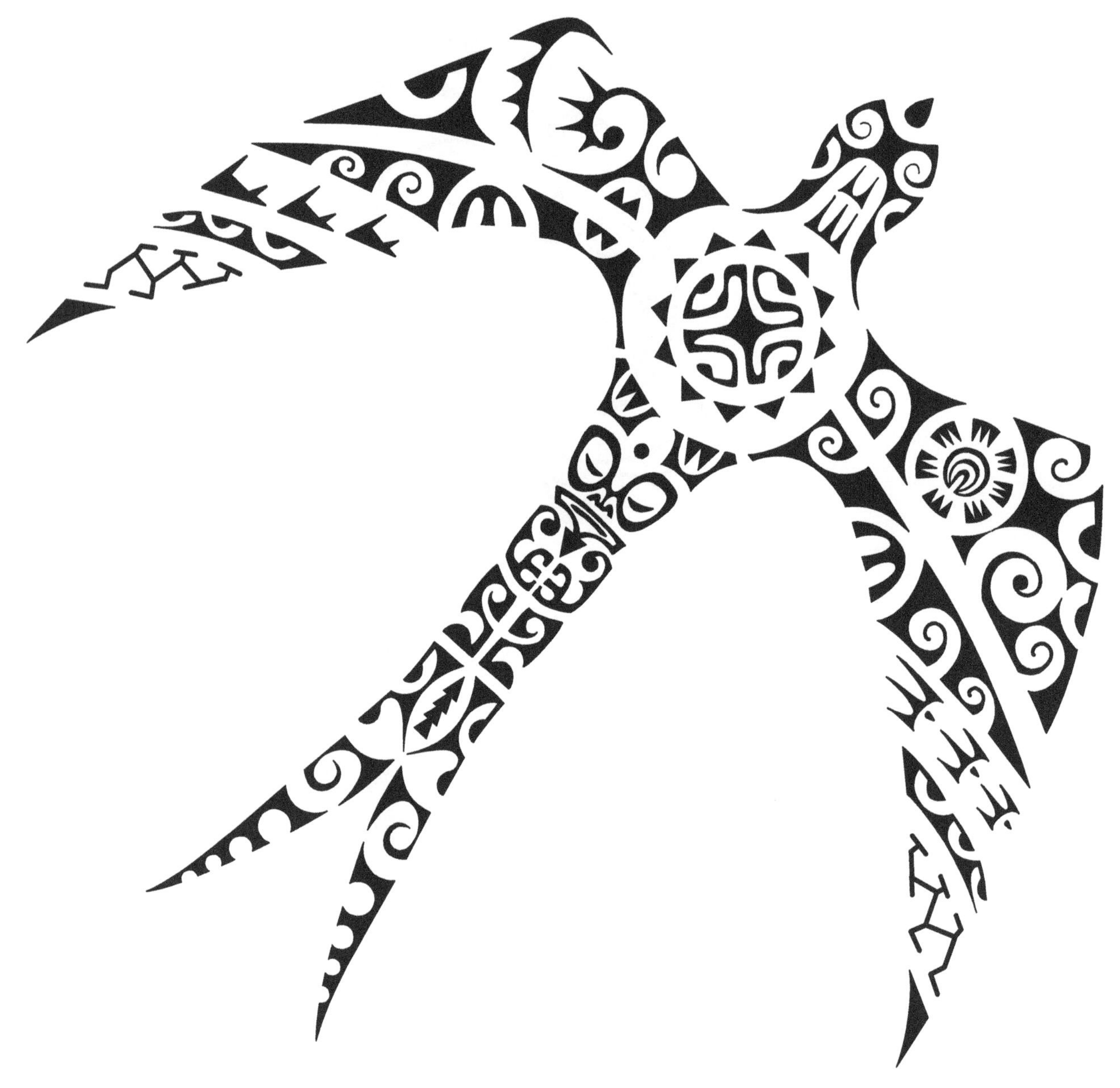

LIFE TRAVELLER

The frigate travels long distances over the ocean.
This design represents the travel of a life,
searching for harmony
under the protection of a tiki.

STENCIL: t067

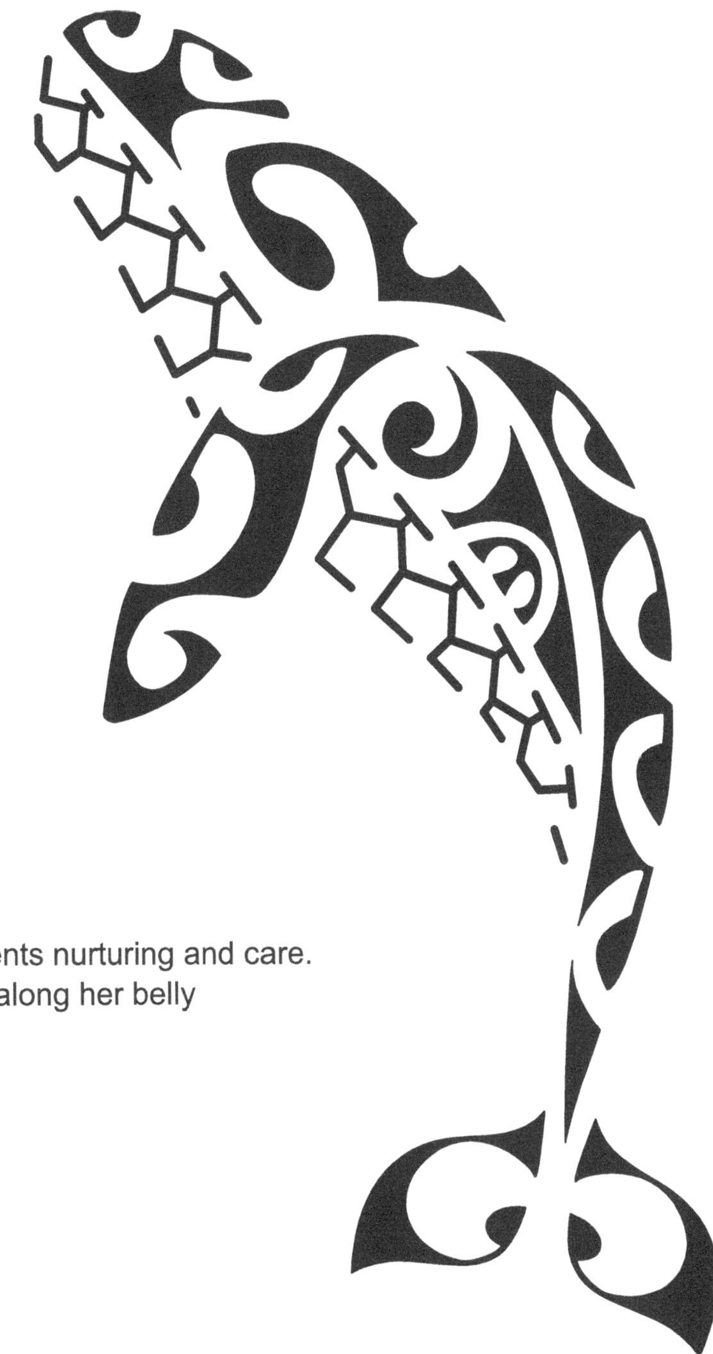

NURTURING

The whale represents nurturing and care. The row of ani ata along her belly represents family.

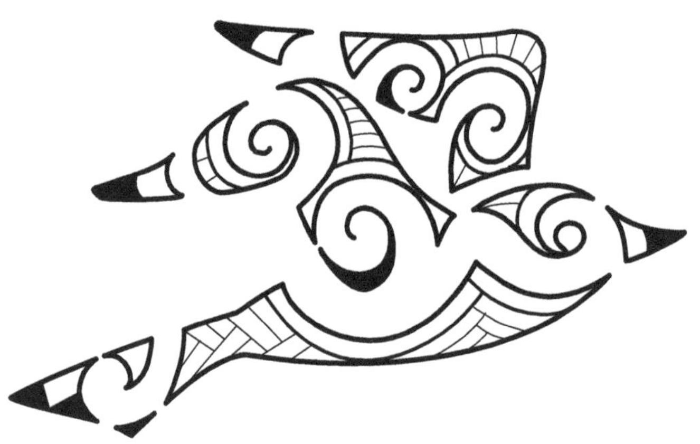

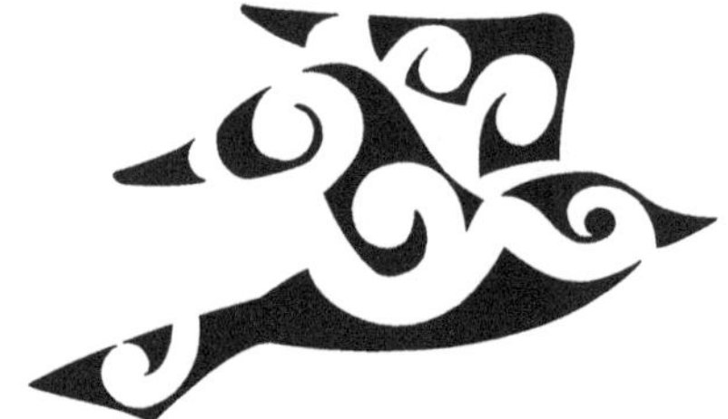

SAFE VOYAGE

Seagulls never fly too far
from the land.
That's why they often represent
safe return from voyages.

STENCIL: t069 - t070

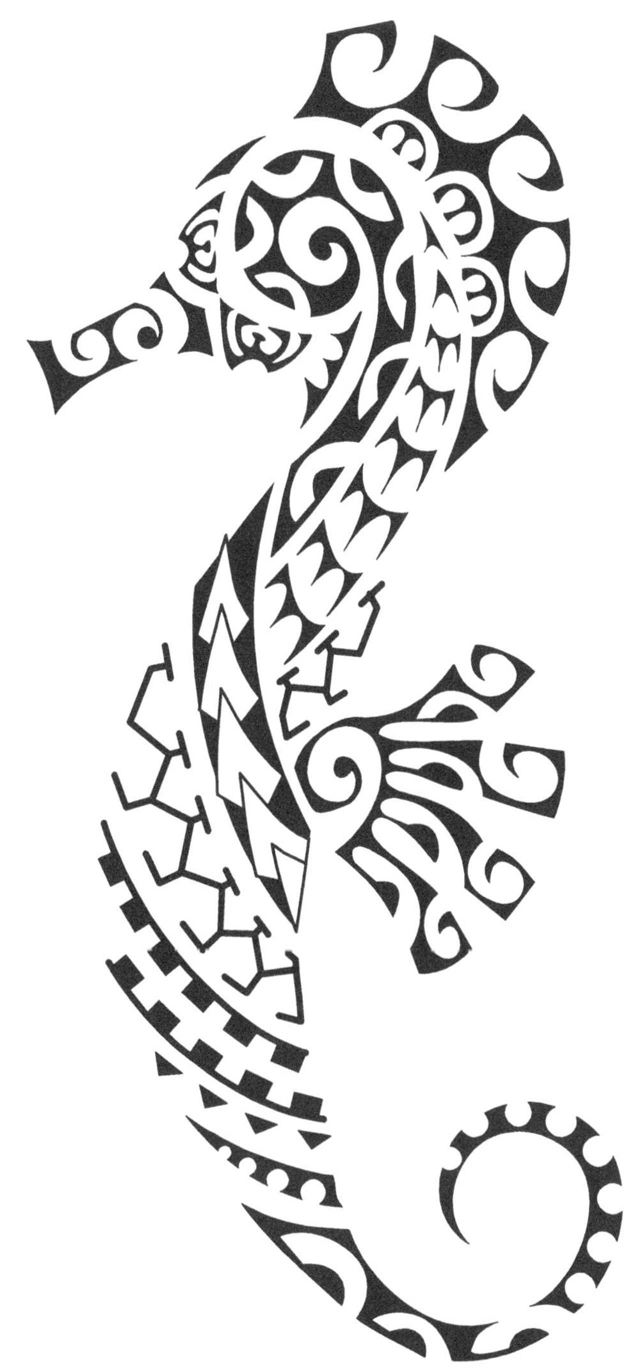

FATHER

The seahorse is a symbol for family man.
The elements here represent family
as the way to overcome adversities.

STENCIL: t071

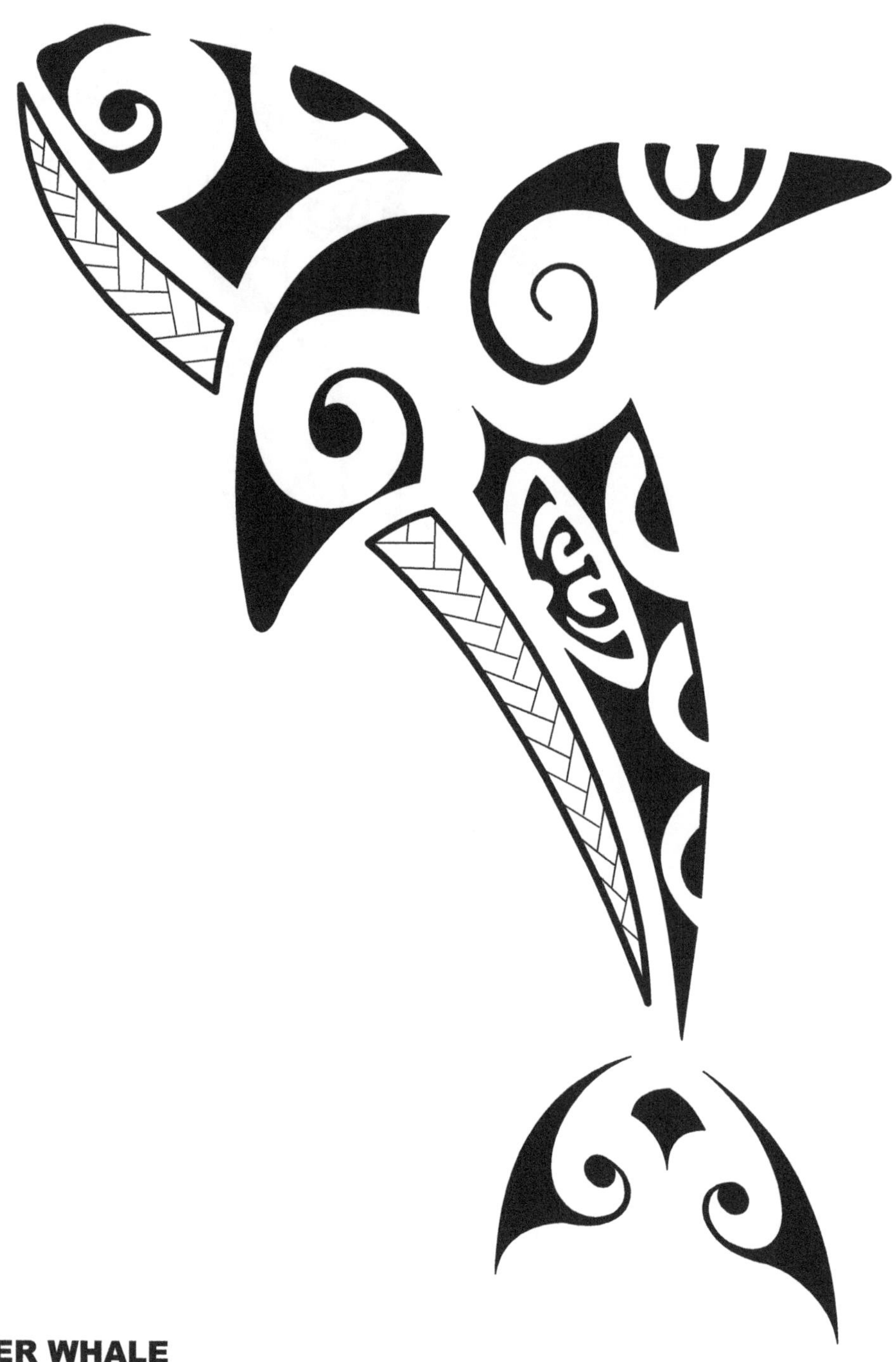

KILLER WHALE

The killer whale, or orca, symbolizes protection for family, represented here by the braid motif along the belly.

STENCIL: t072

JELLYFISH

The jellyfish has several meanings,
but the most important one
that leads to harmony
comes from its behaviour:
to follow the stream,
adapting to the flow of life.

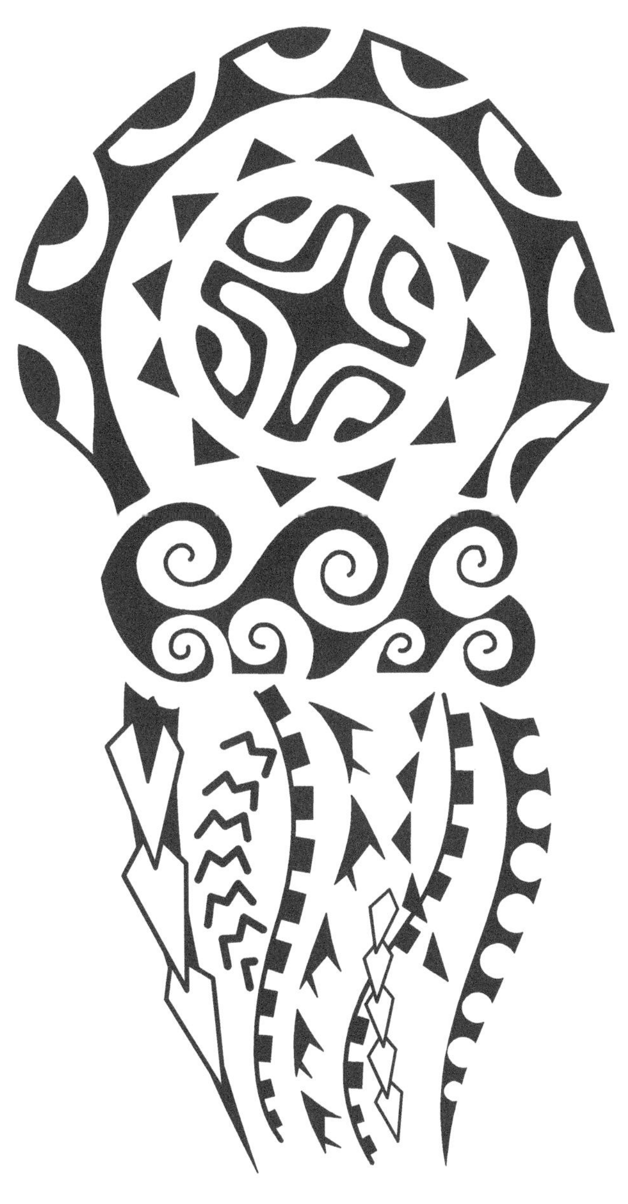

STENCIL: t073

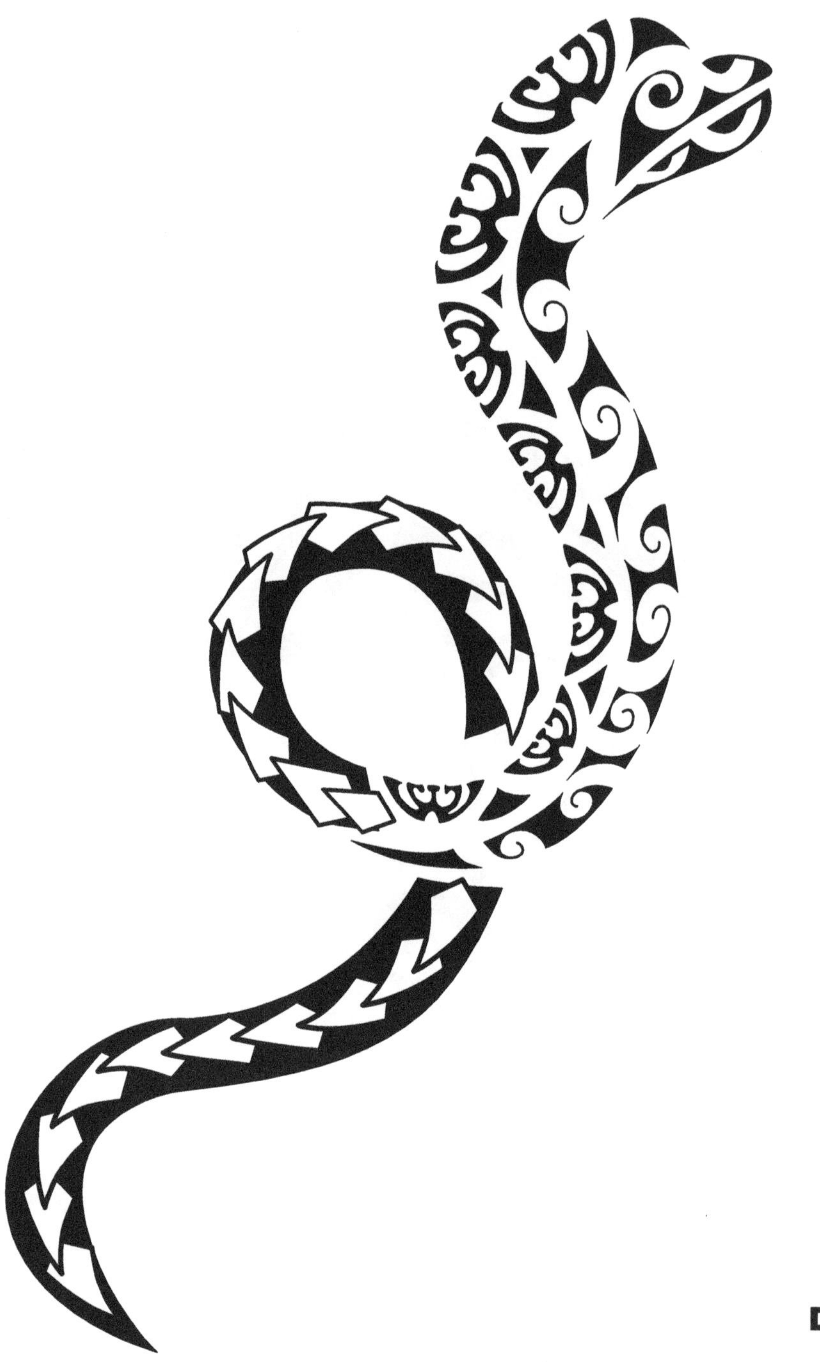

DANGER

Moray eels are dangerous animals.
They are tenacious and difficult to catch
and that's why they are often used
to represent adversities, danger.

STENCIL: t074

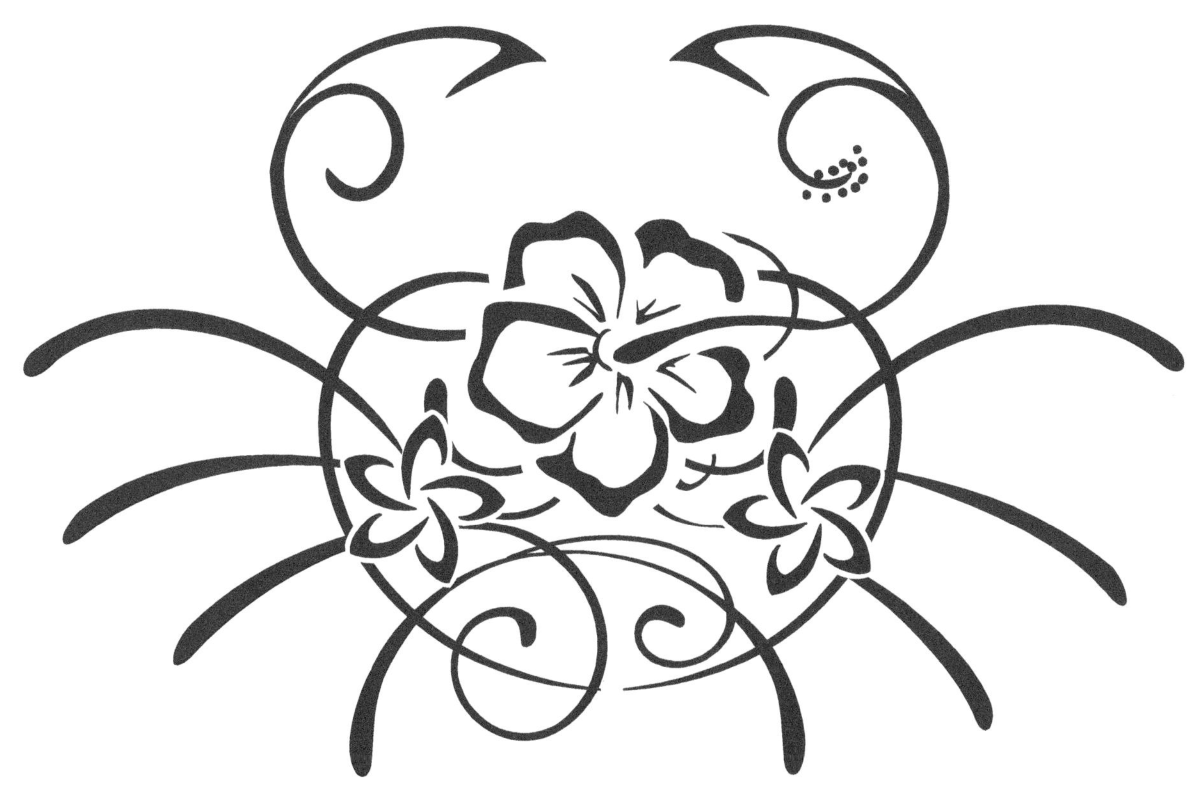

CHILDREN

This crab contains a flower of hibiscus
and two flowers of frangipani
to symbolize a mother protecting her two children
and her love for them.

STENCIL: t075

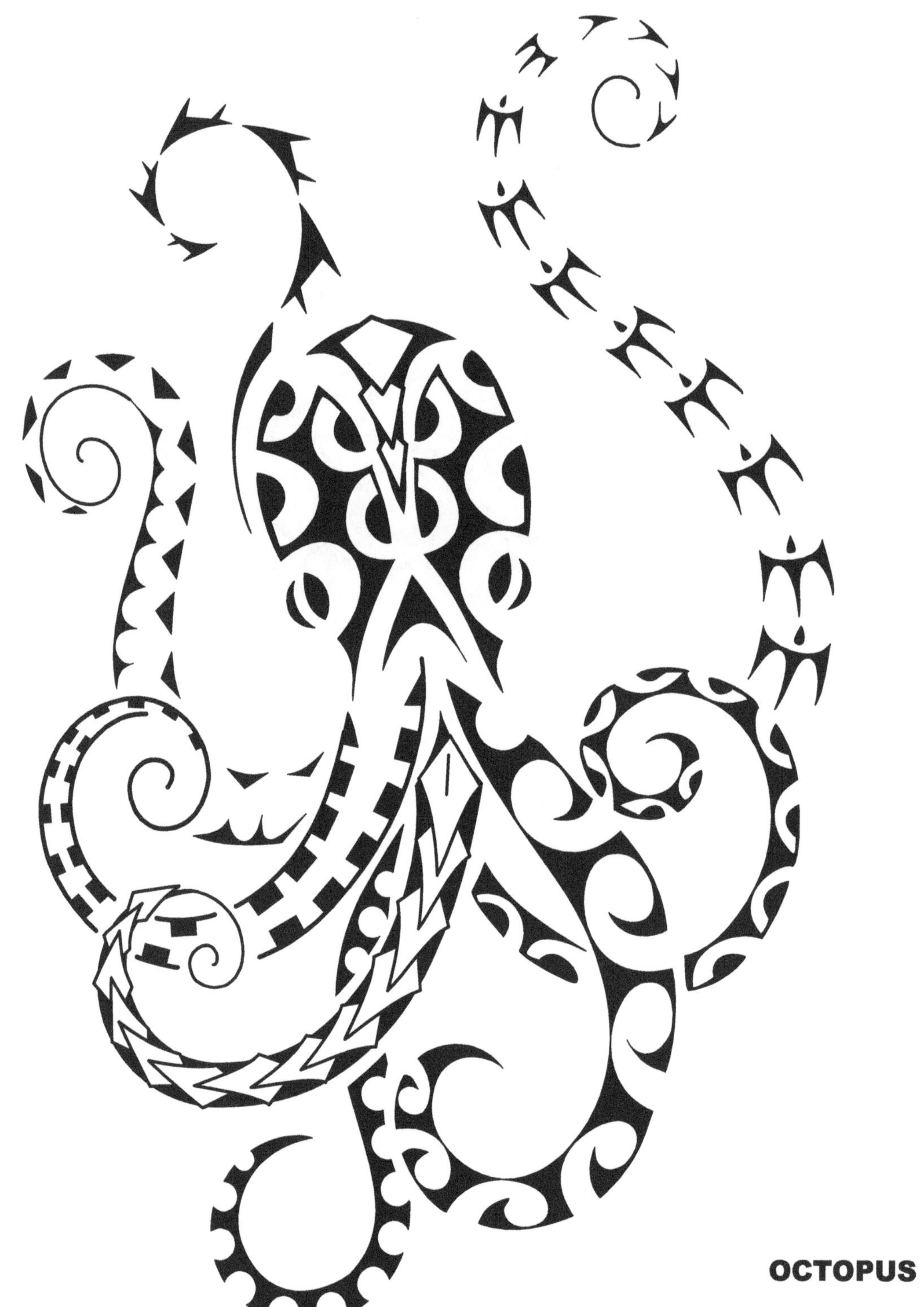

OCTOPUS

The octopus is a versatile creature. Master of camouflage, it is adaptable, intelligent and tenacious.

STENCIL: t076

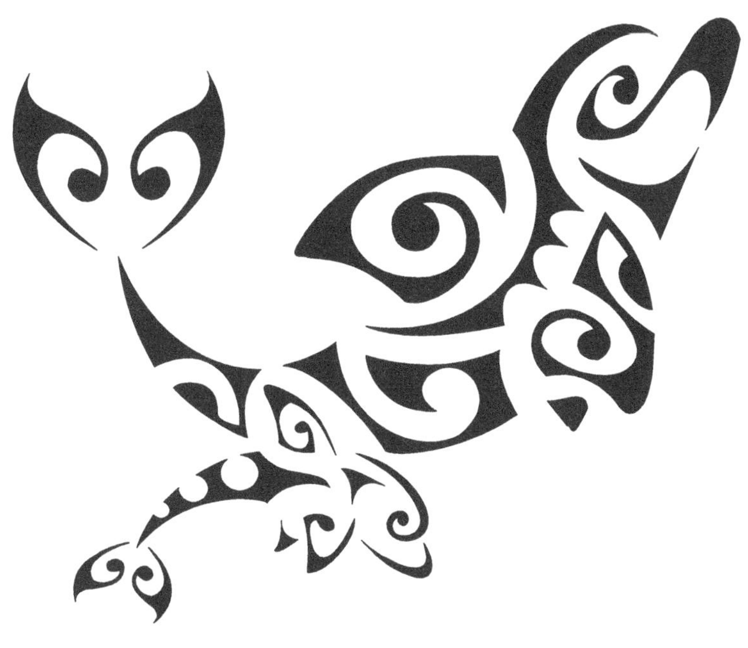

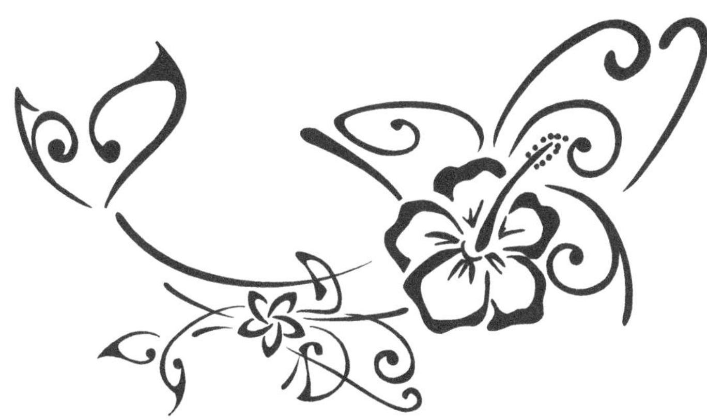

PARENT

Two versions of the same design,
one bolder and one more feminine,
to represent a parent fostering a child.

STENCIL: t077 - t078

BALANCE

The seahorse clings
to the kelp not to be carried away by the waves,
but it takes advantage of streams to move
without struggling against them.

STENCIL: t079

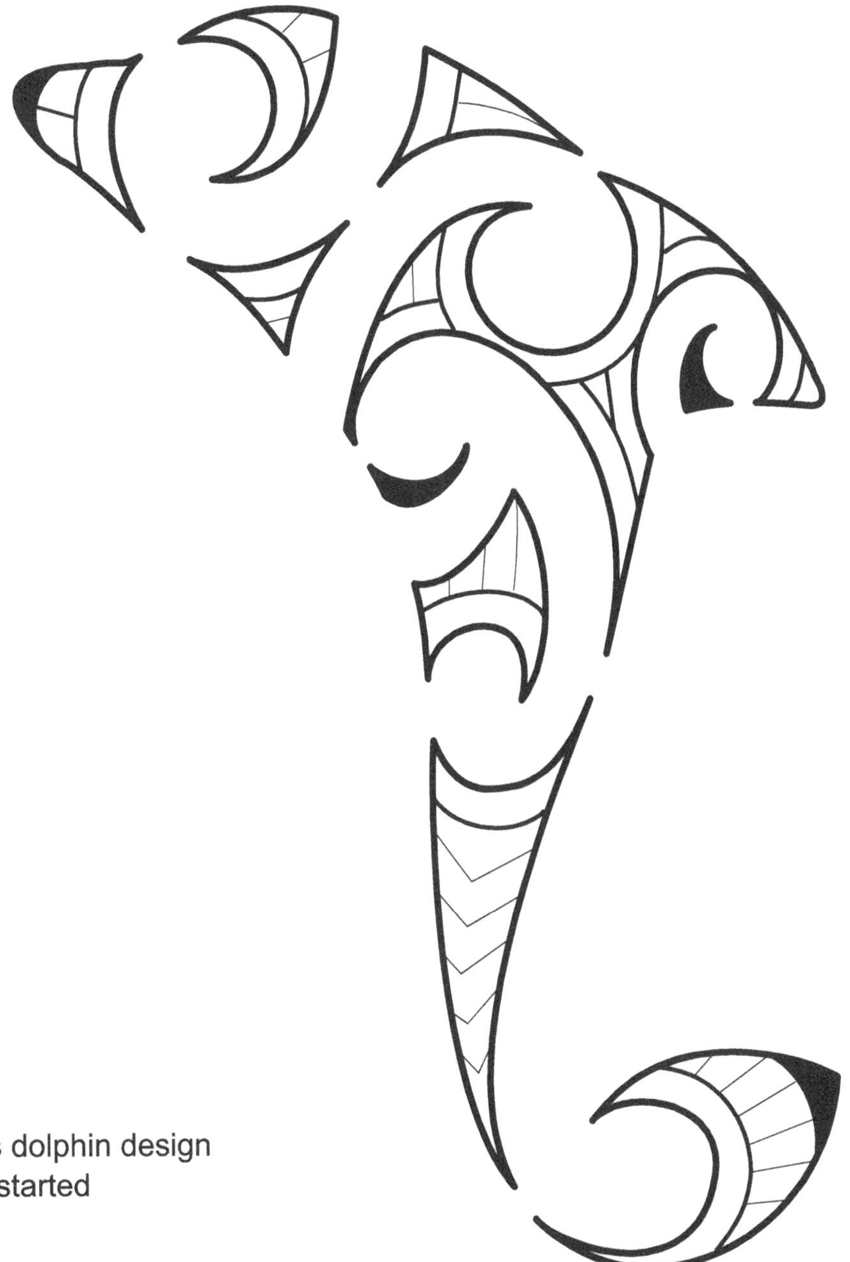

NEW LIFE

The korus in this dolphin design show a new life started from tenacity.

STENCIL: t080

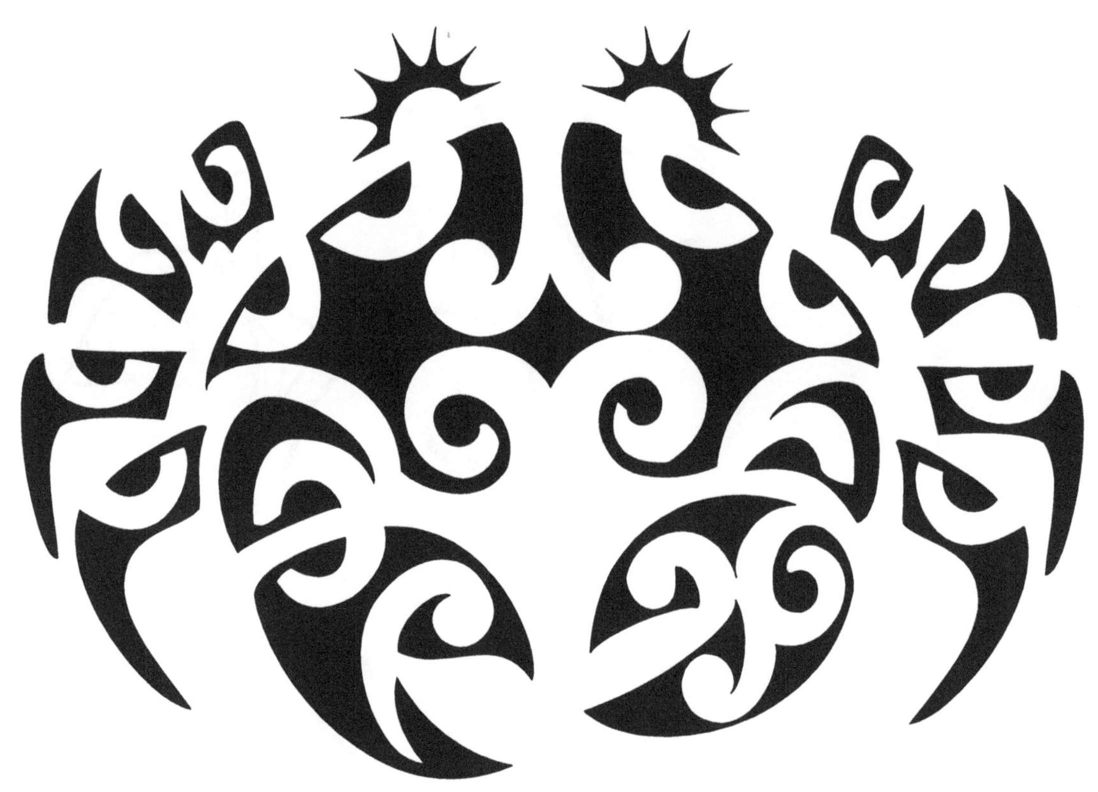

ACHIEVEMENTS

Protection, tenacity and determination
to reach prosperity and joy
through changes.

STENCIL: t081

CUTTLEFISH

Small Maori styled cuttlefish representing tenacity.

STENCIL: t082

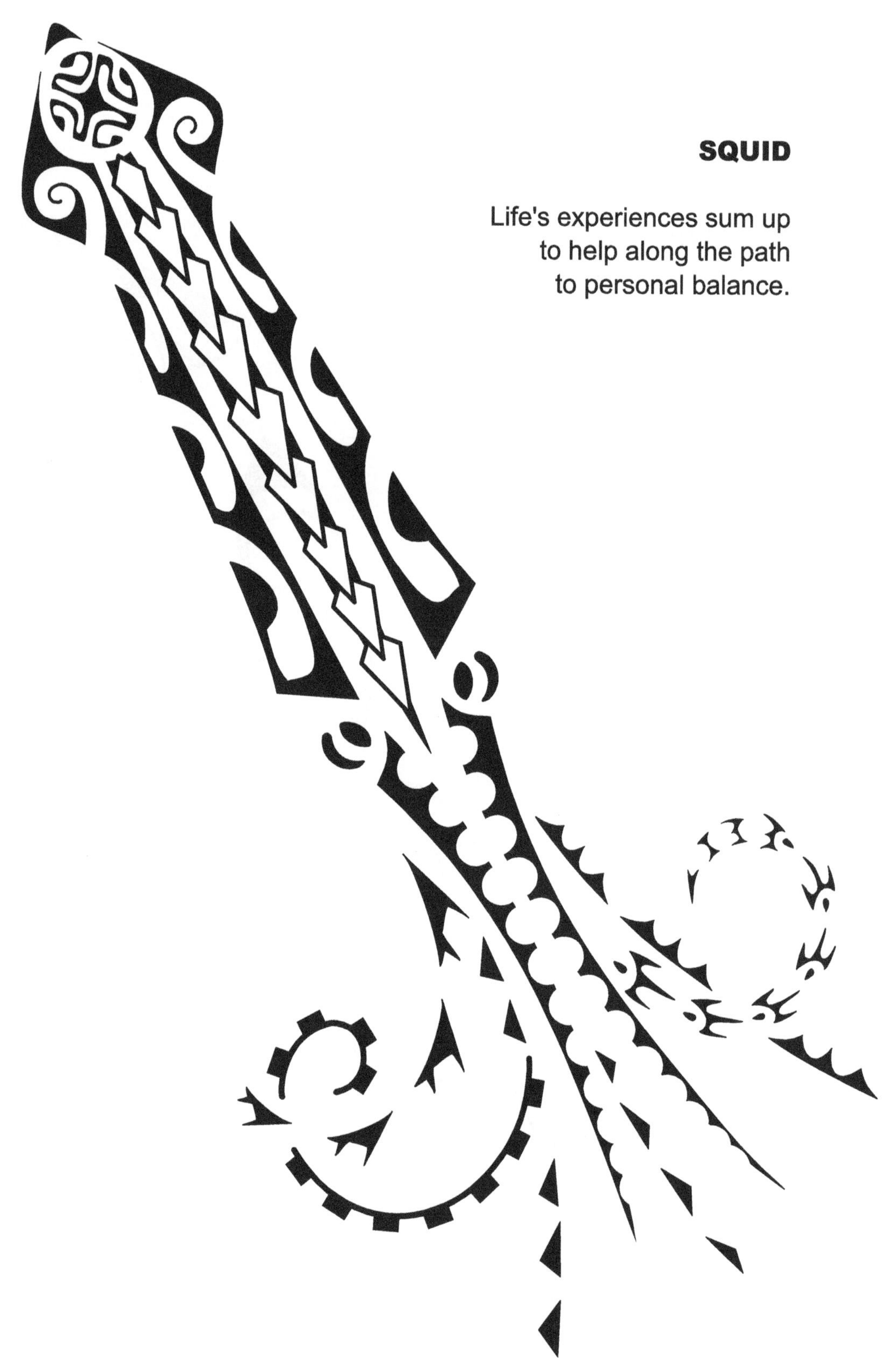

SQUID

Life's experiences sum up
to help along the path
to personal balance.

STENCIL: t083

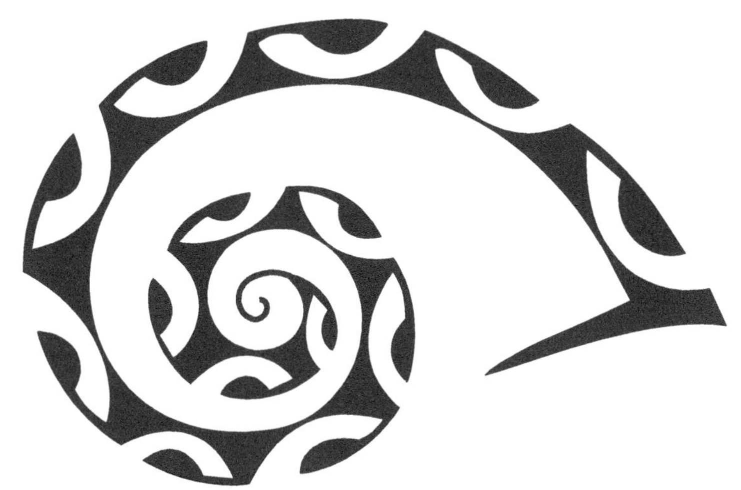

SEA SHELLS

Sea shells simbolyze intimacy, safe shelter, prosperity.

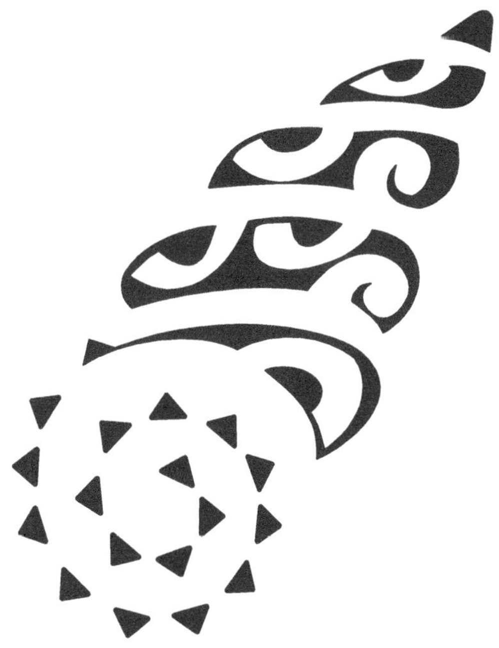

STENCIL: t084 - t085

VOYAGER

The path to knowledge is never easy, never straight, but it's always worth taking the risk of leaving on such a voyage.

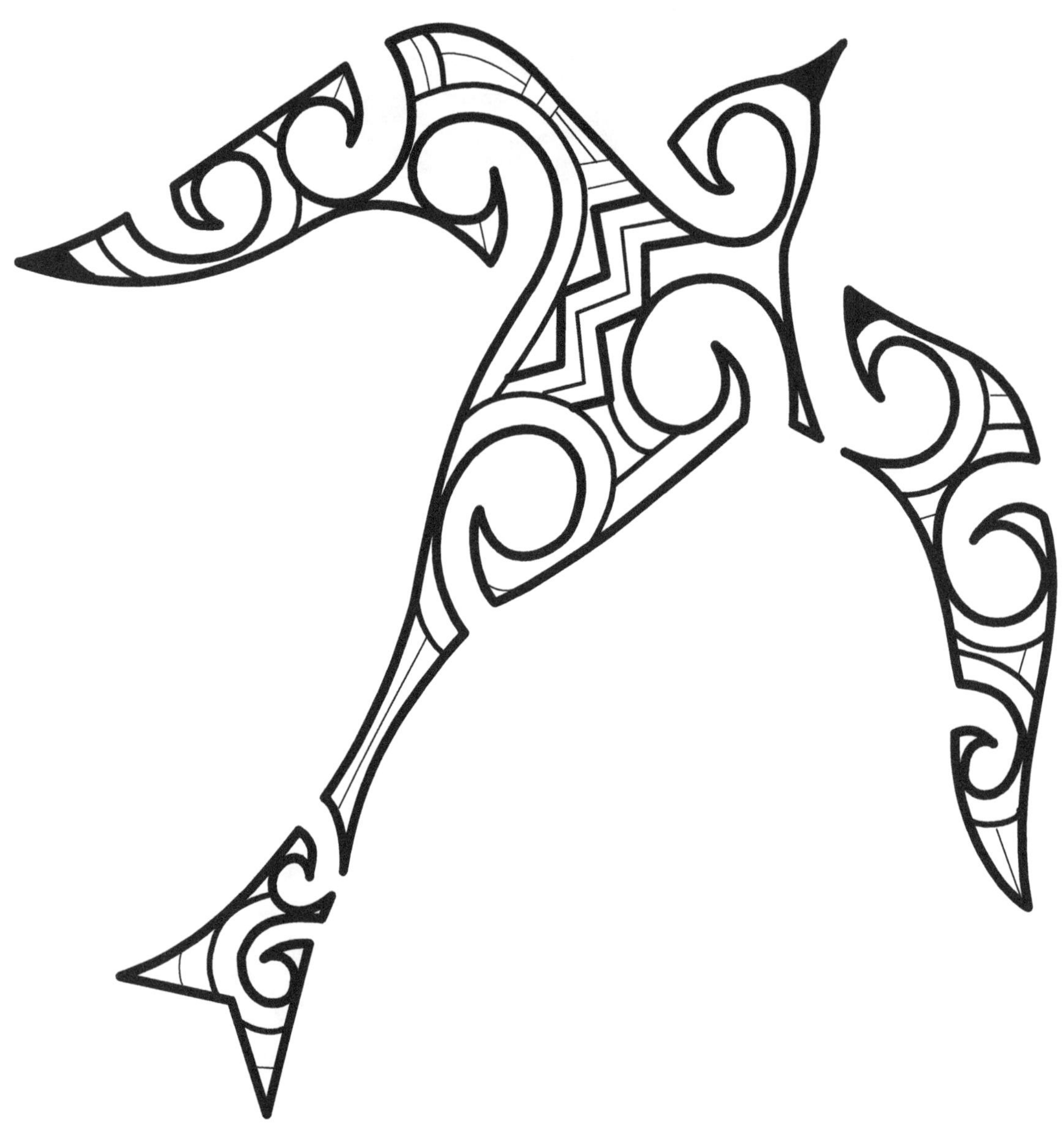

STENCIL: t086

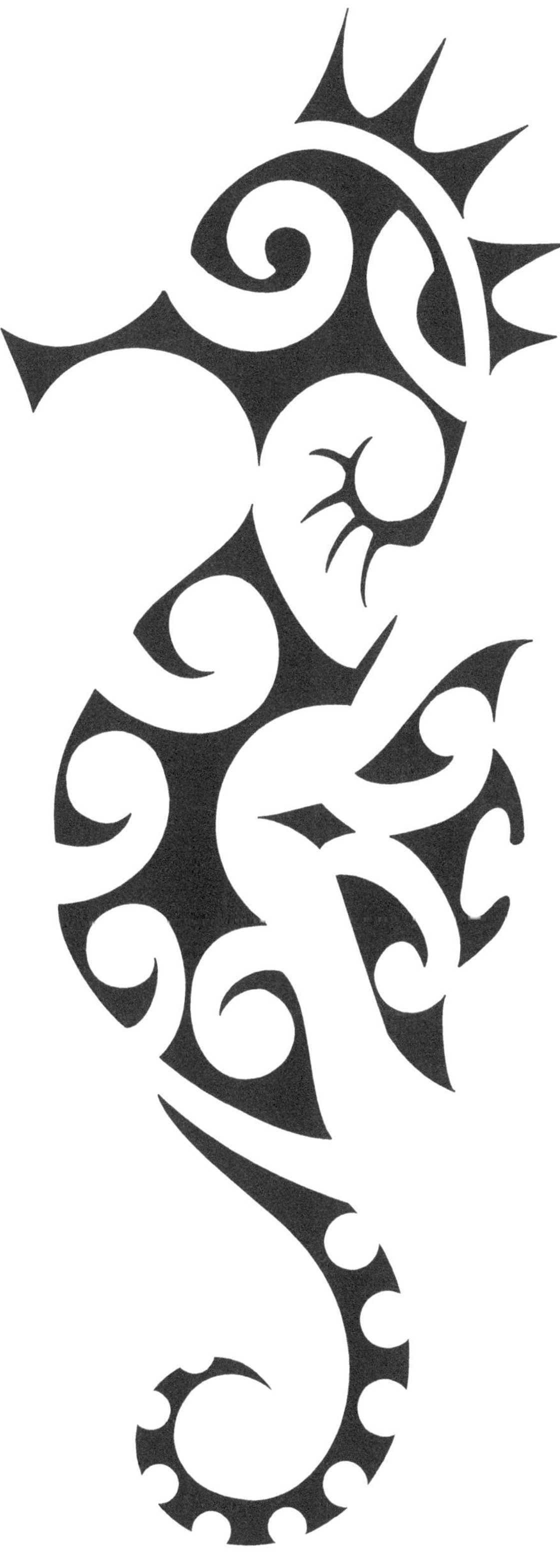

LOVE

Love requires patience, tenacity and adaptability and the prize is freedom.

STENCIL: t087

PROTECTED

The tiki among the waves on the shell of this crab is a symbol of protection among changes.

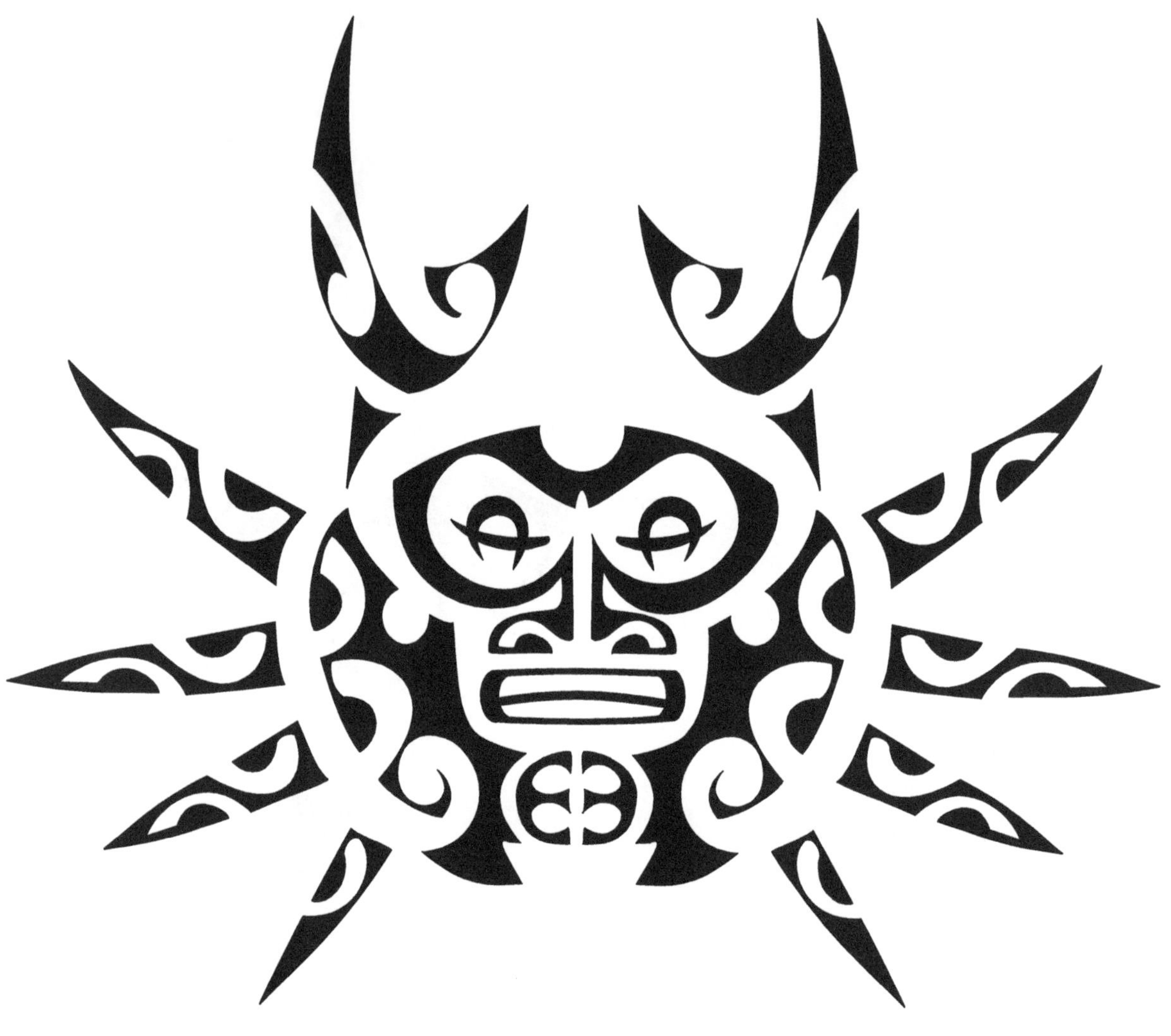

STENCIL: t088

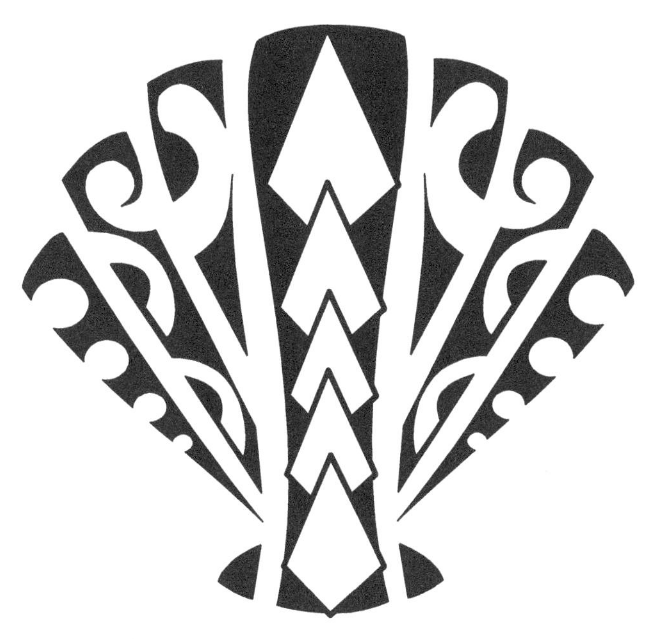

FEMININITY

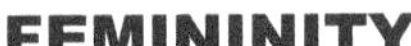

Bivalve shells are symbols of femininity. Secondary meanings are strength for the shell on top and fertility for the other.

STENCIL: t089 - t090

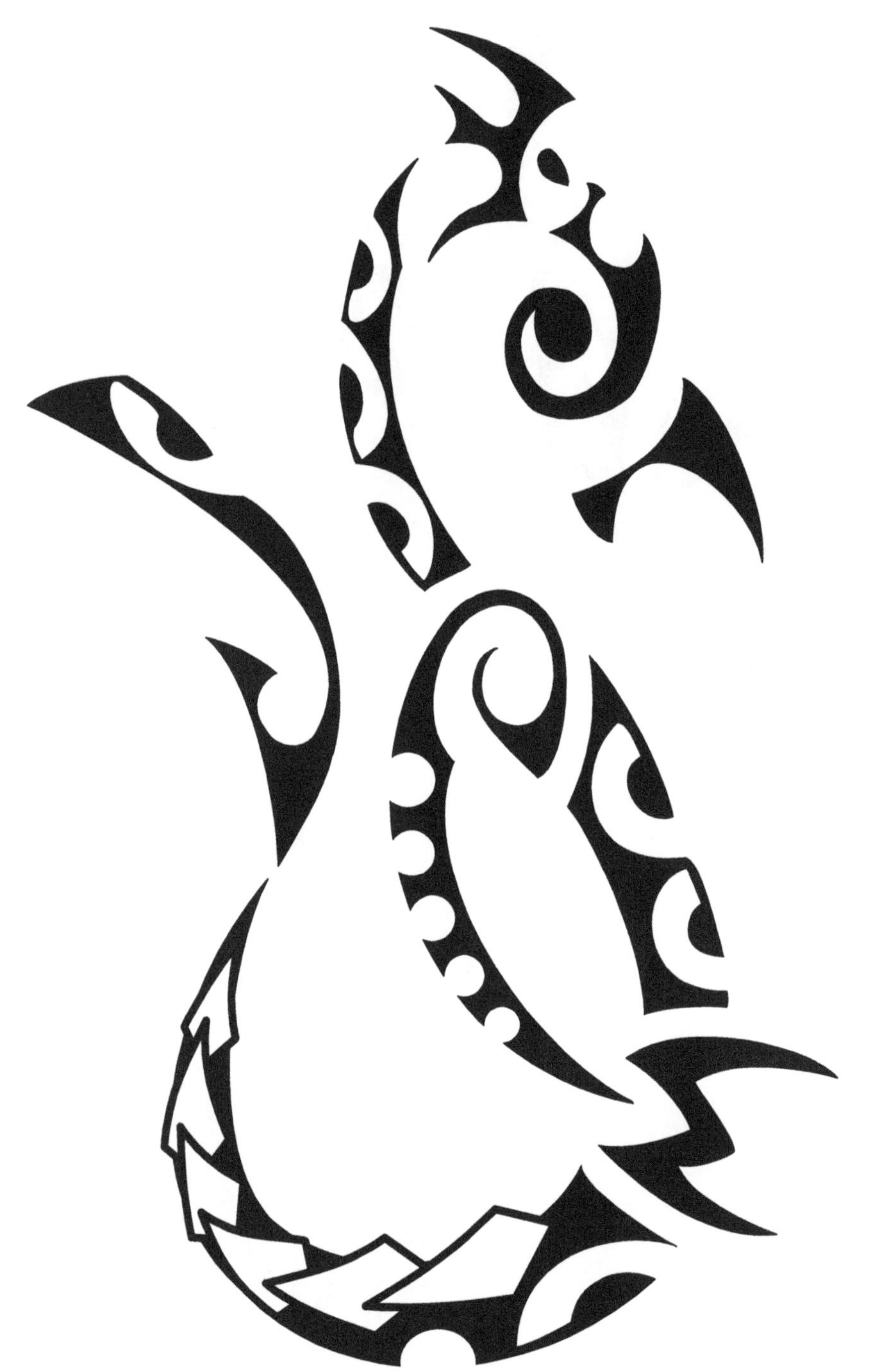

ANCESTOR

The manaia is a deified ancestor protecting the family.

STENCIL: t091

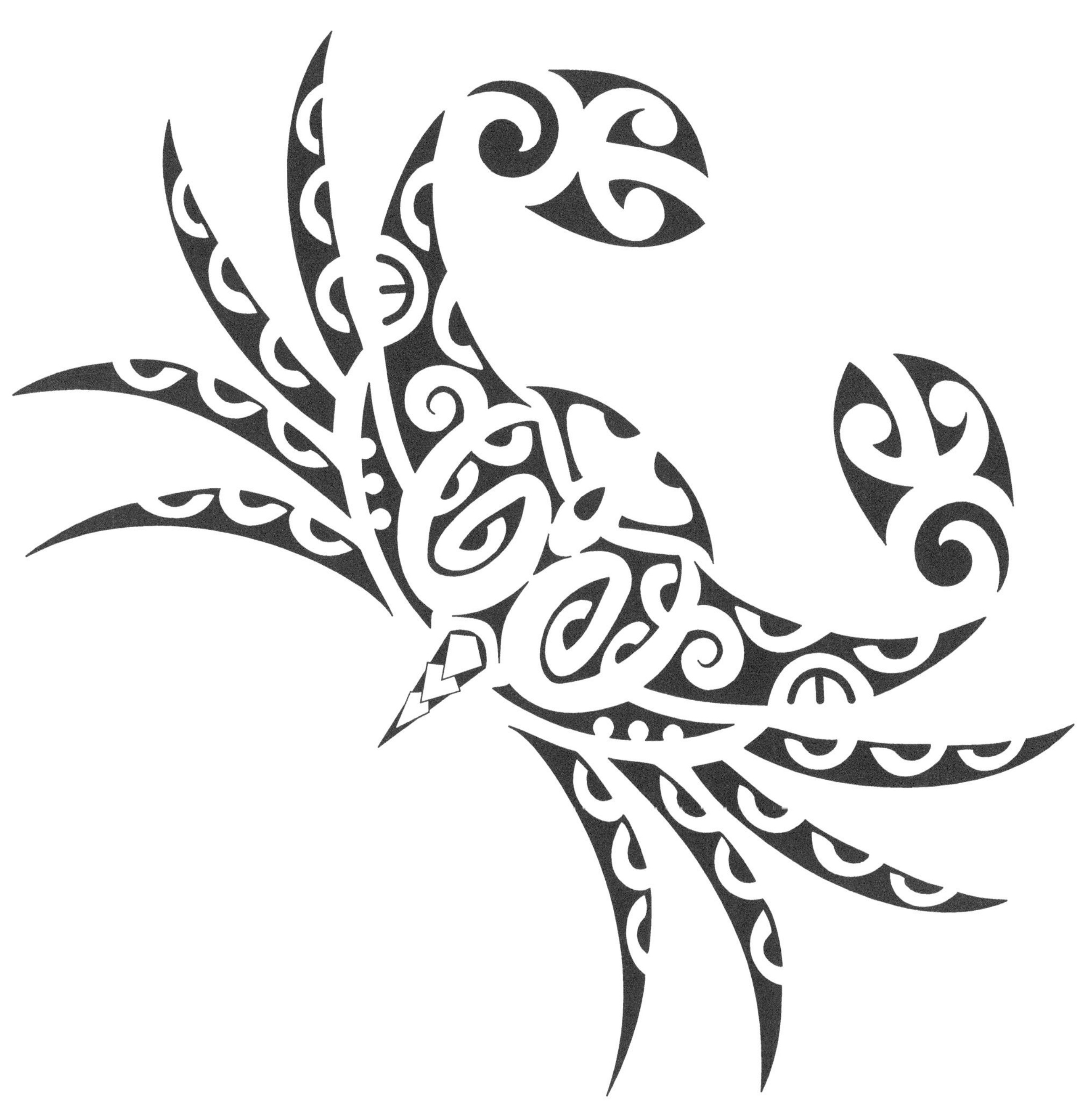

FREEDOM

This crab is formed by a manta swimming through the waves, representing freedom and changes.

STENCIL: t092

t001

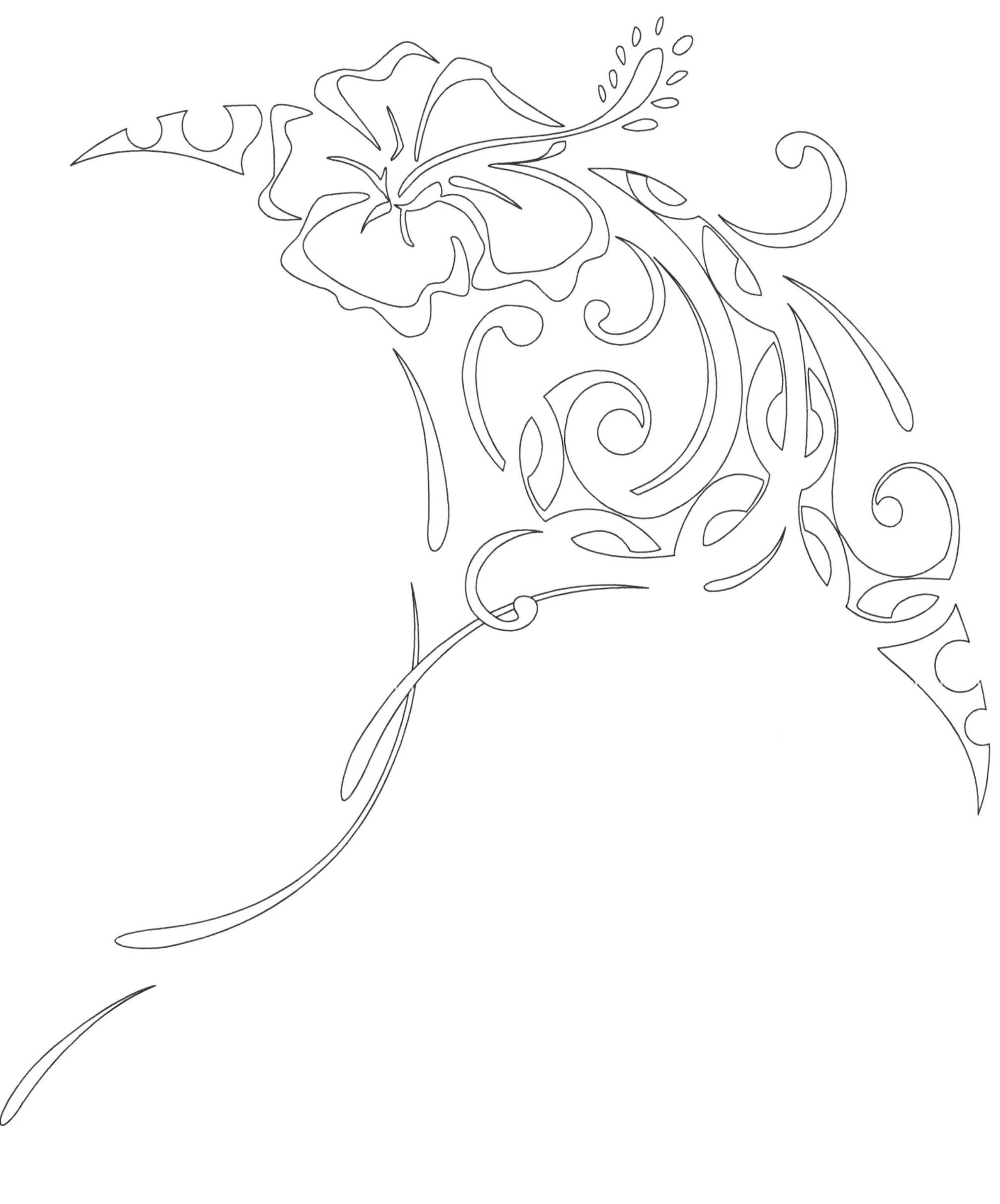

t002

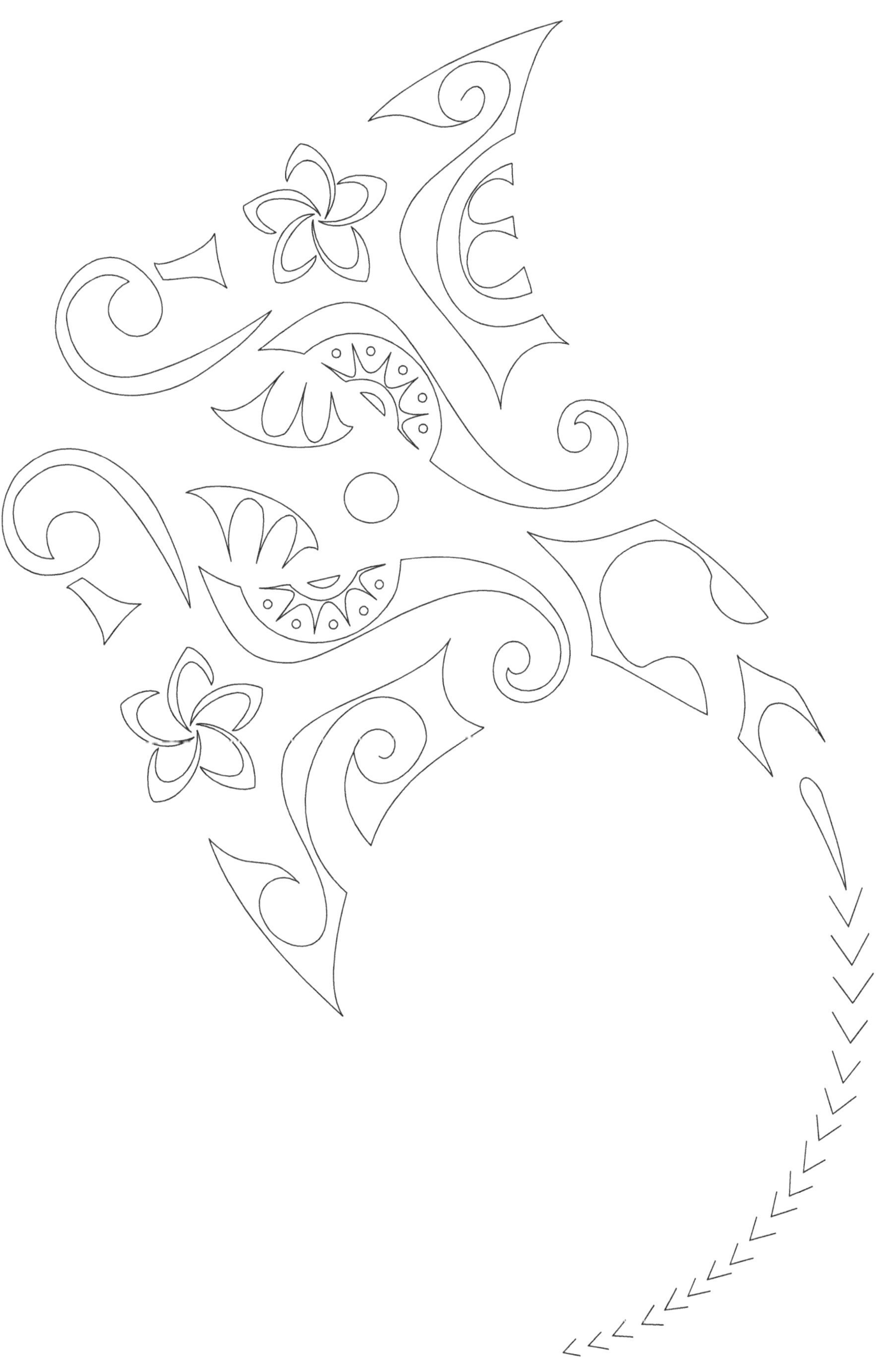

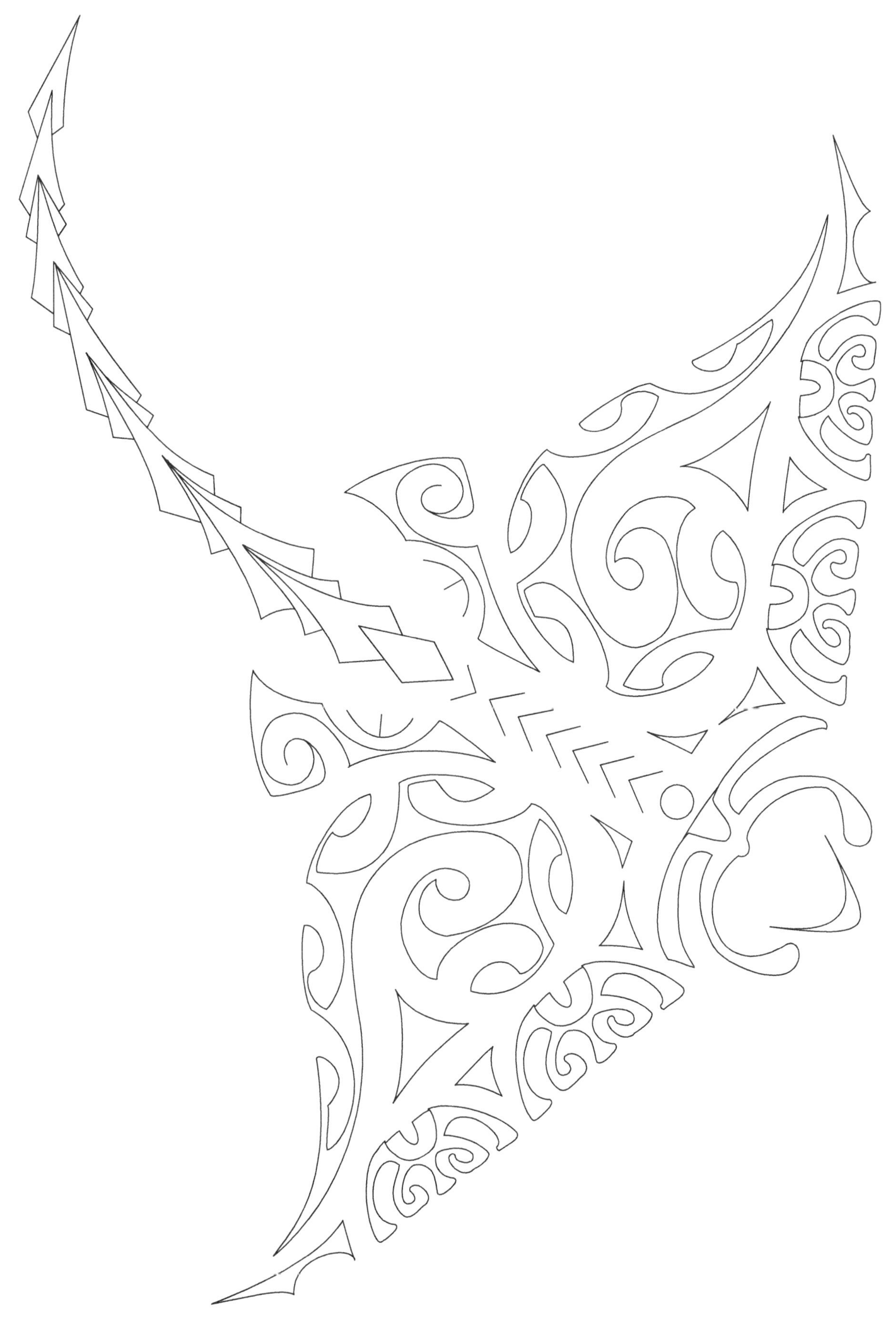

t004

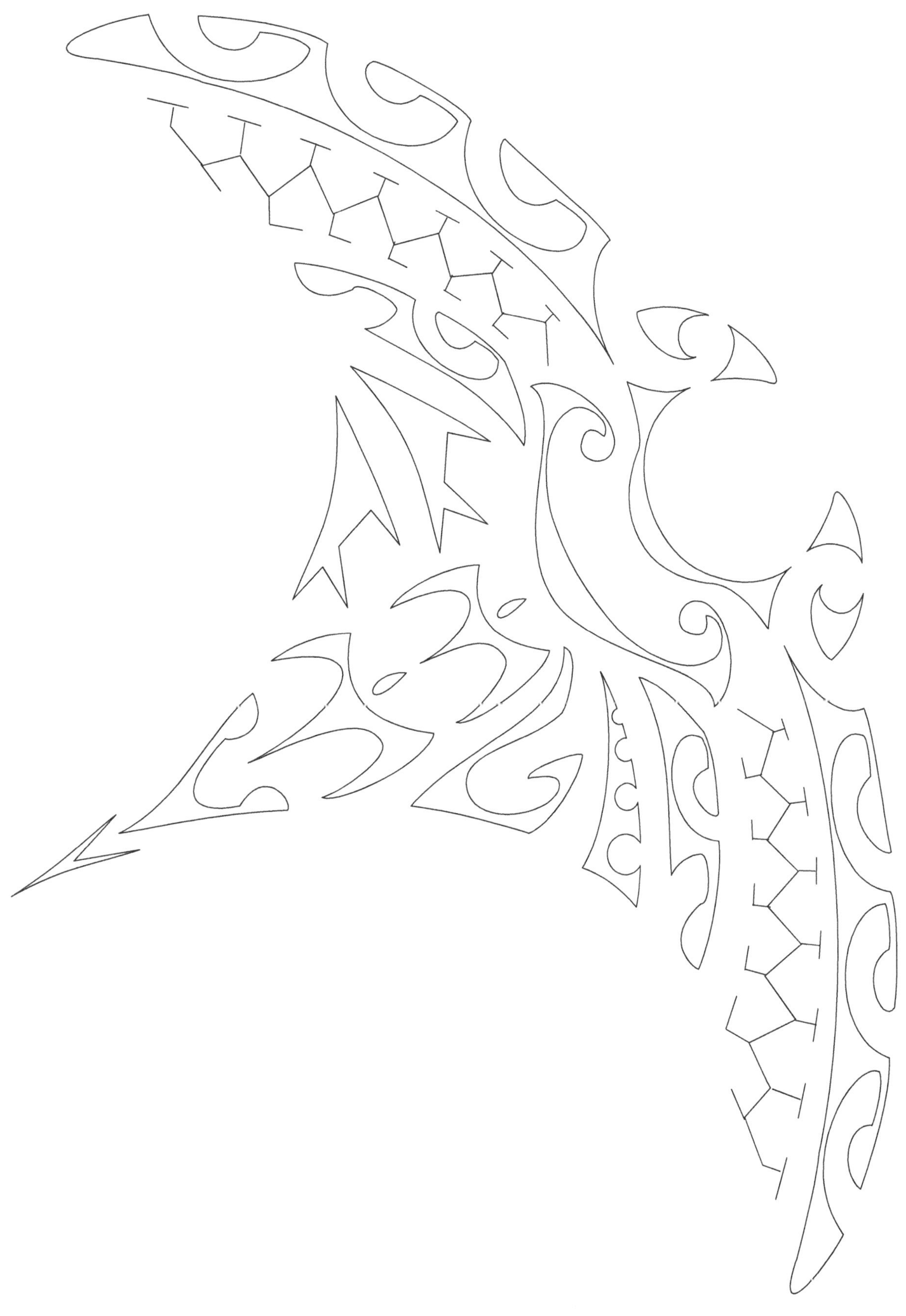

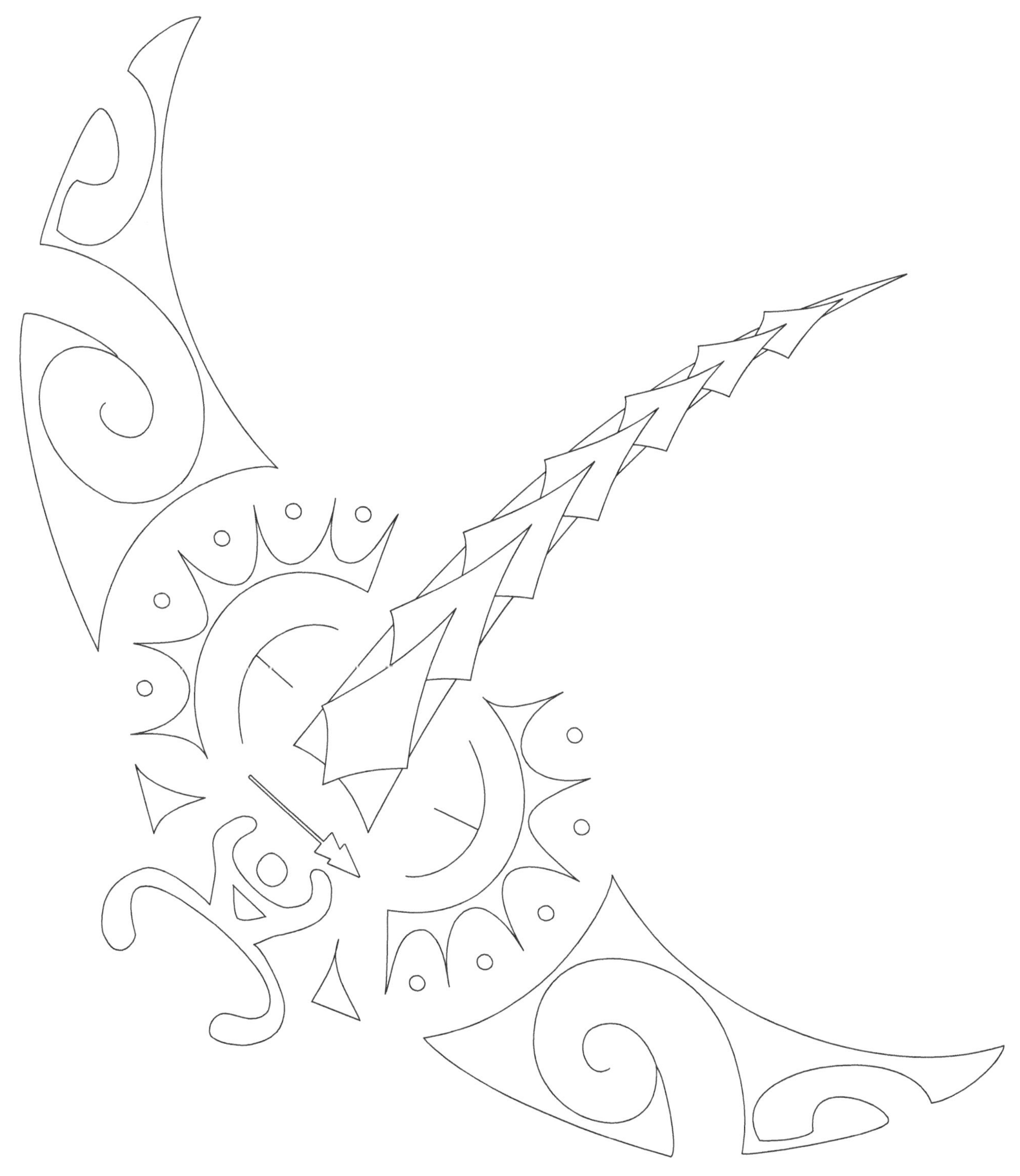

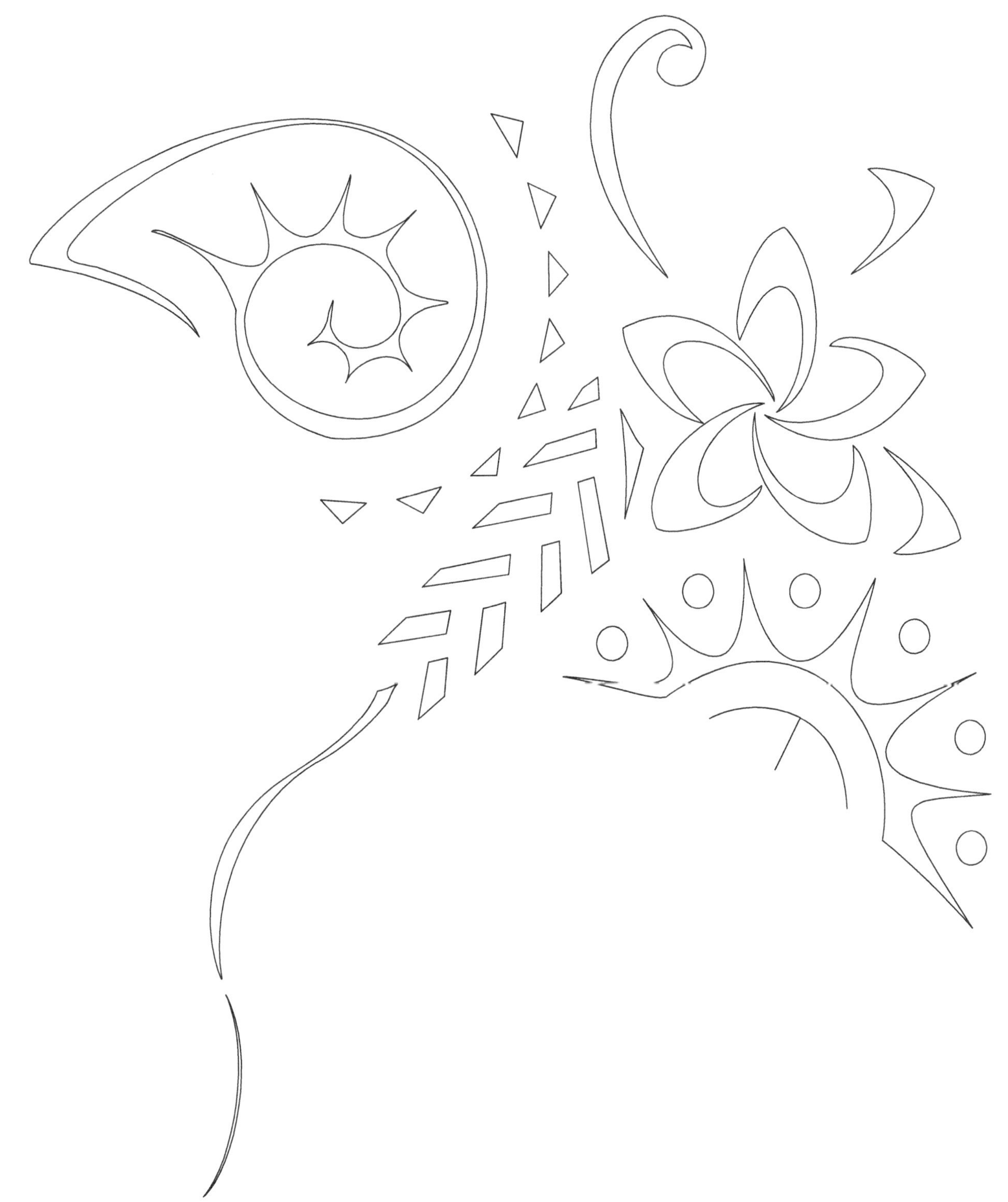

t008

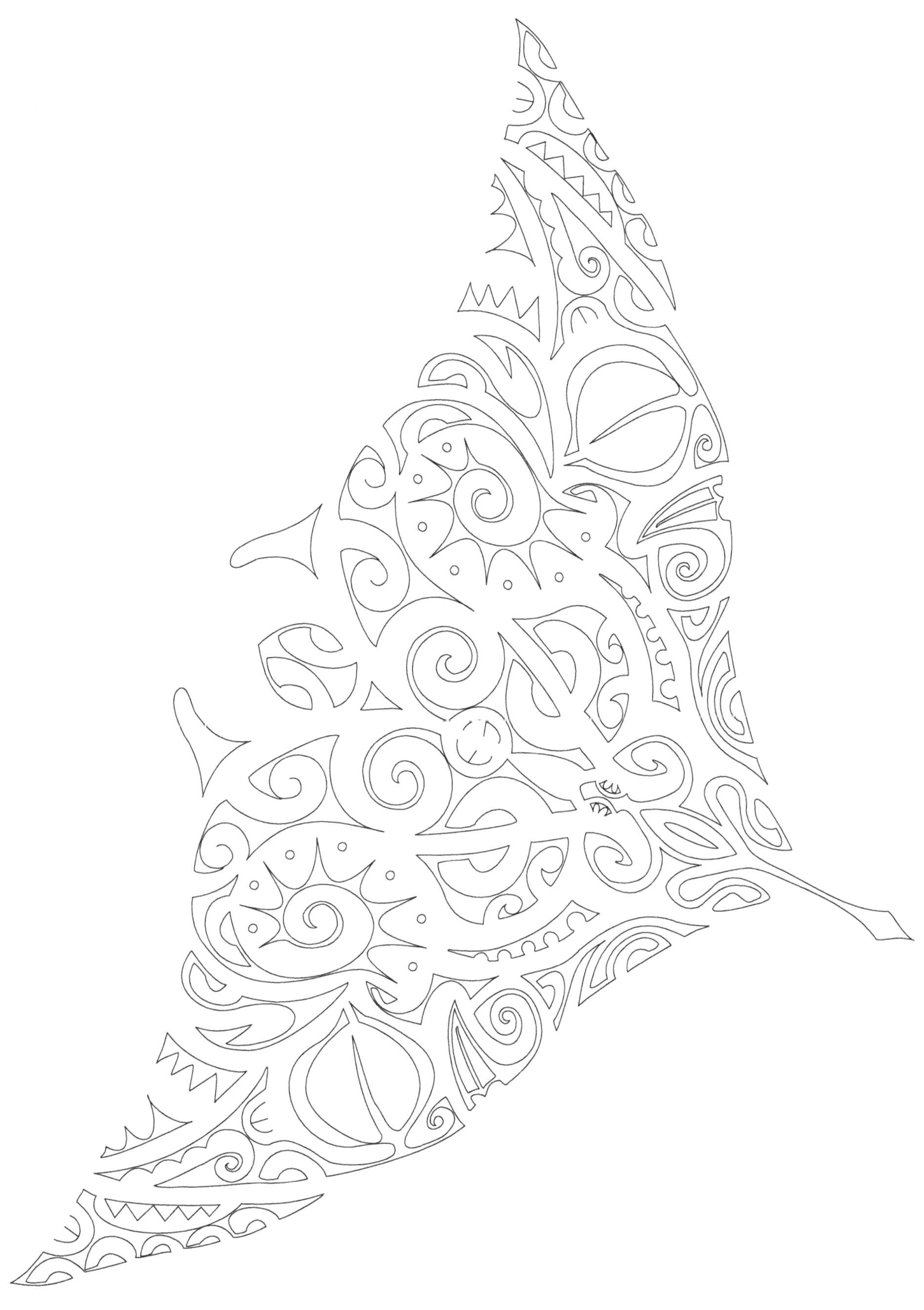

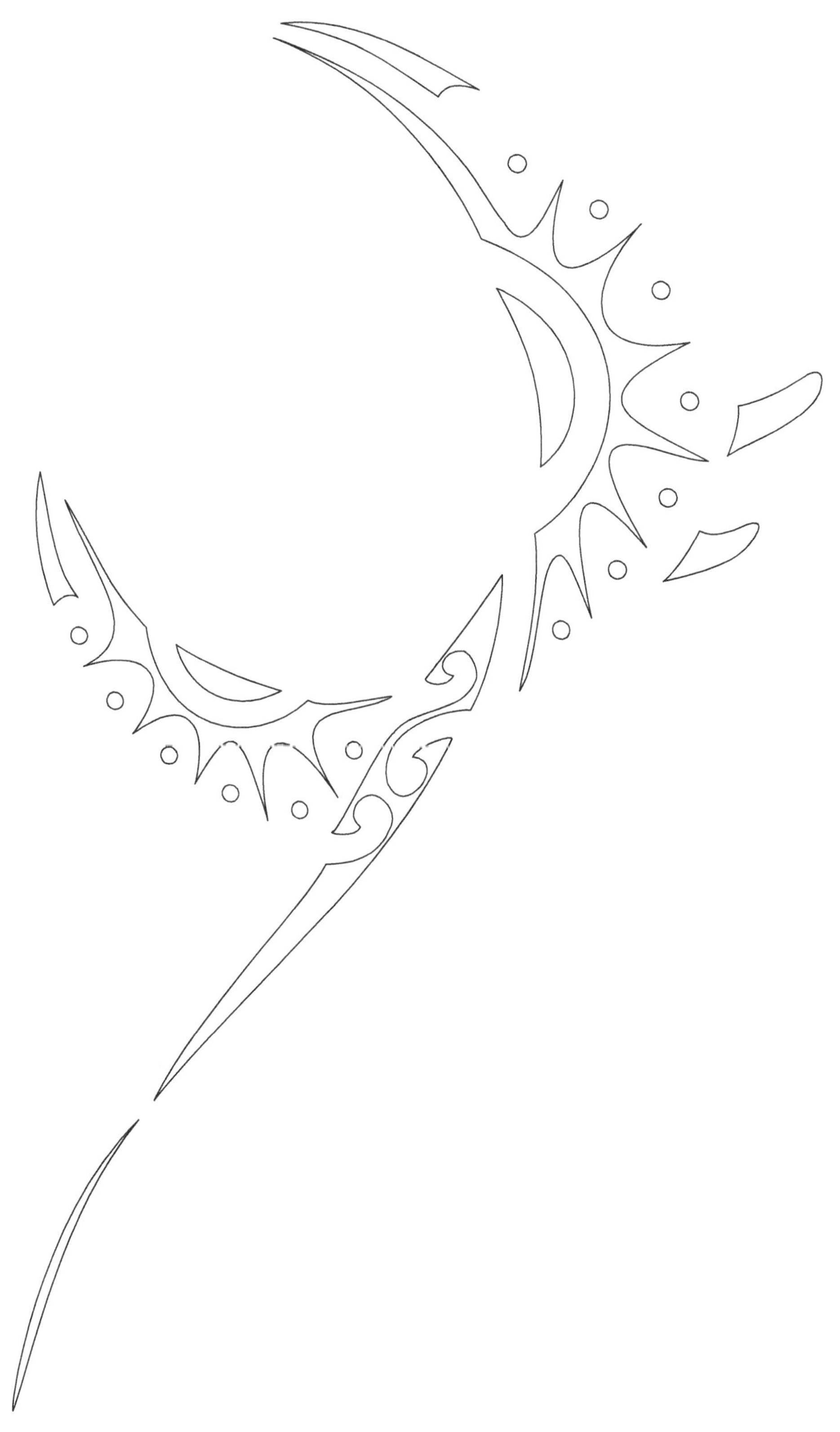

t010

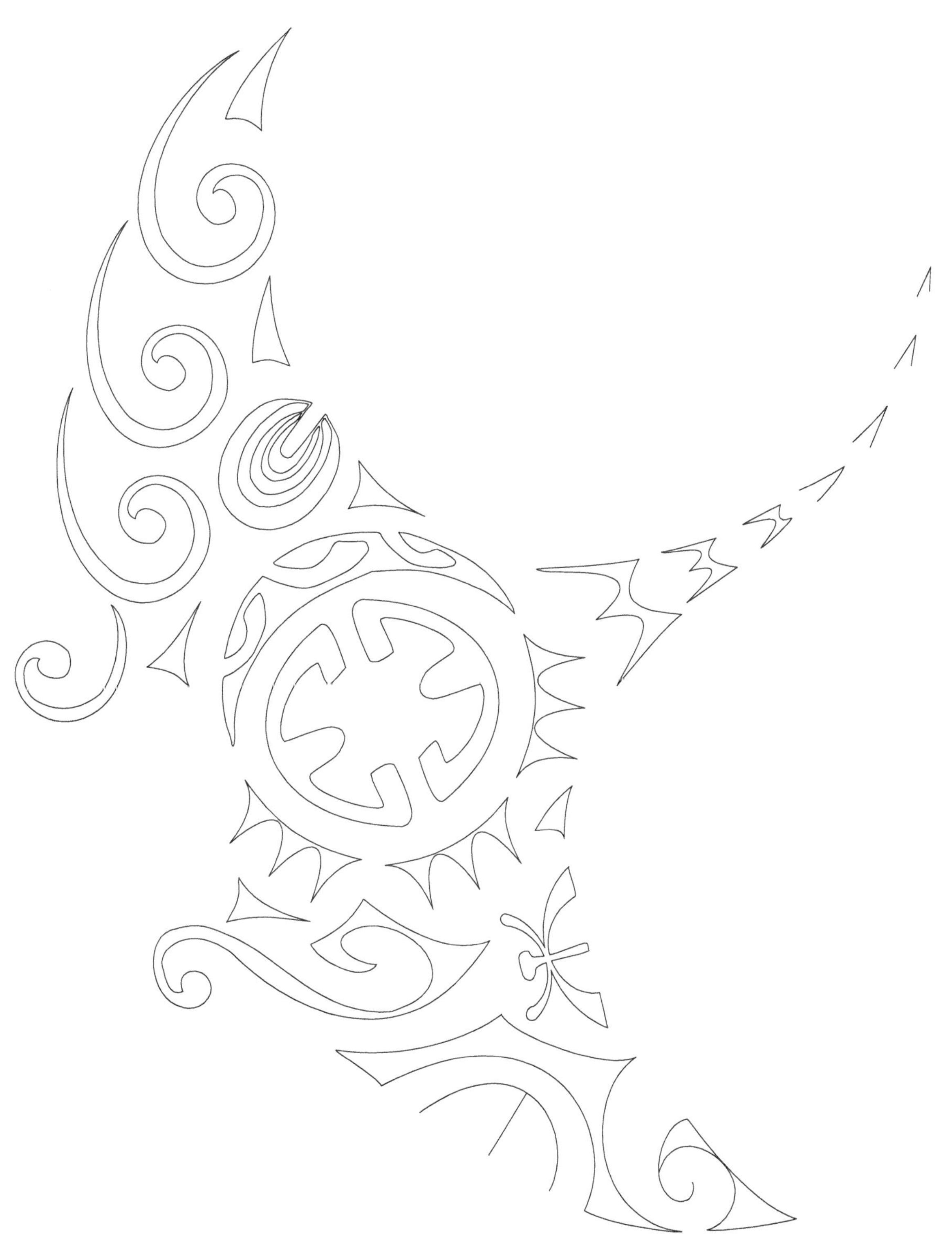

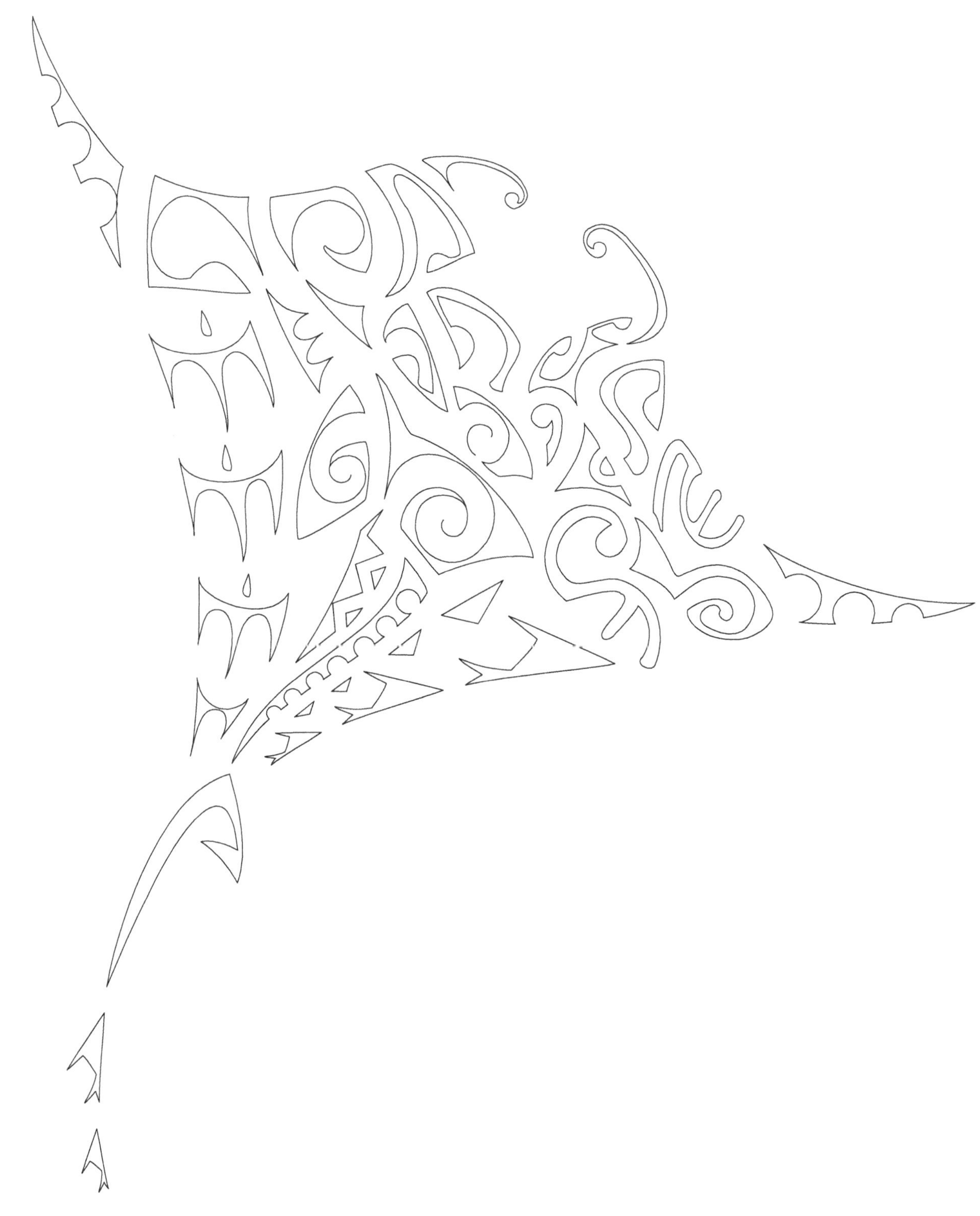

t012

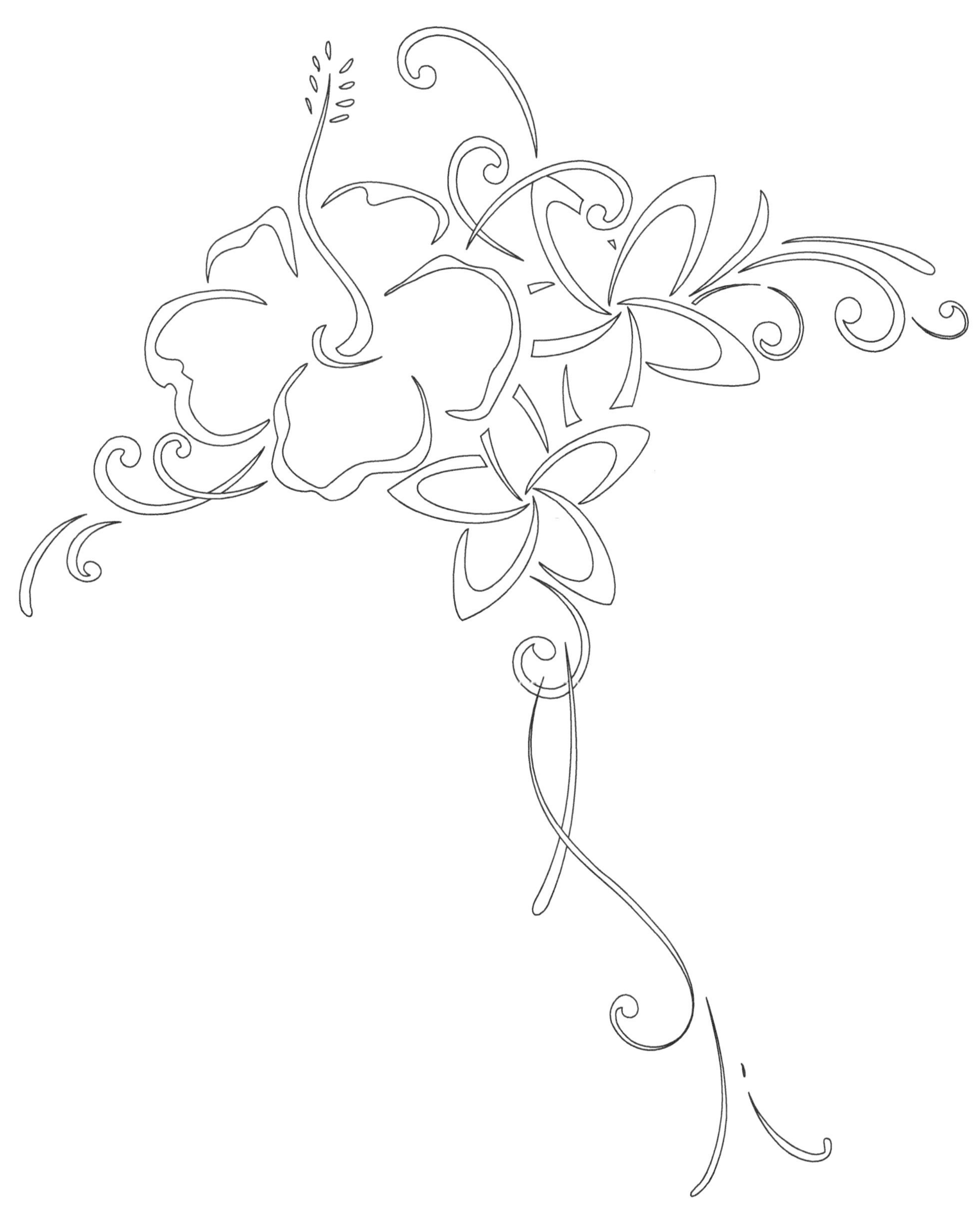

t014

t015

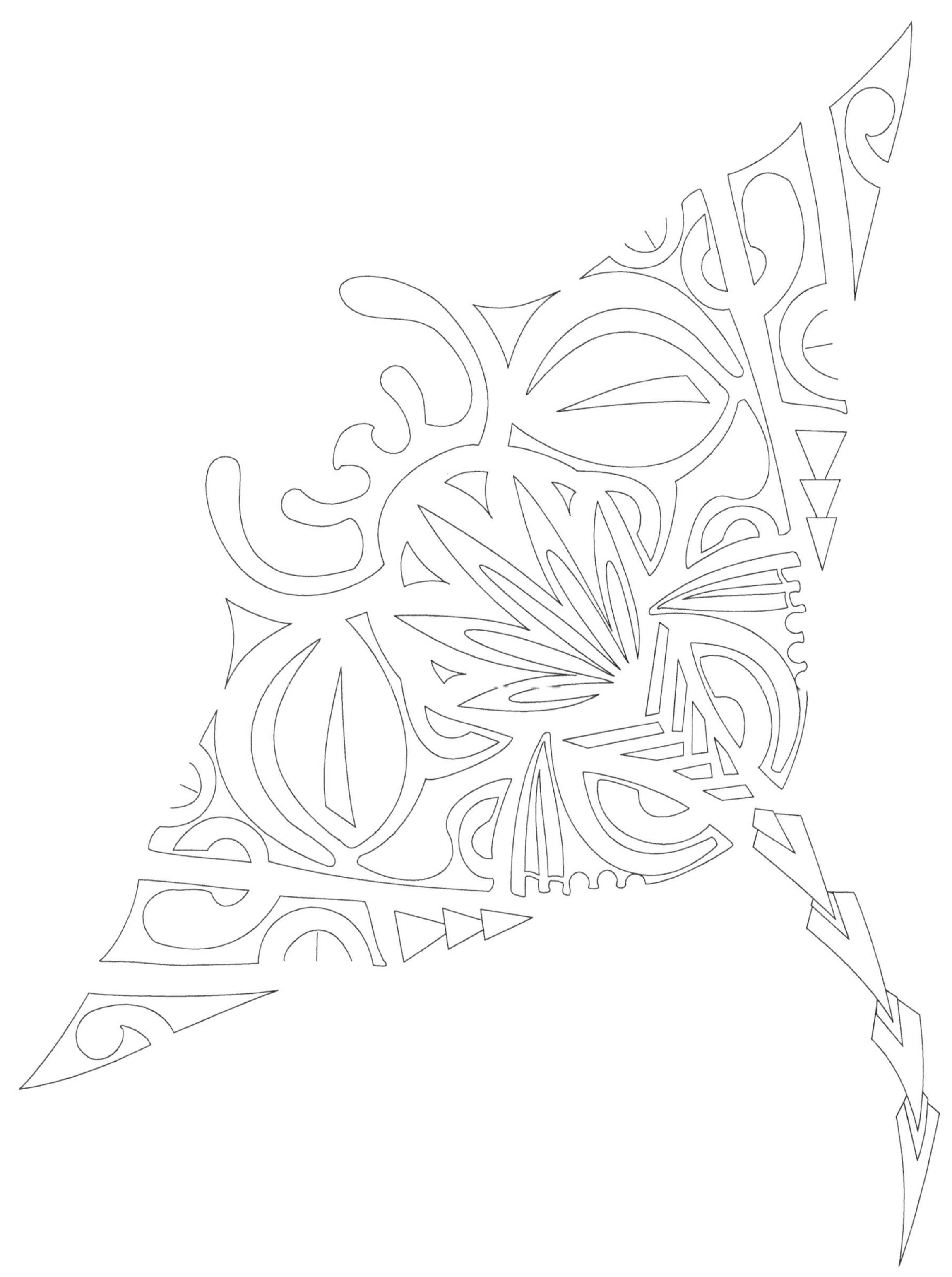

t016

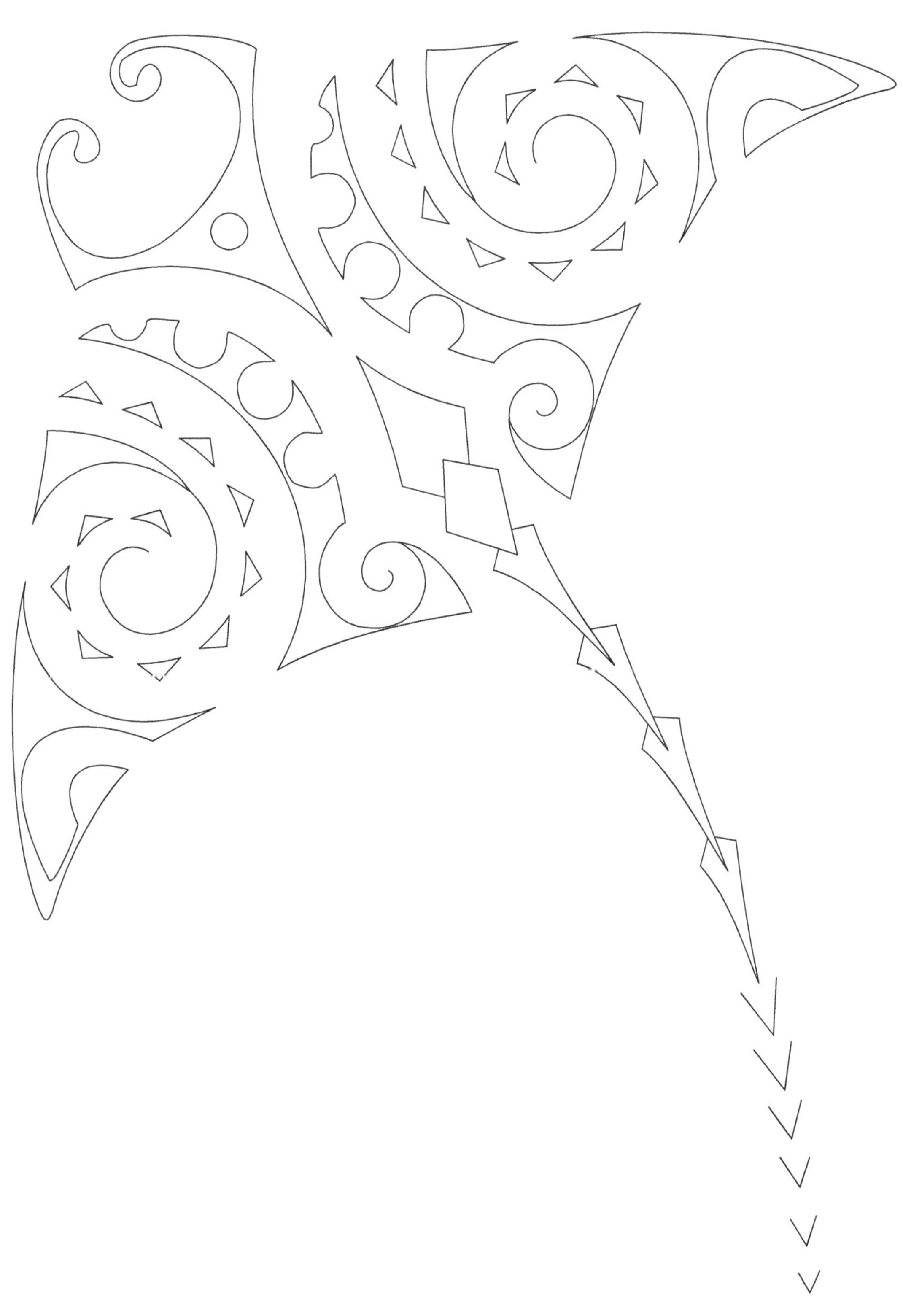

t017

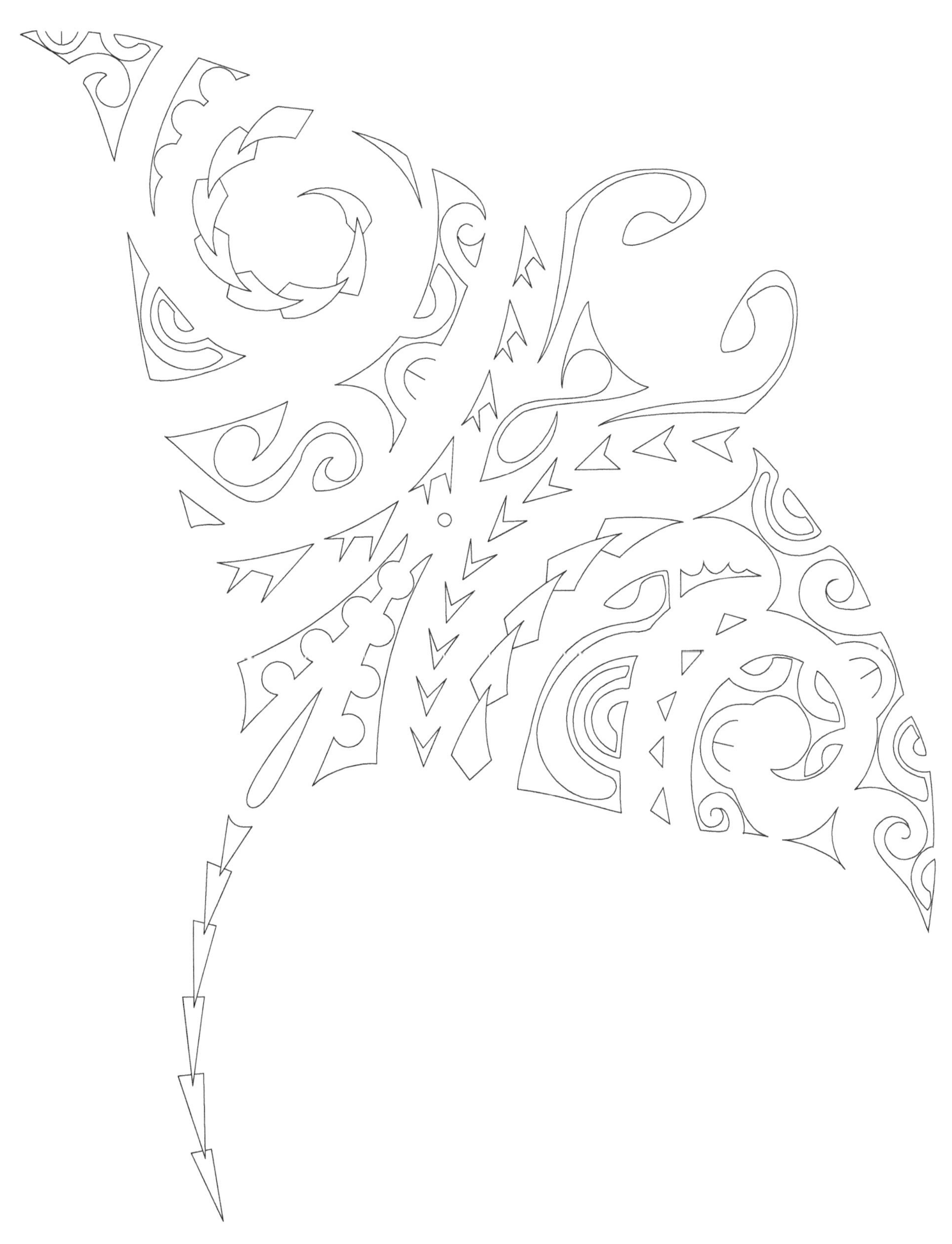

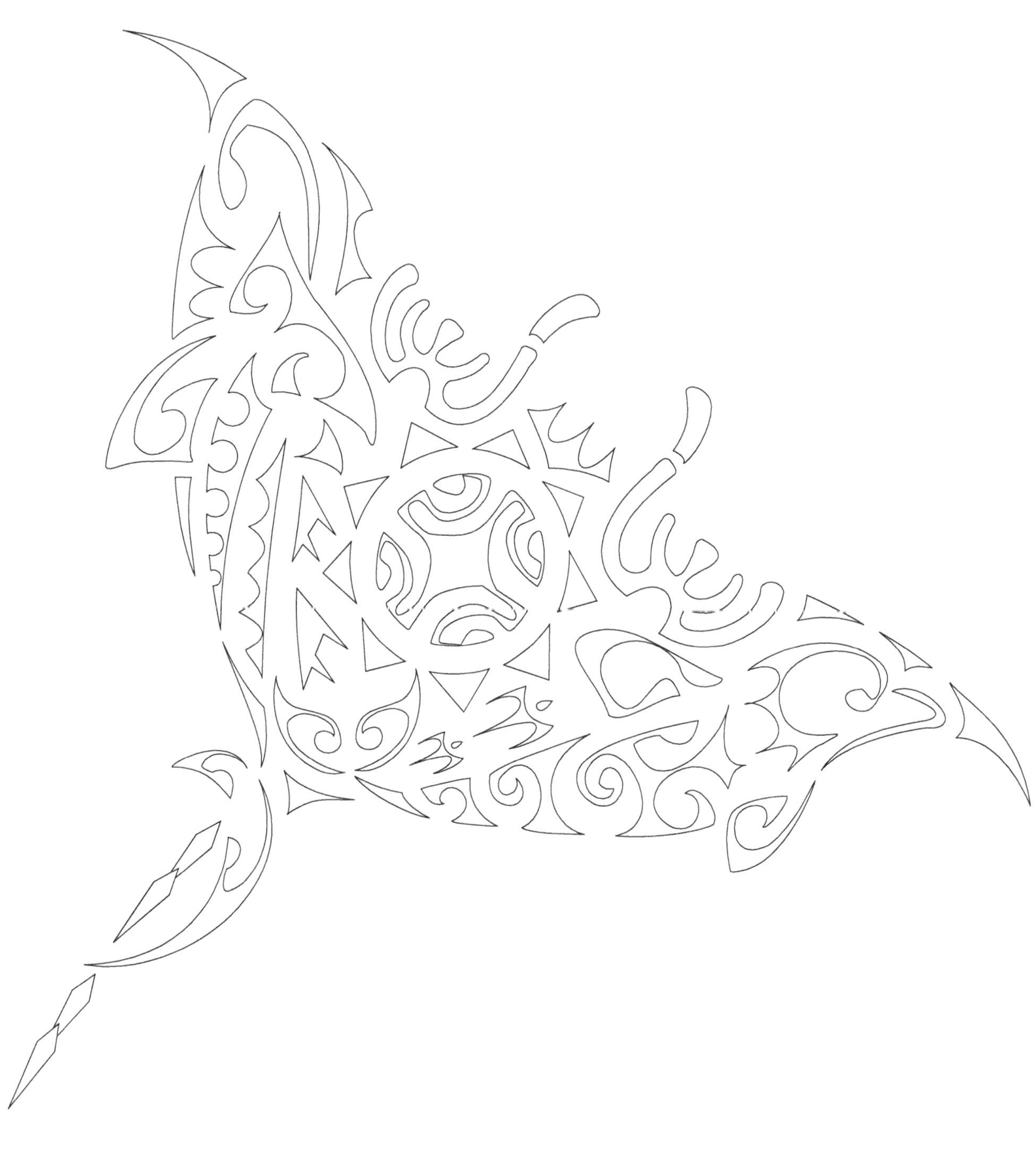

t020

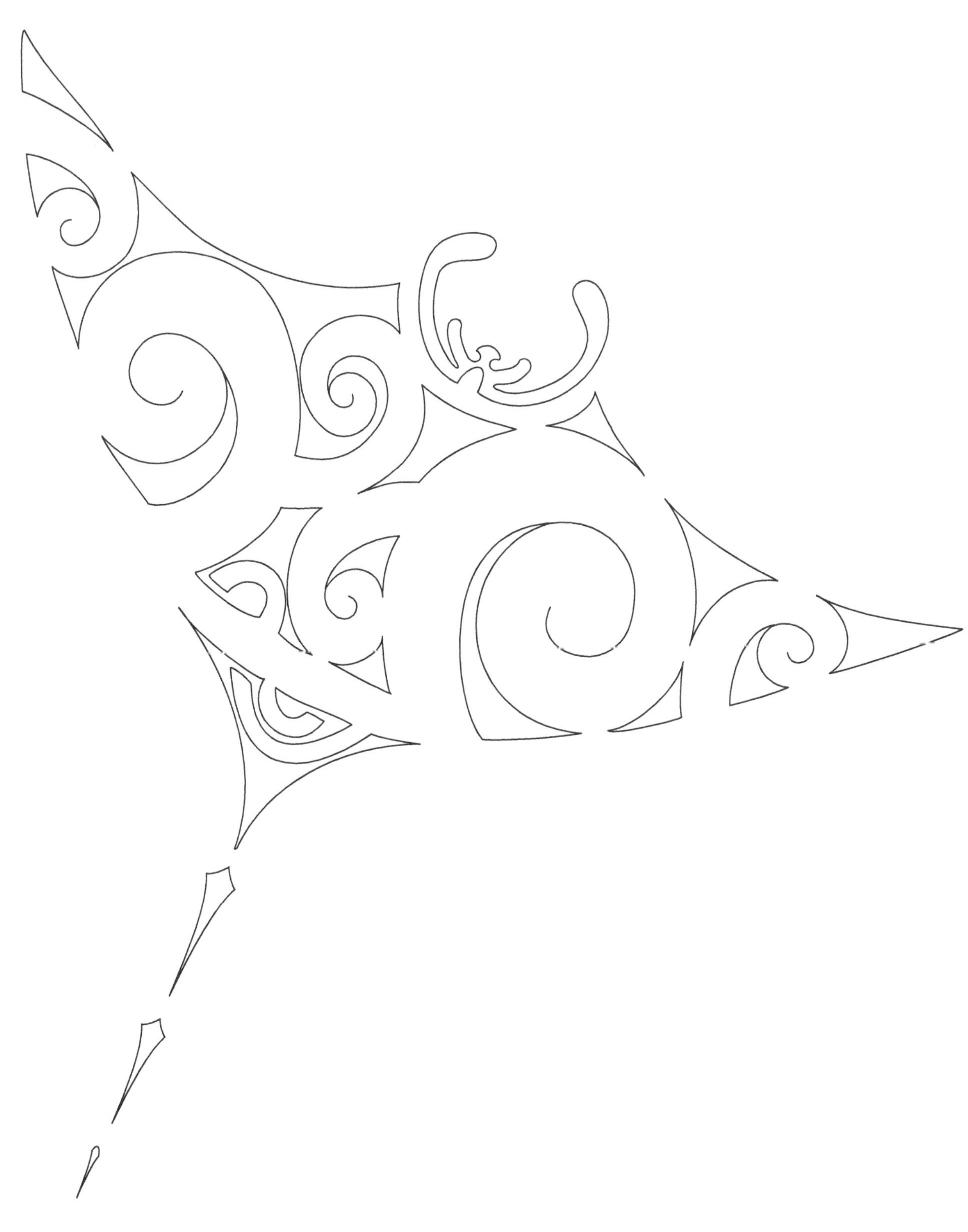

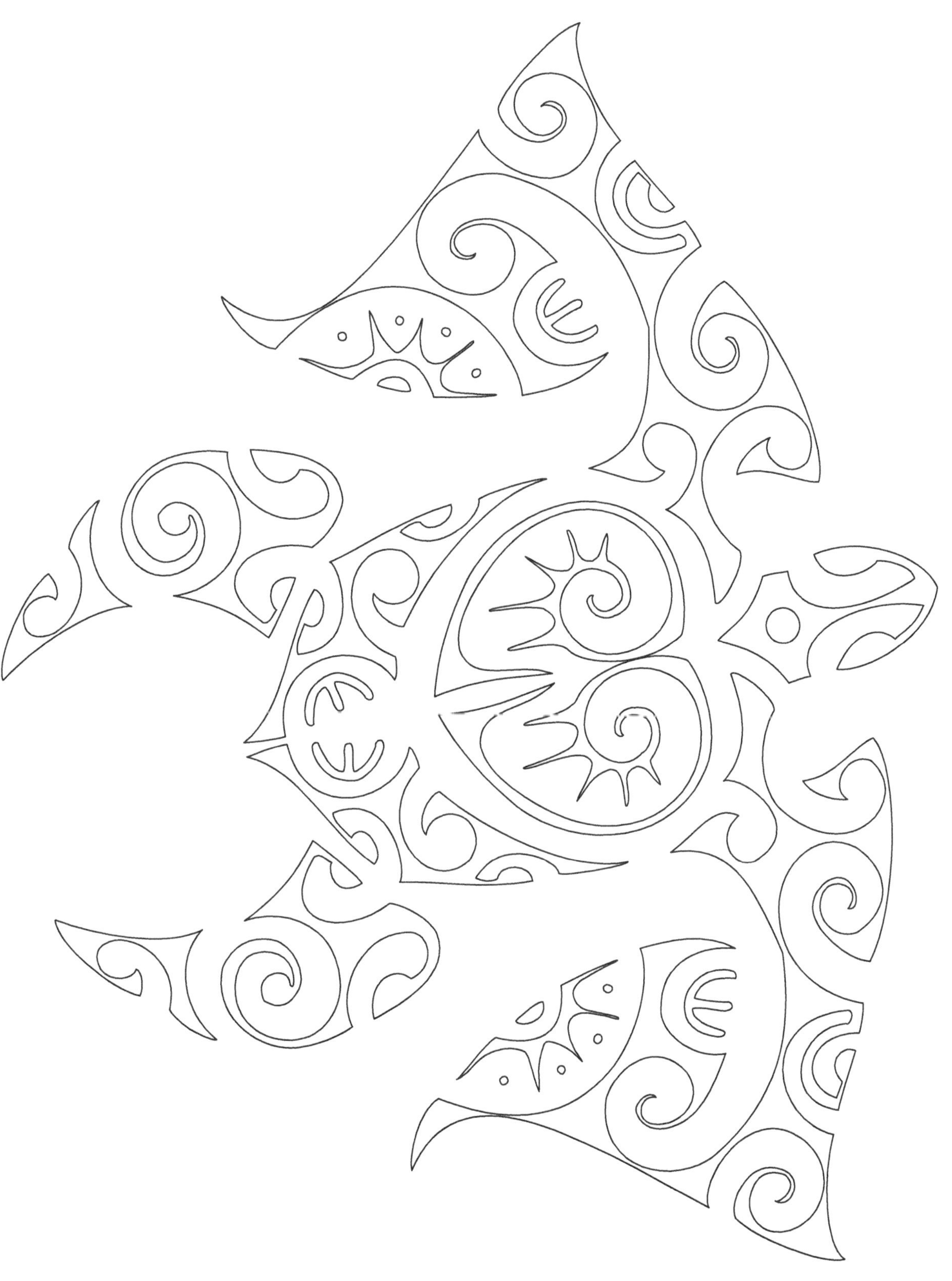

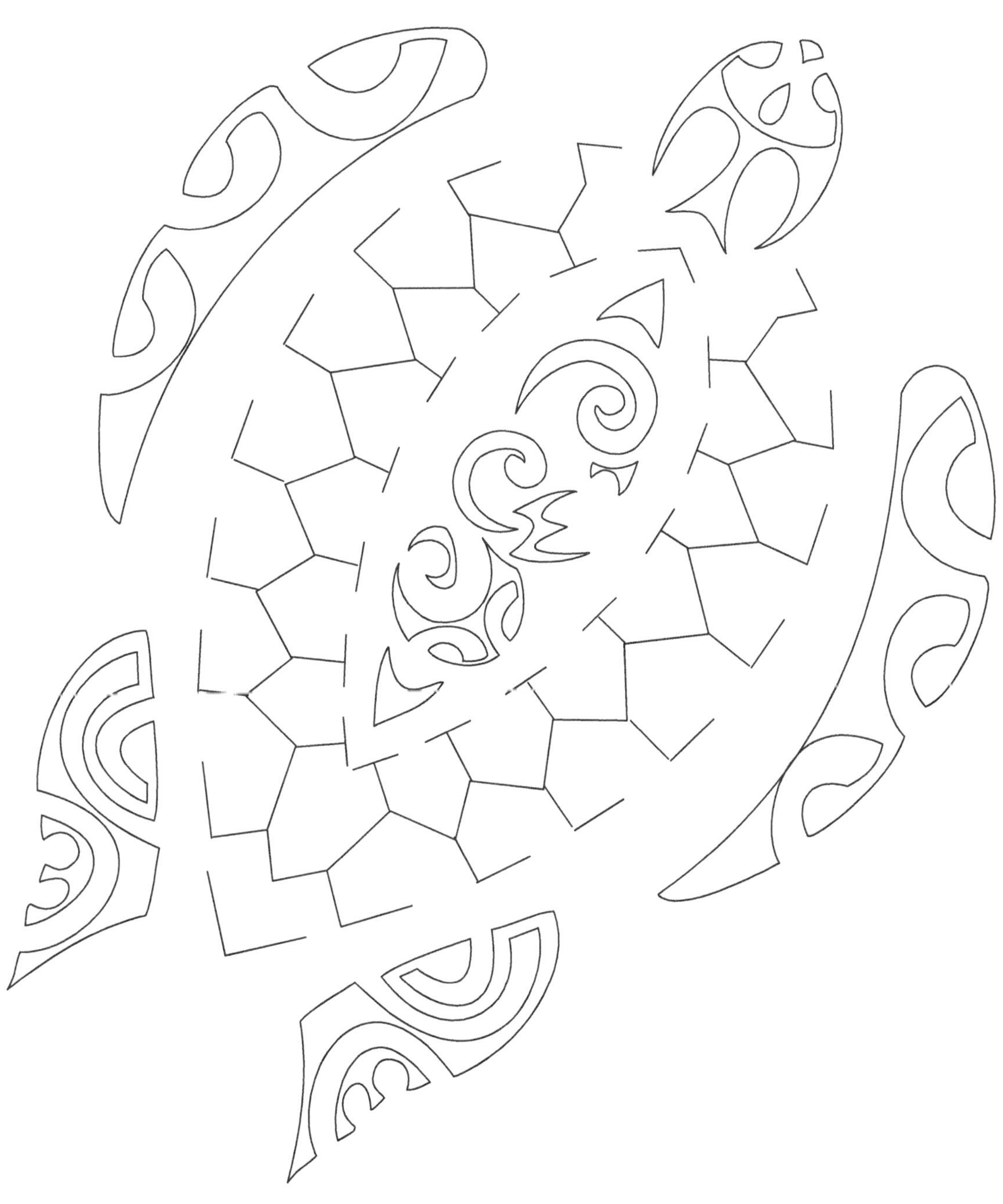

t023

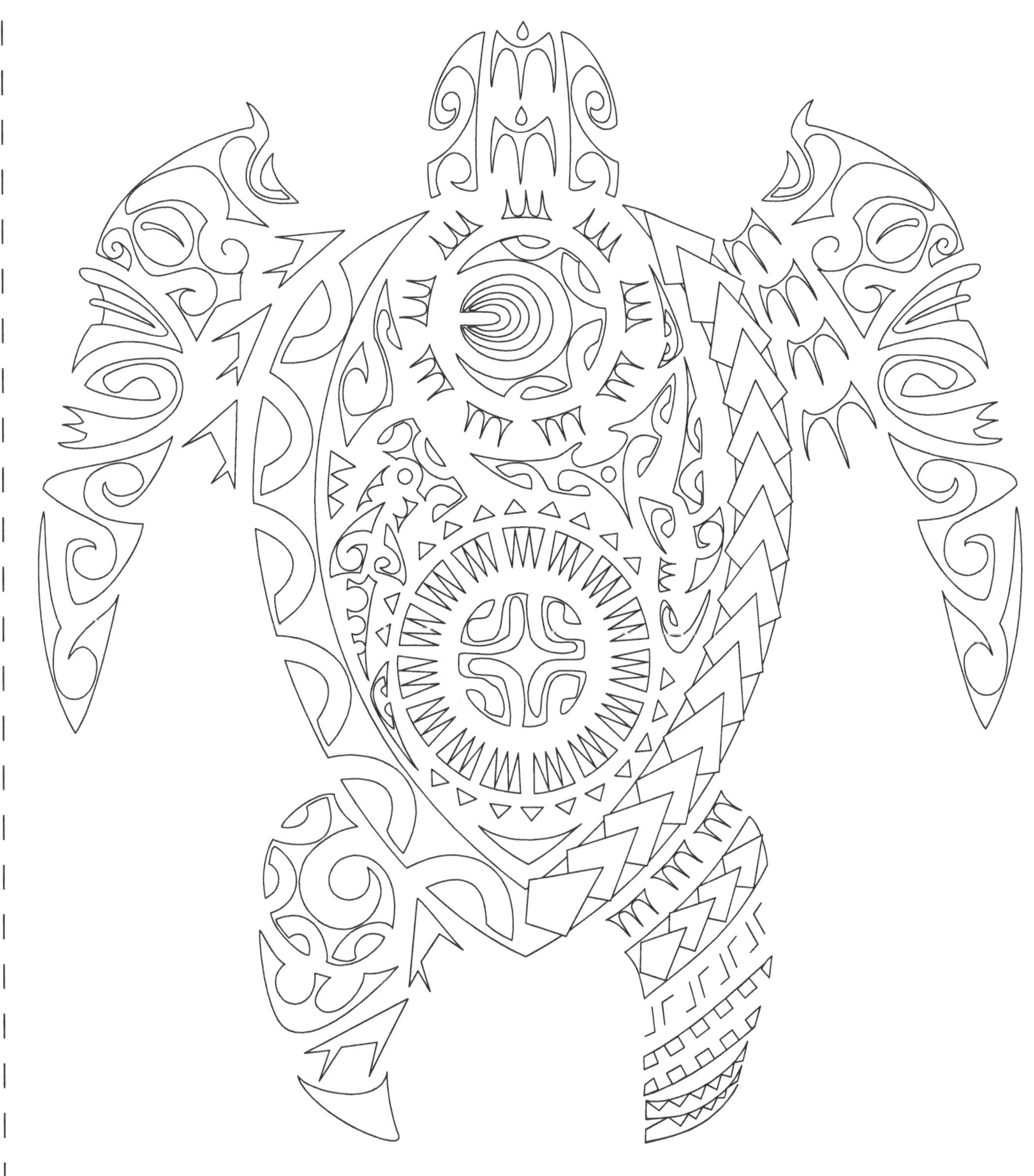

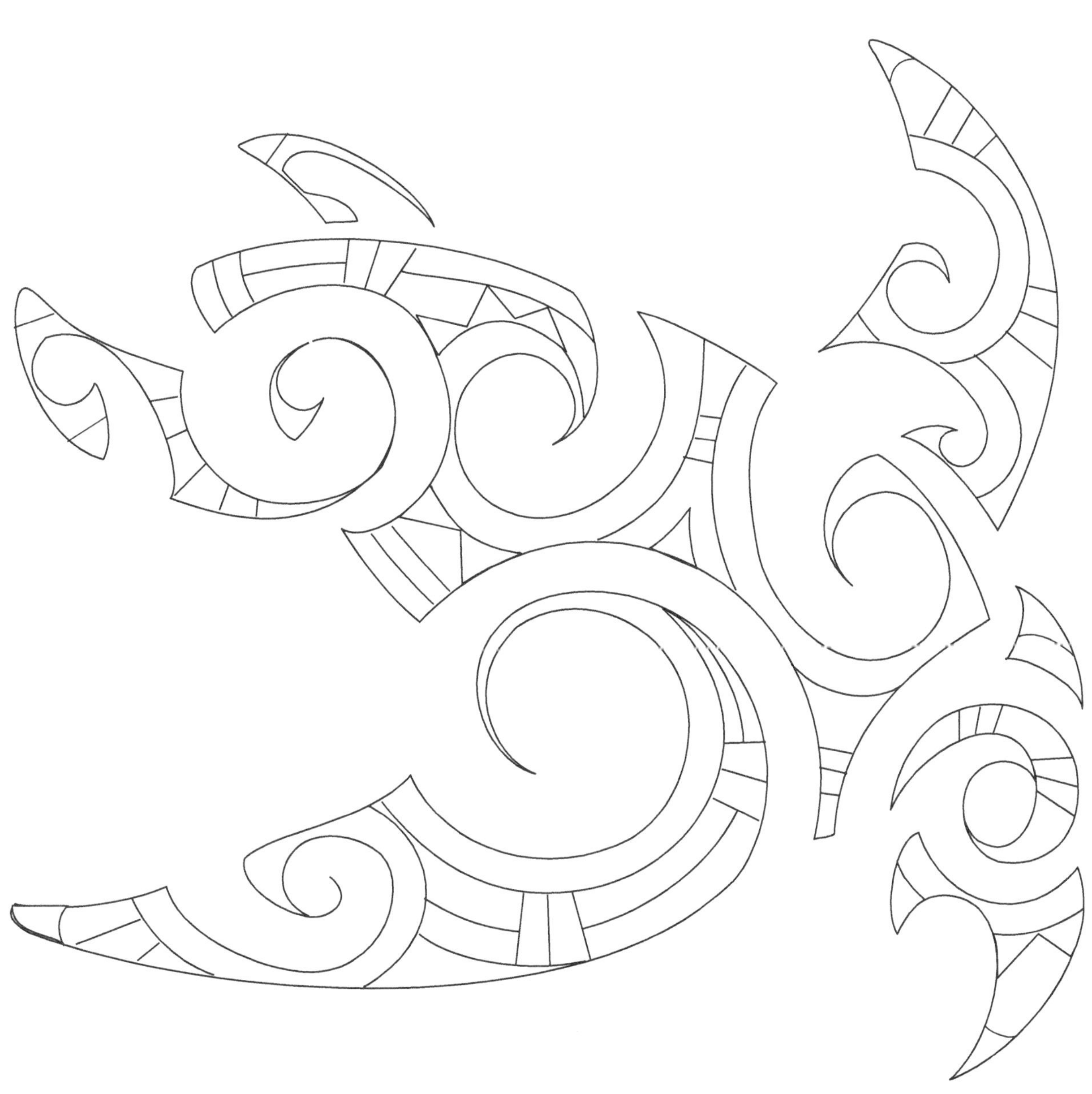

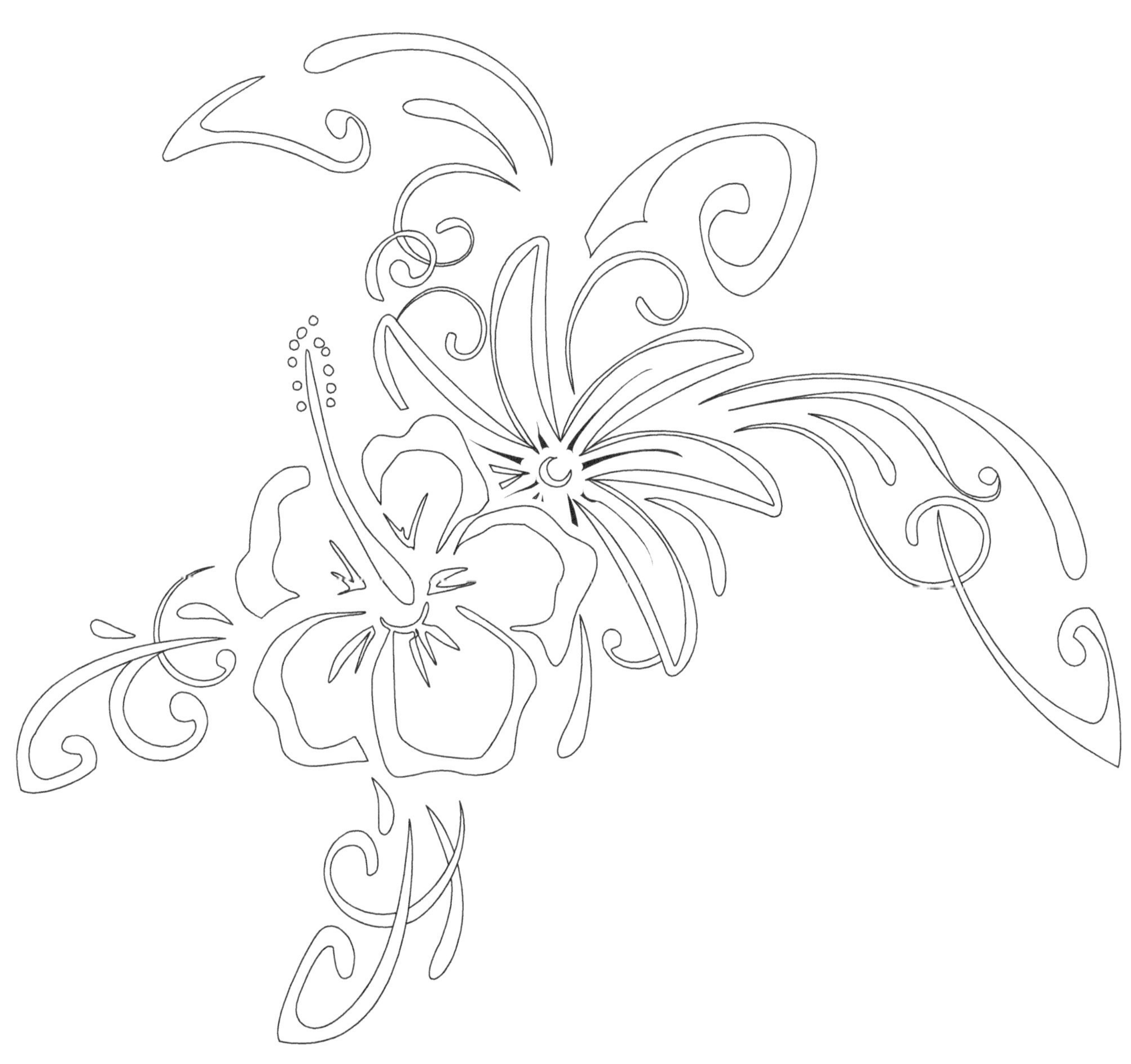

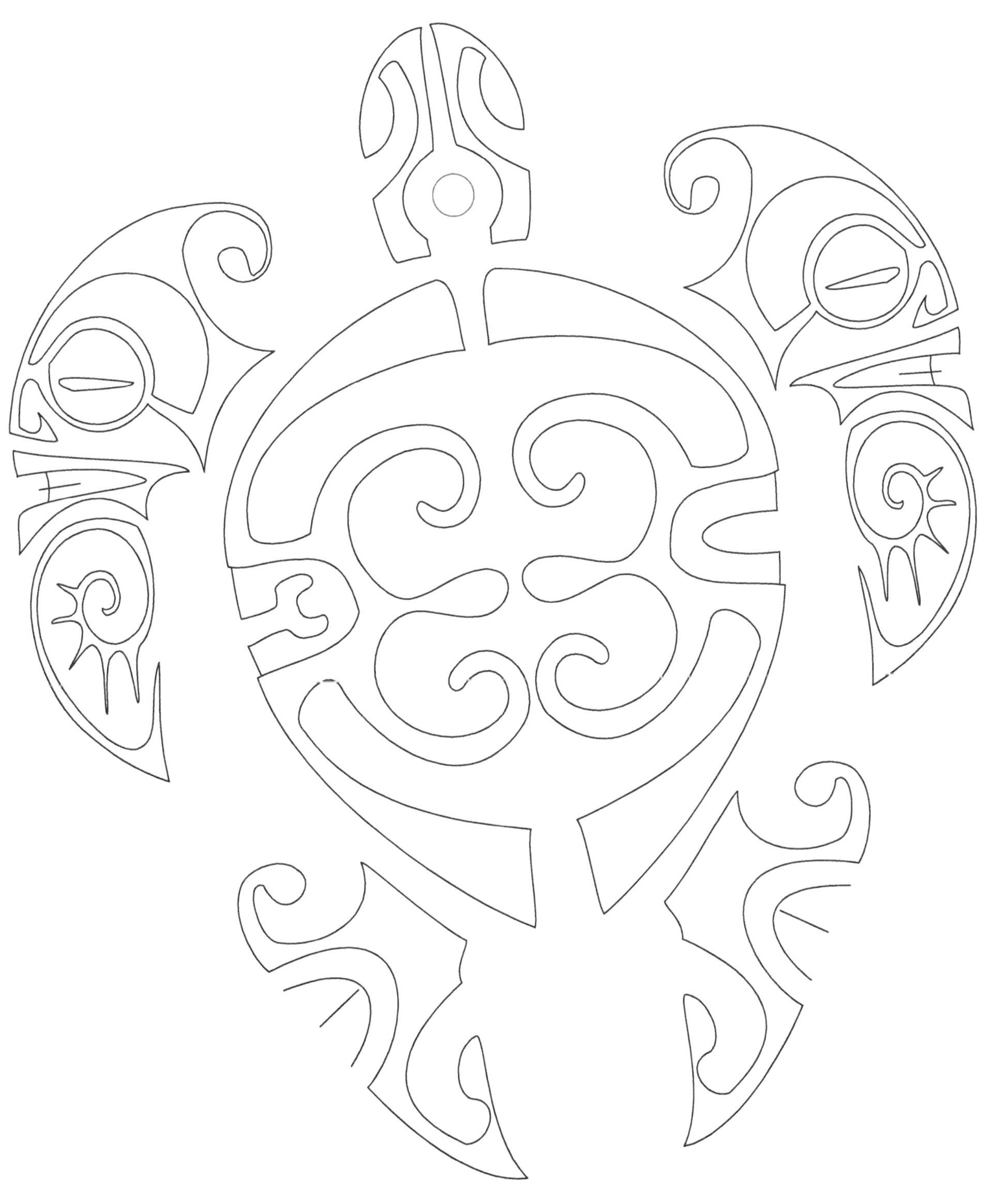

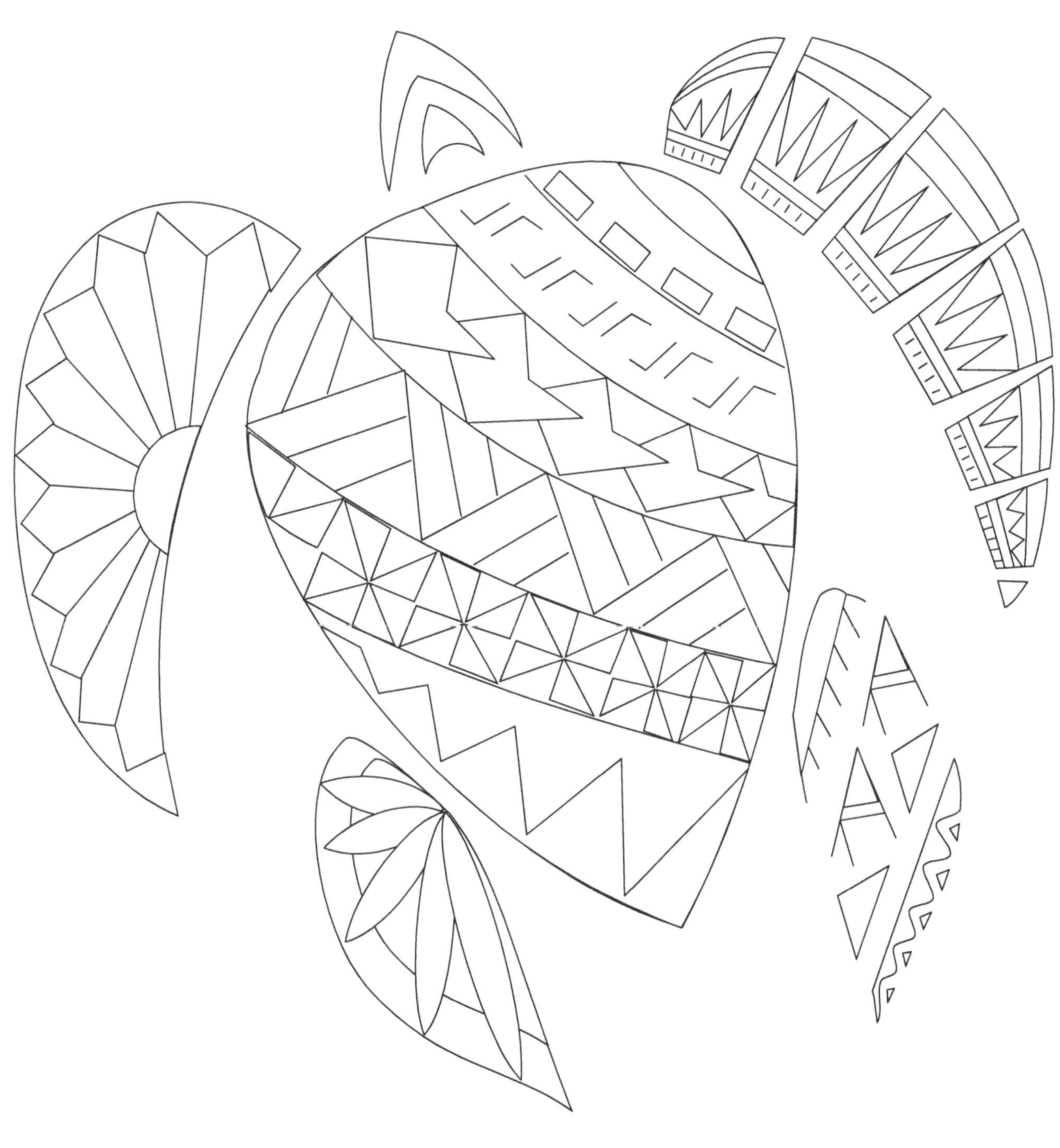

t028

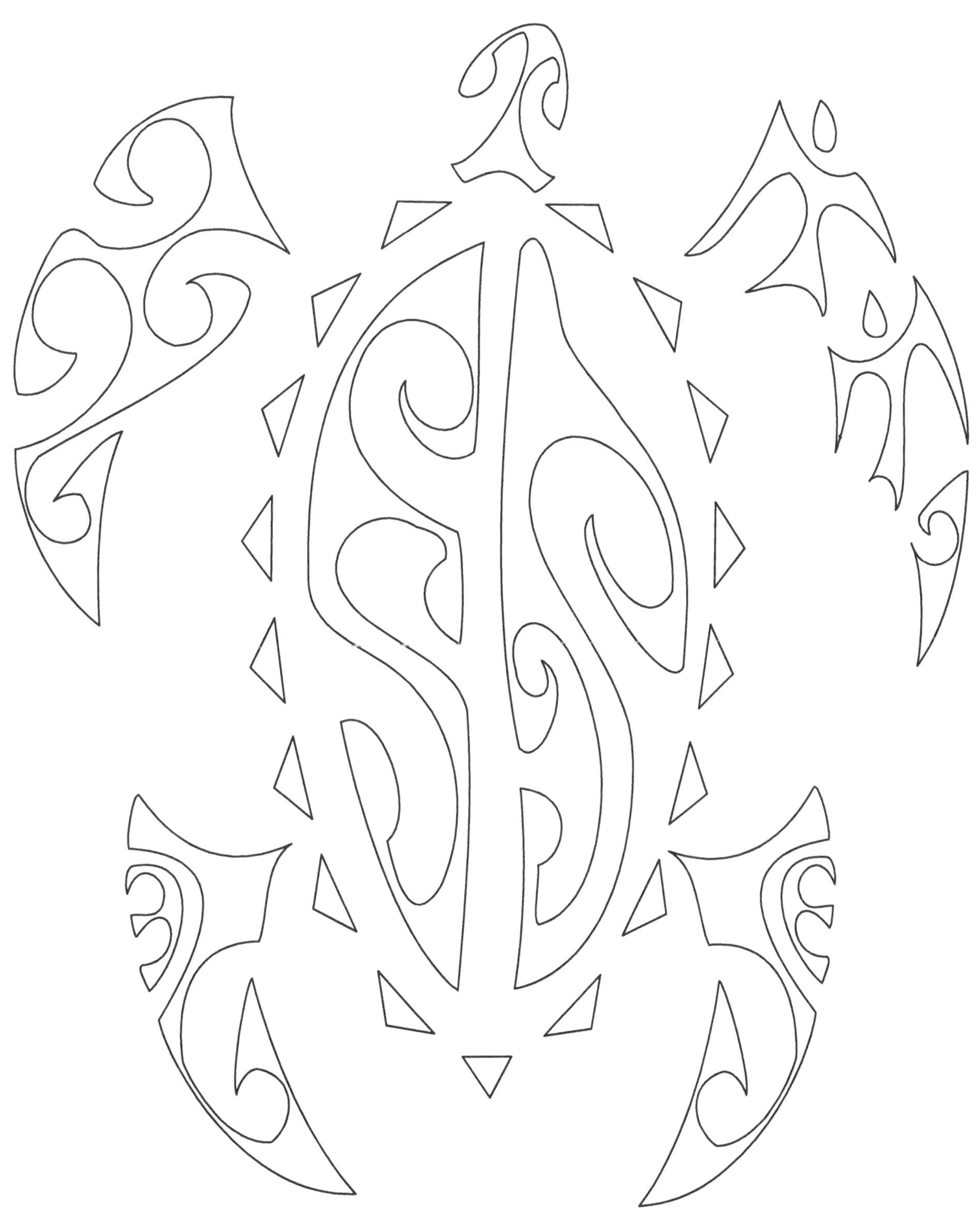

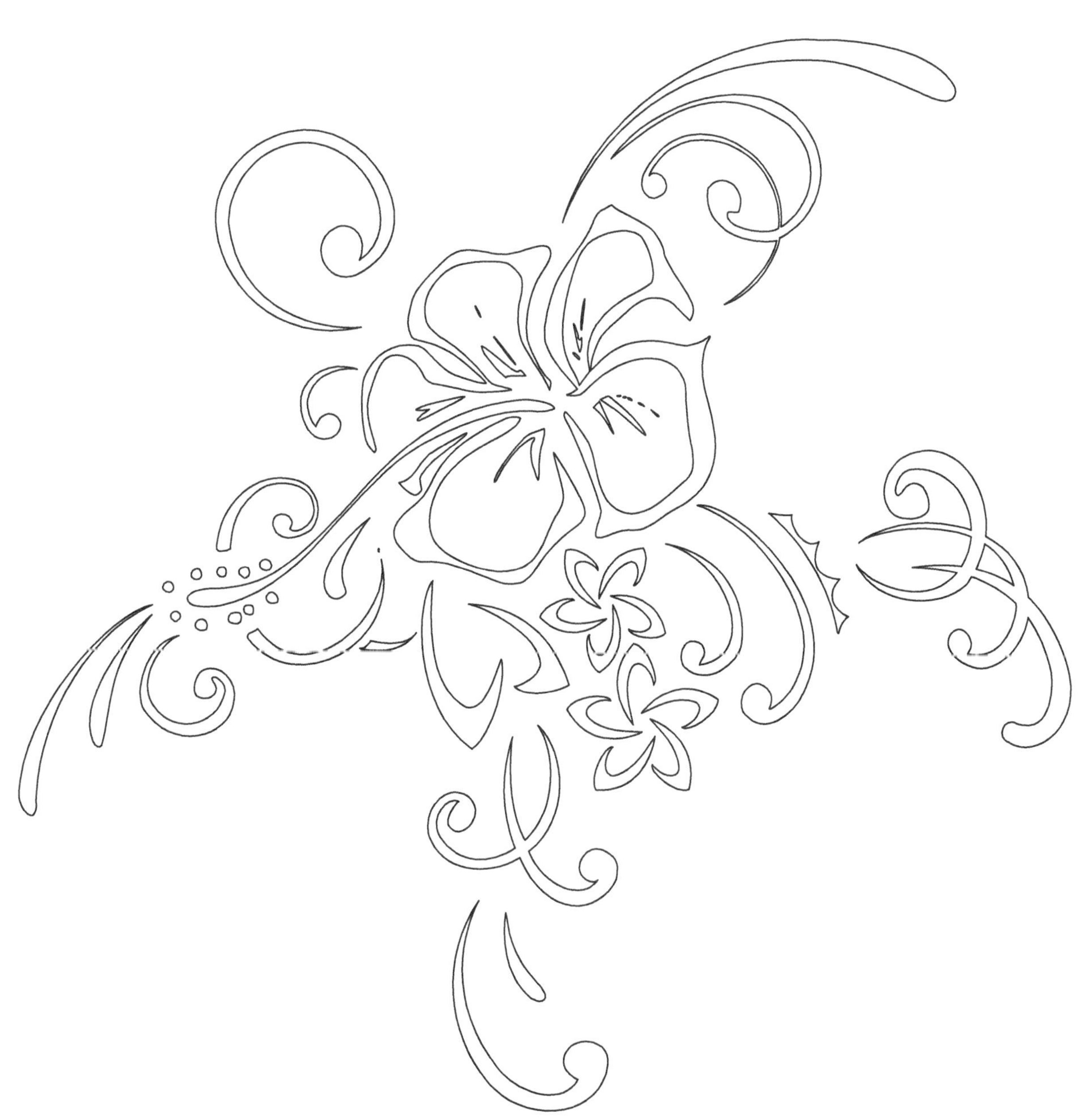

t030

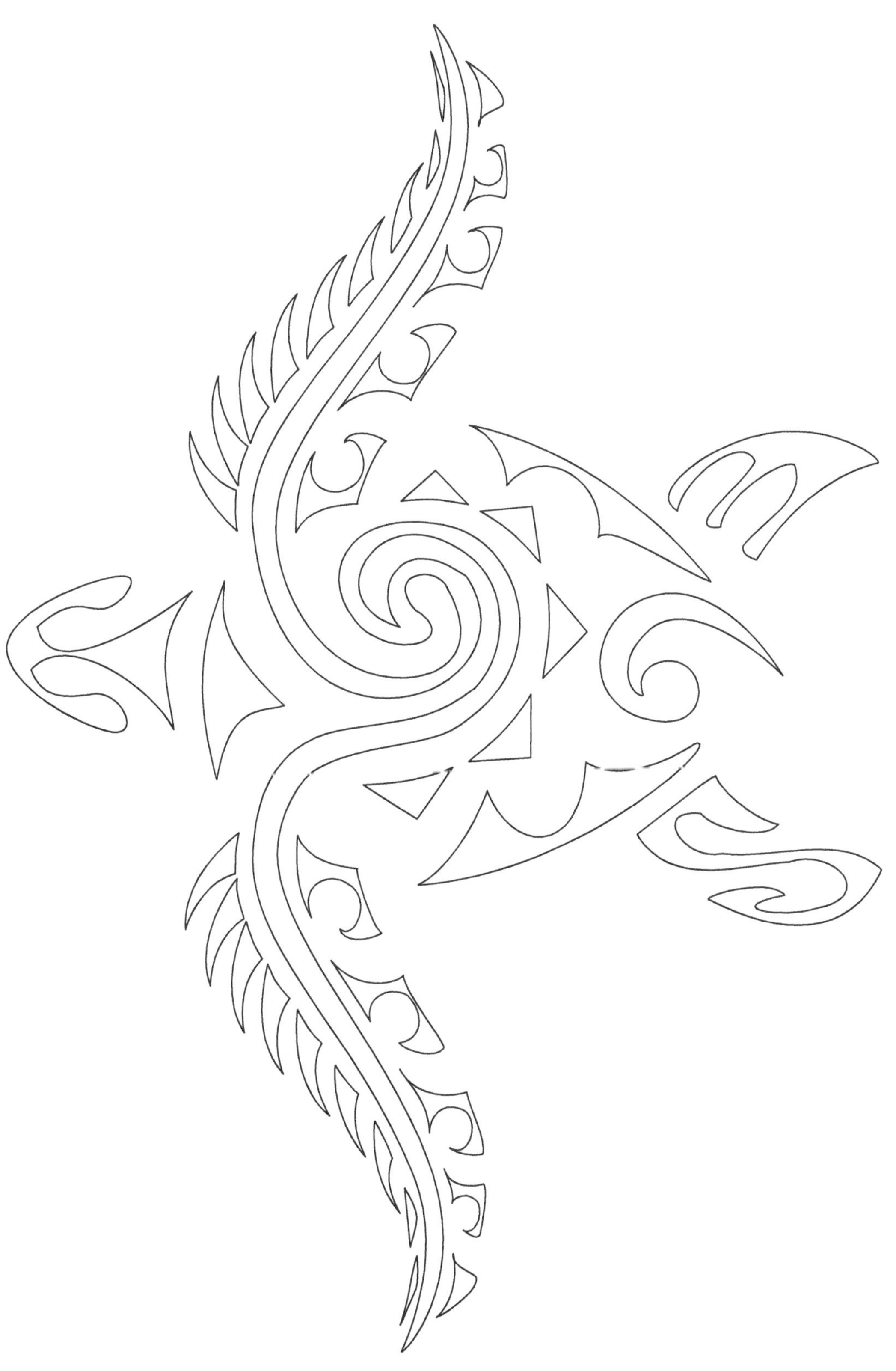

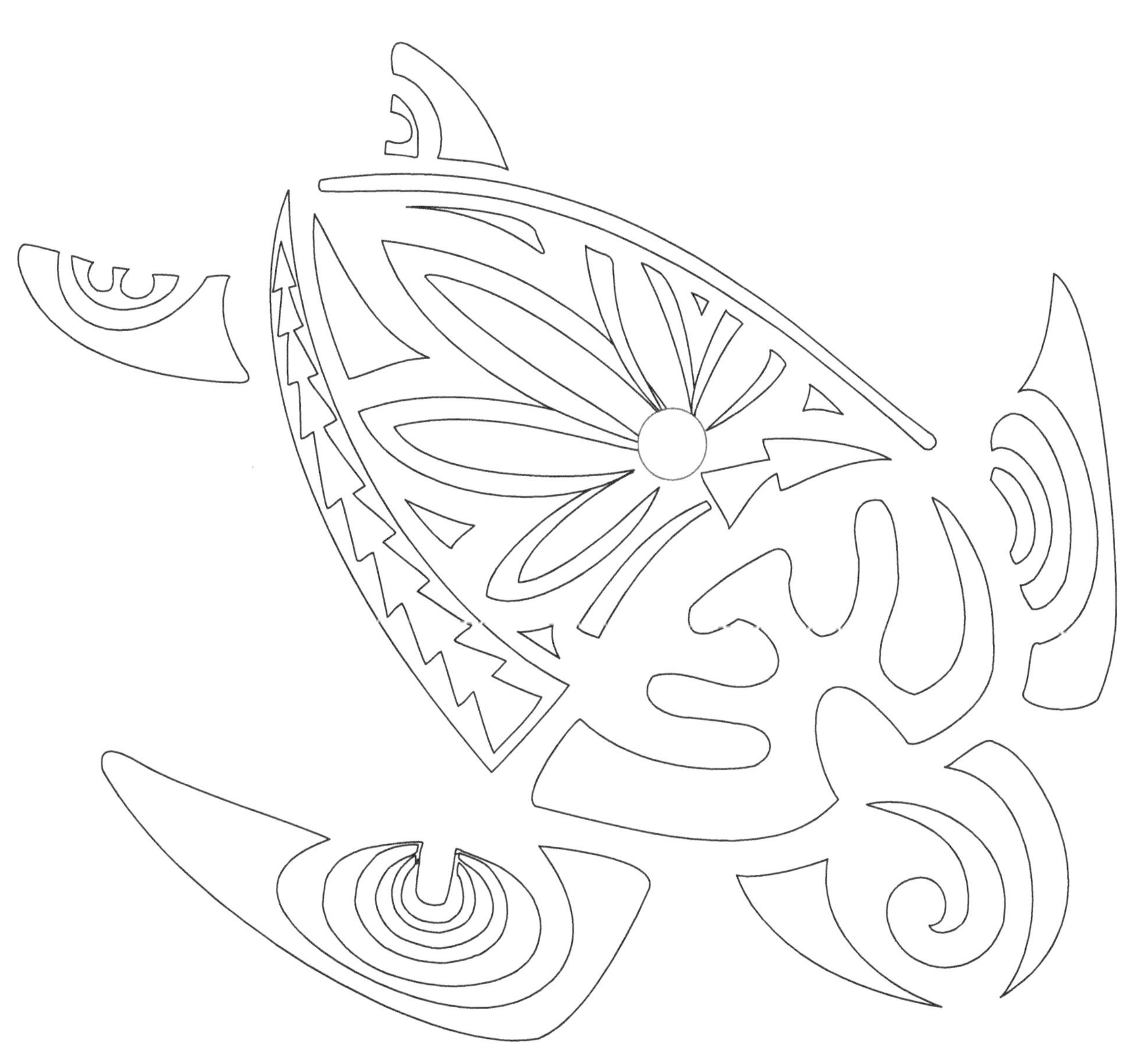

t032

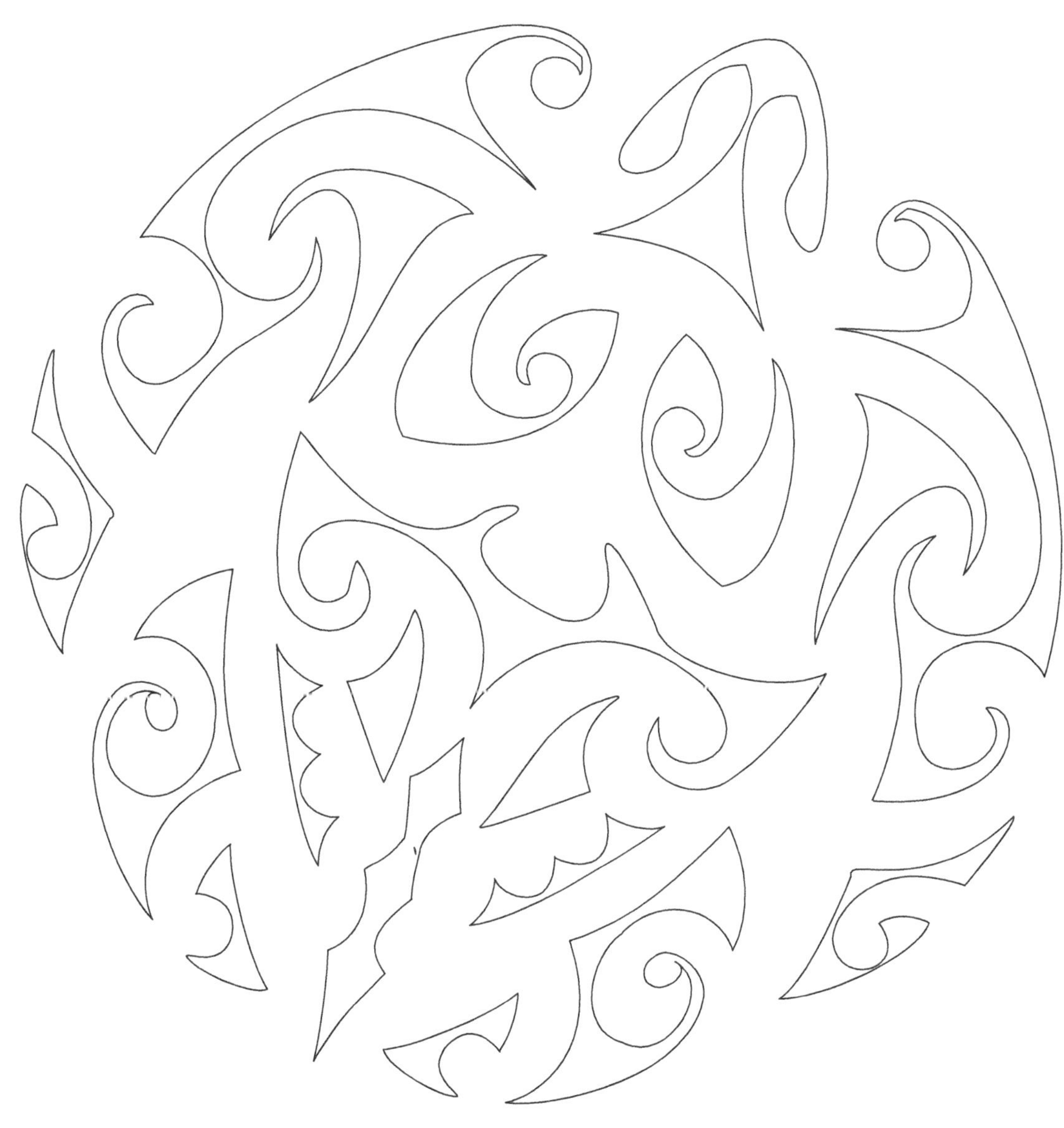

t033

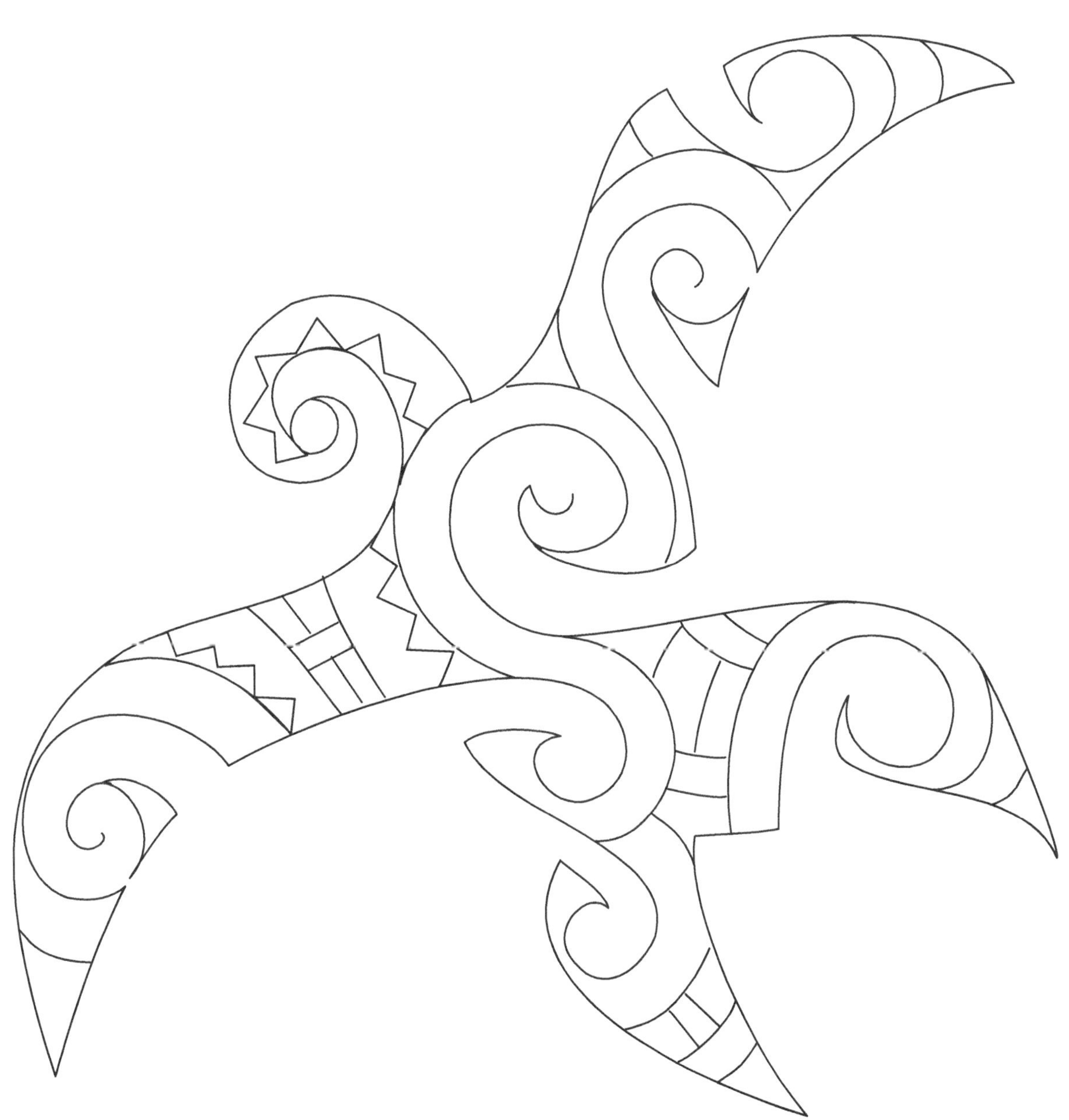

t034

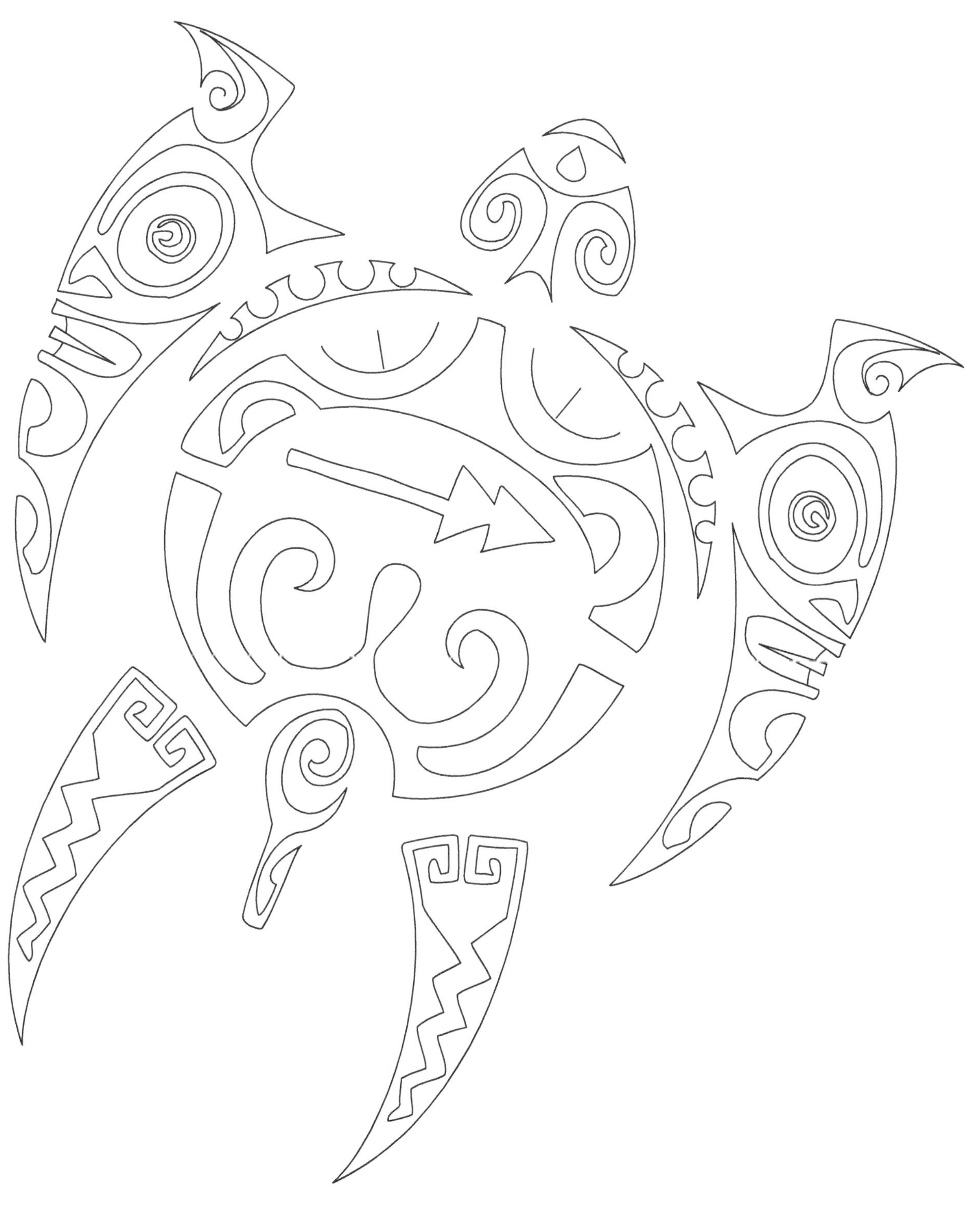

t035

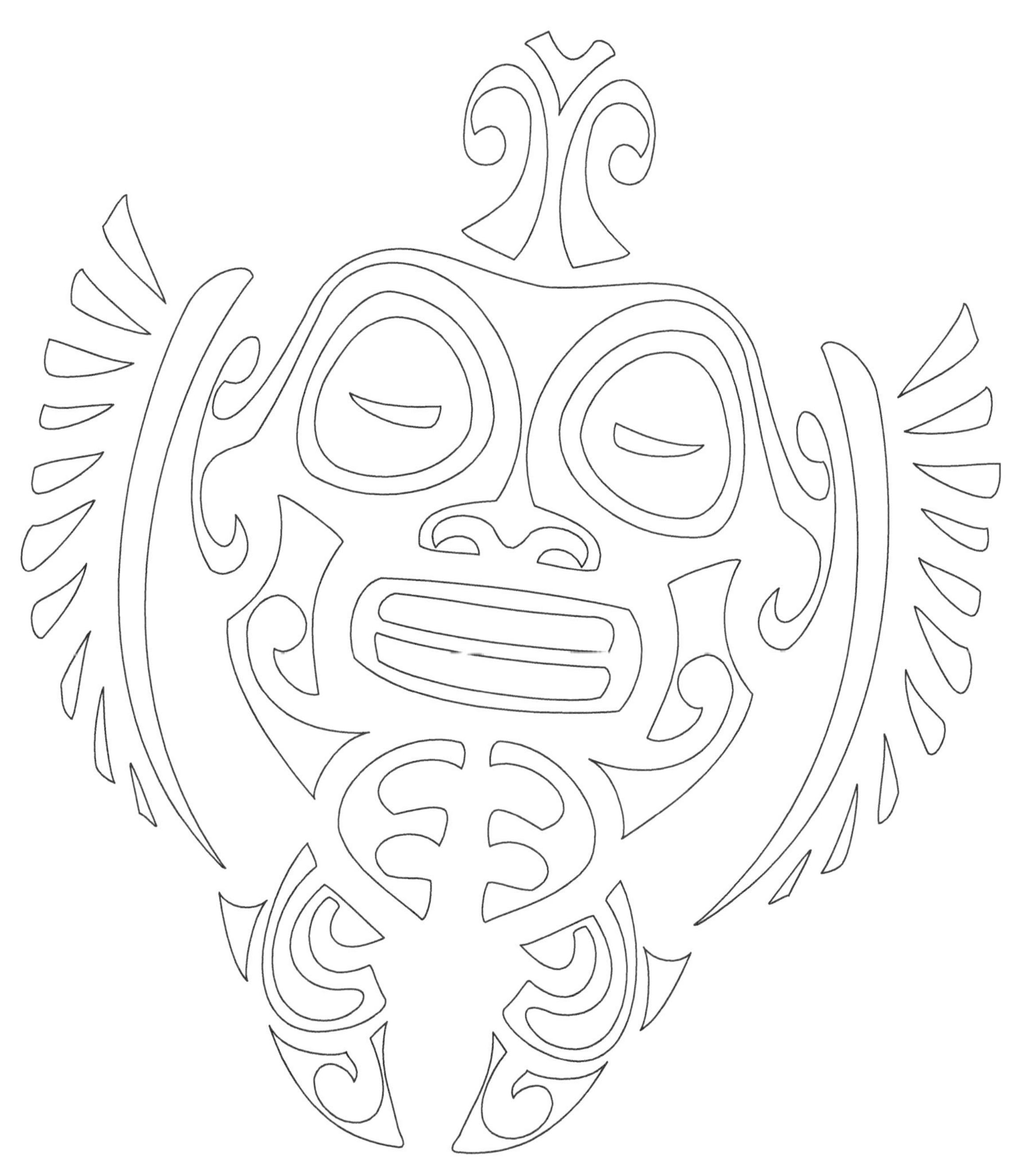

t036

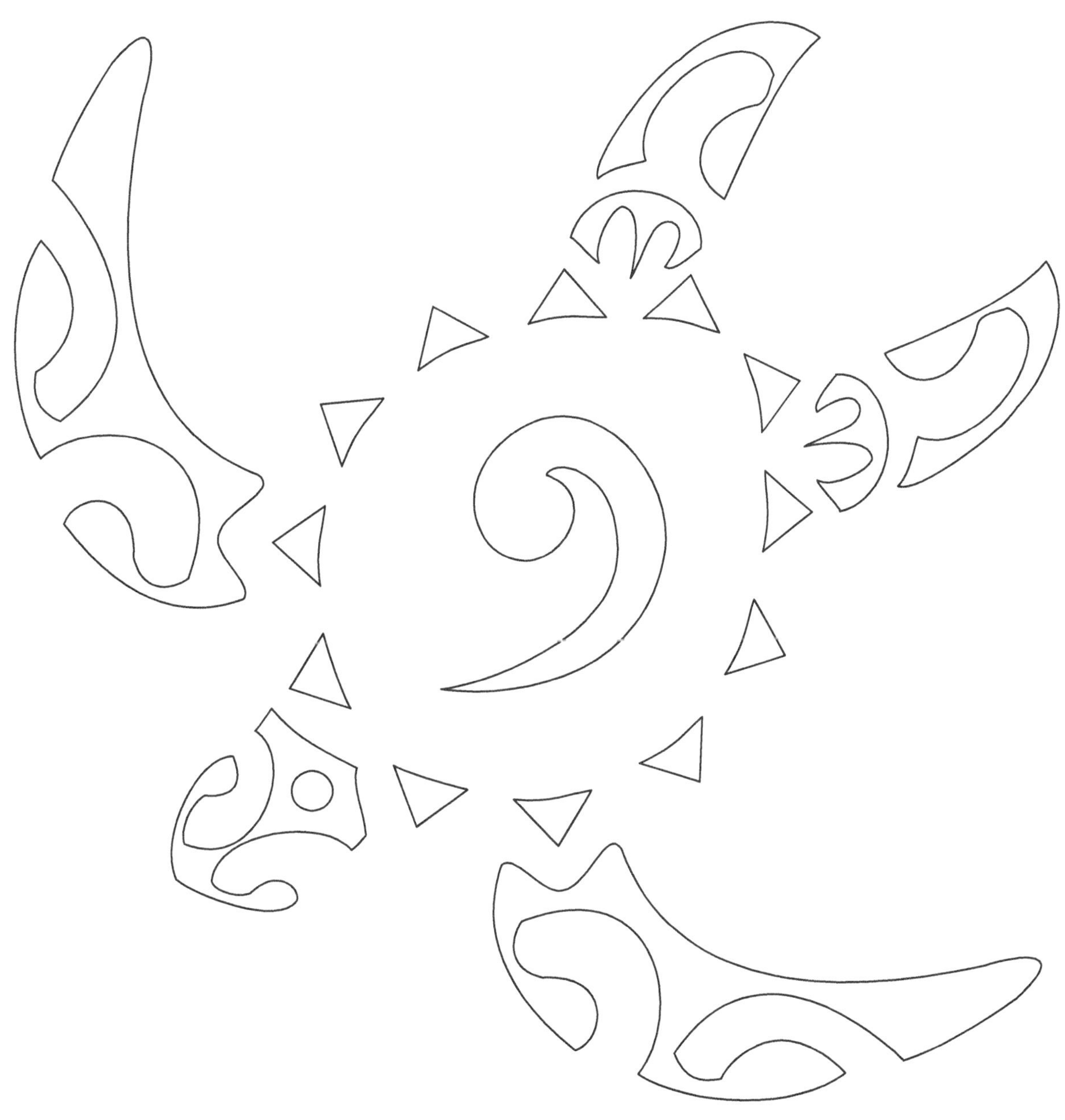

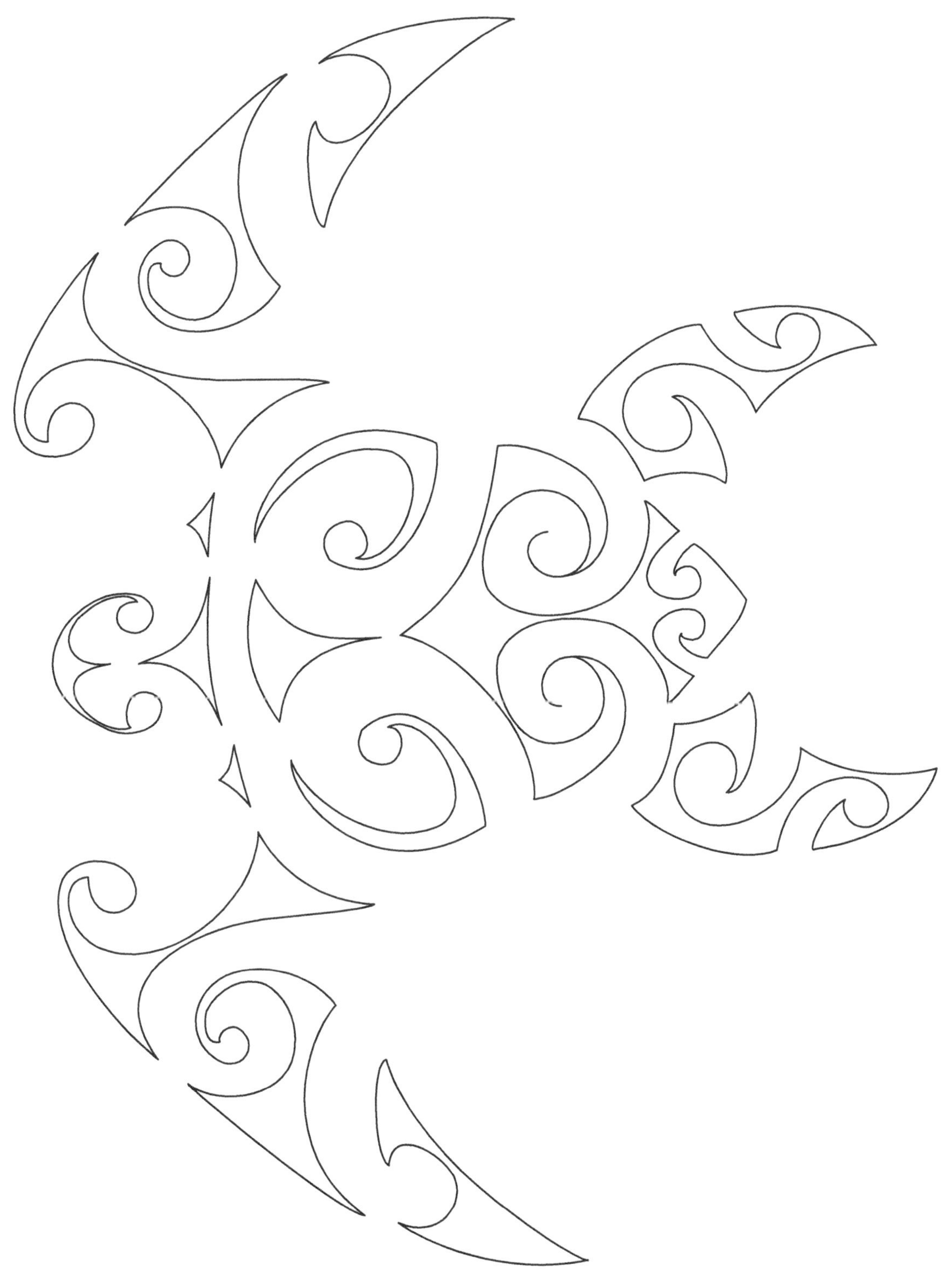

t038

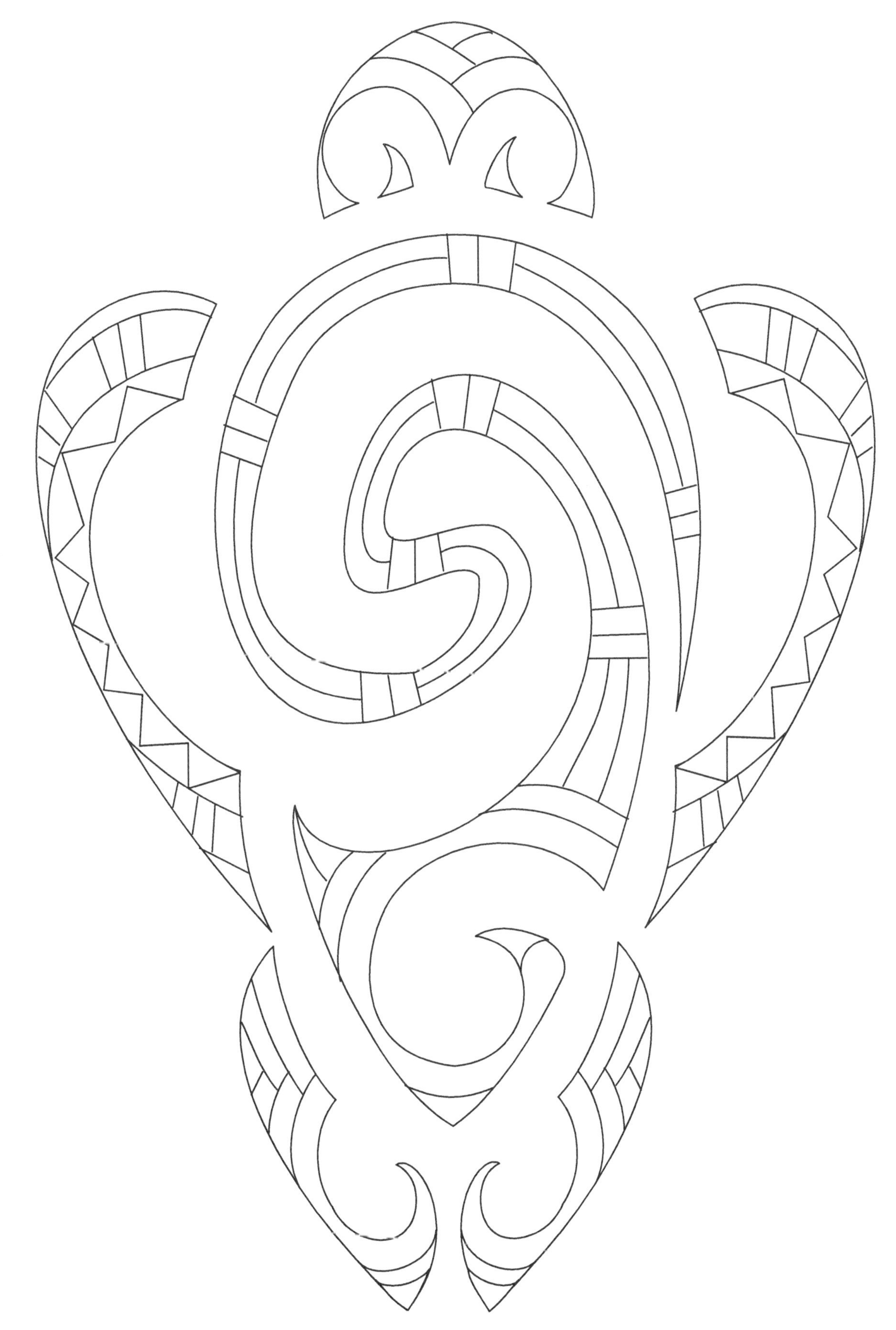

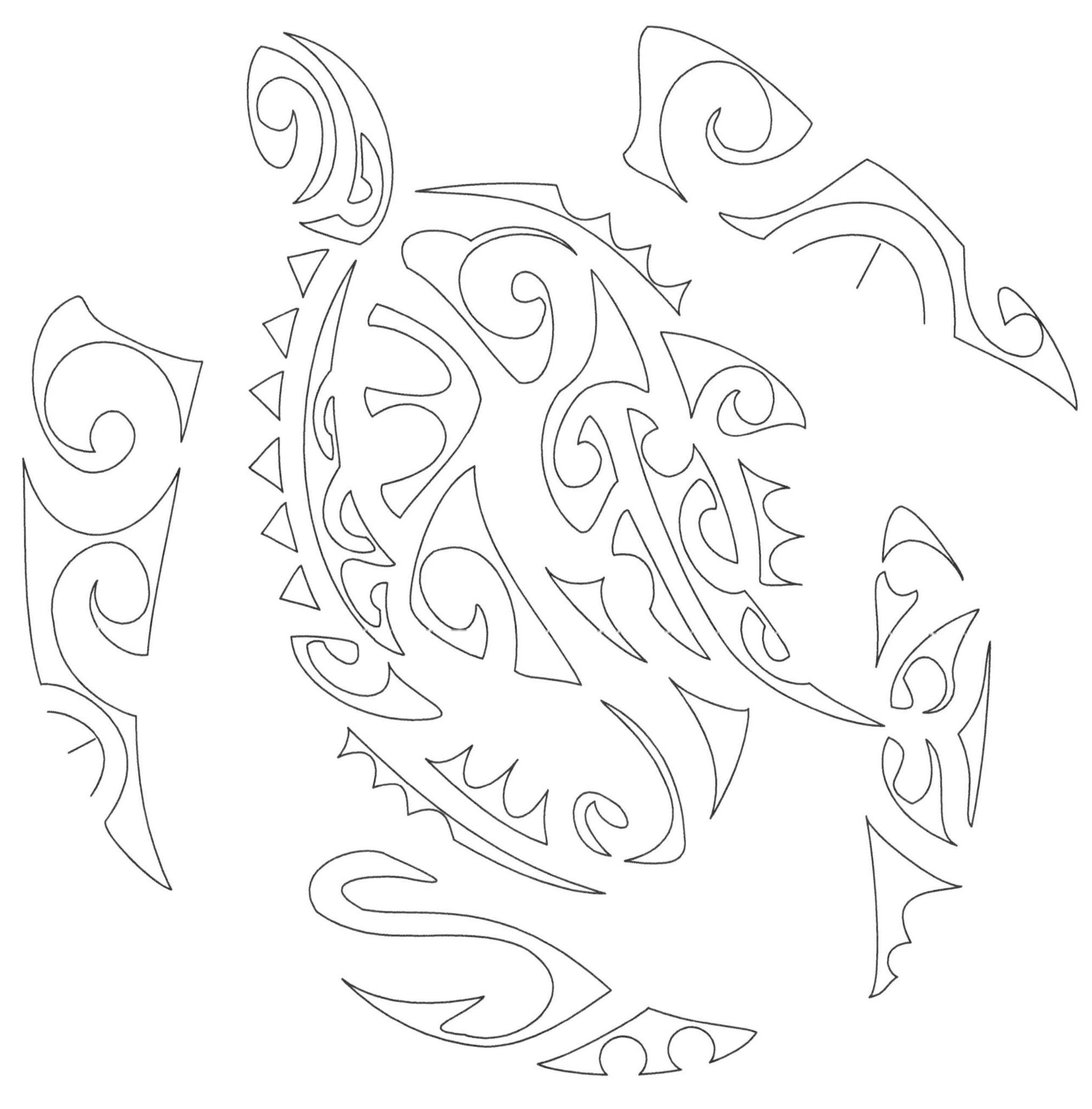

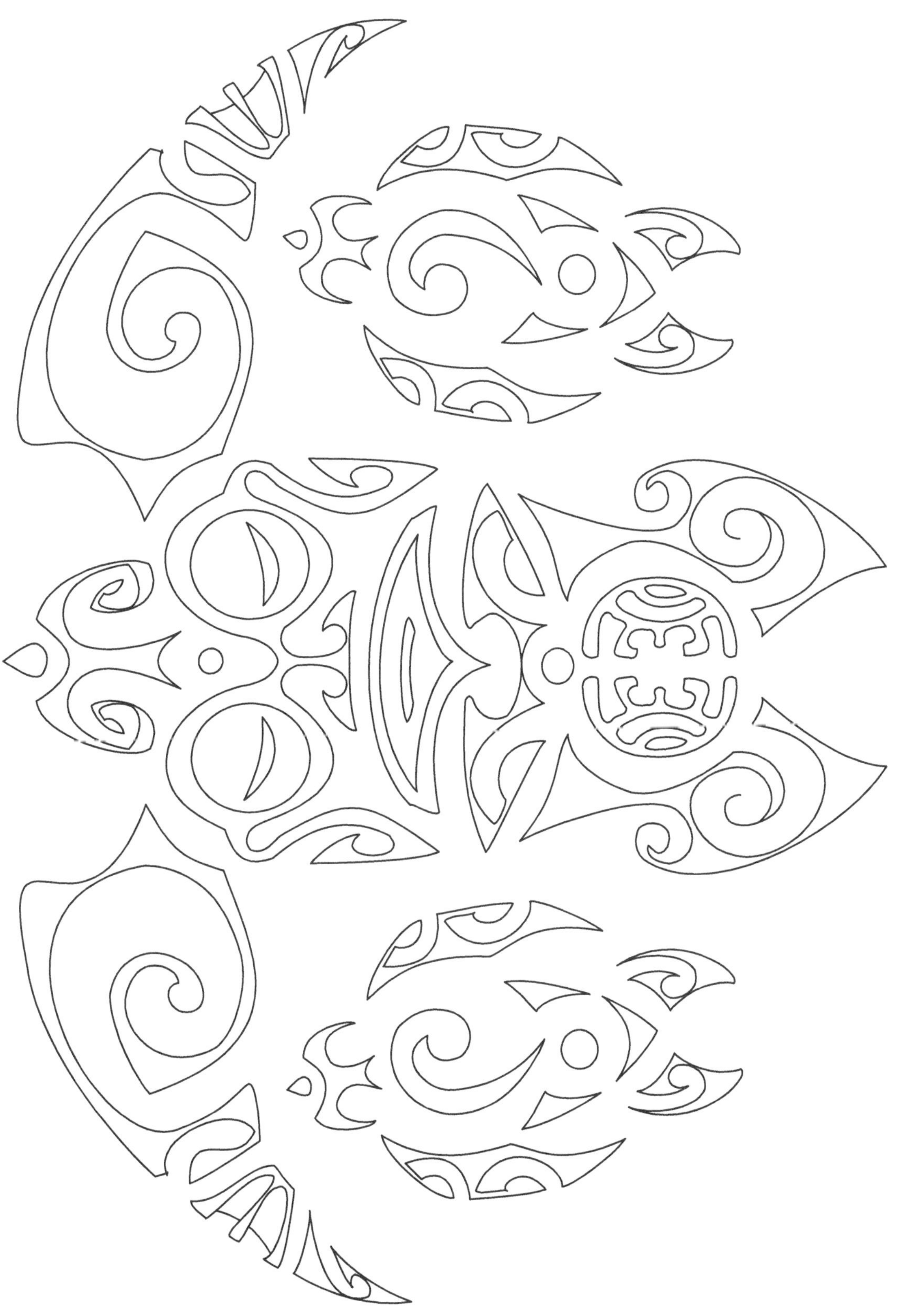

t041

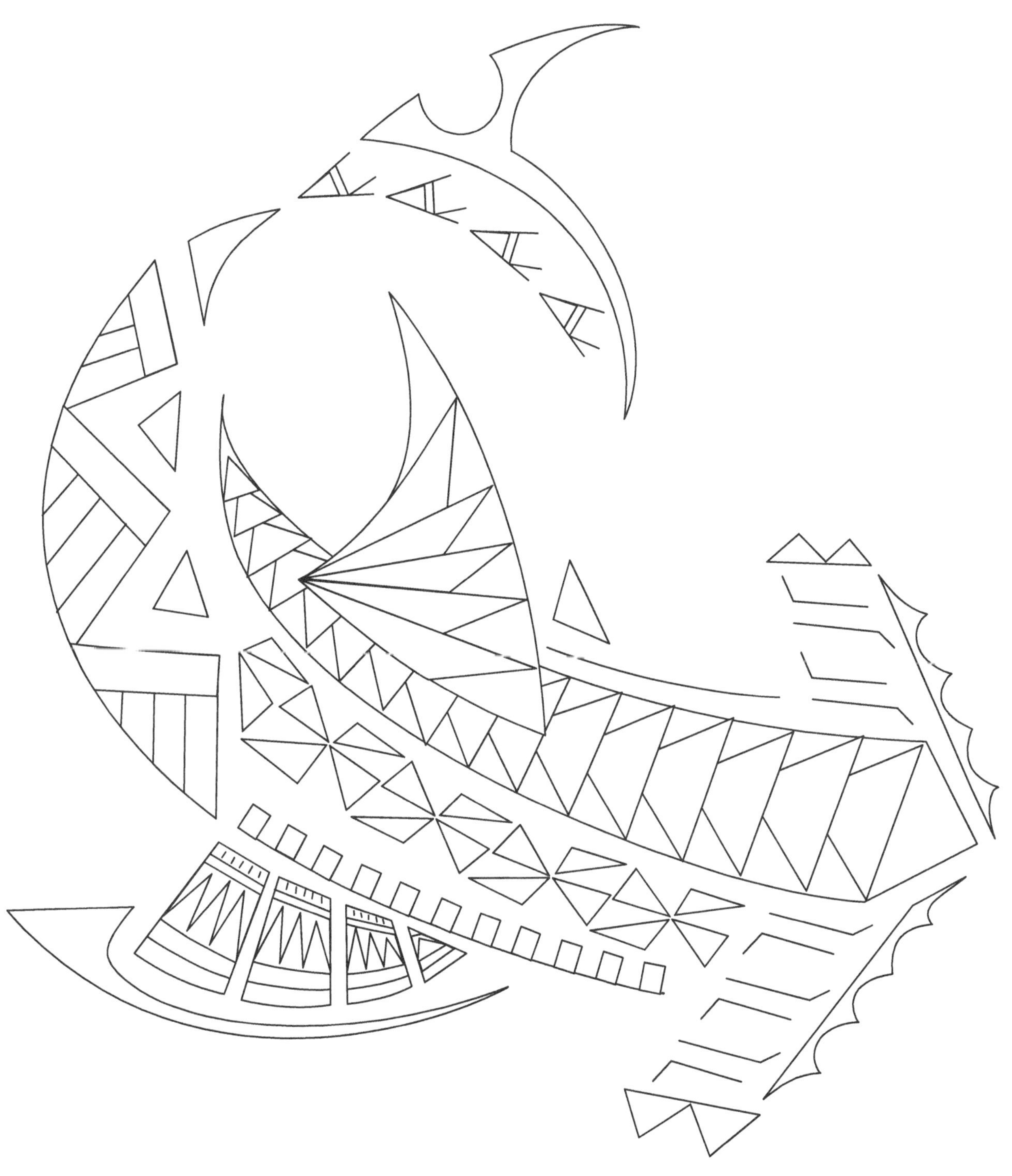

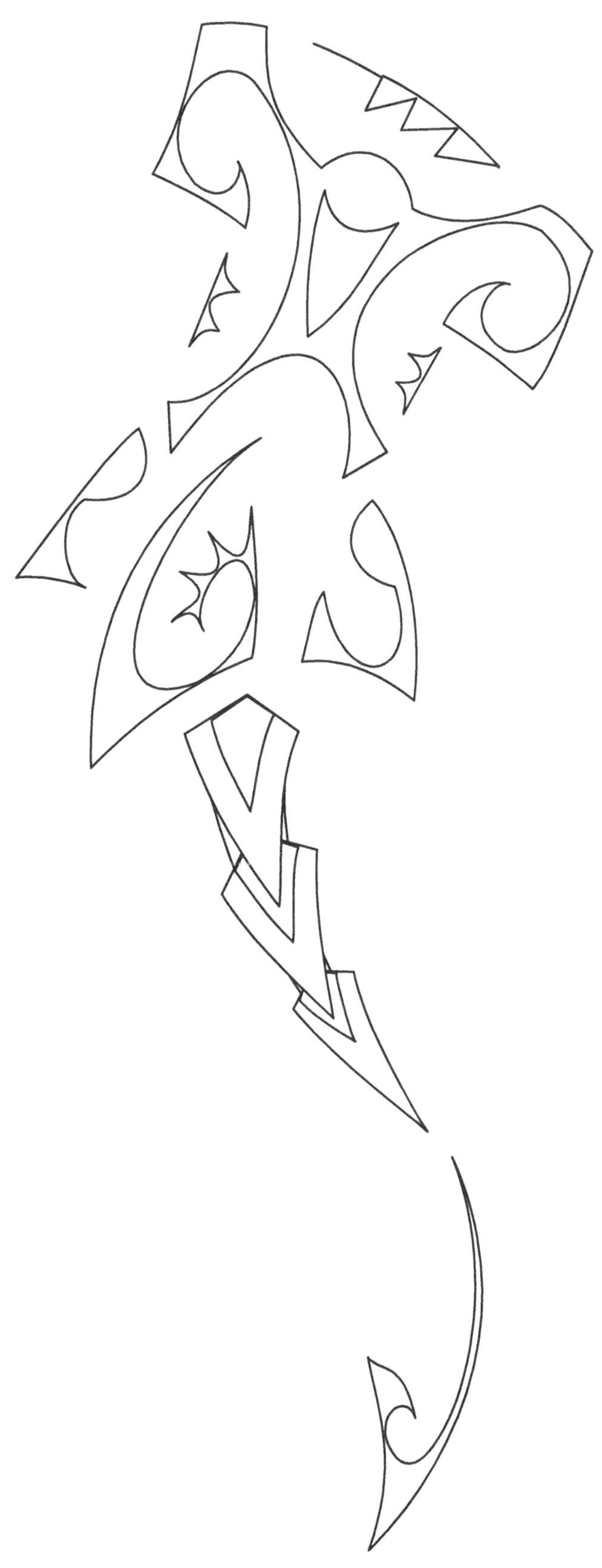

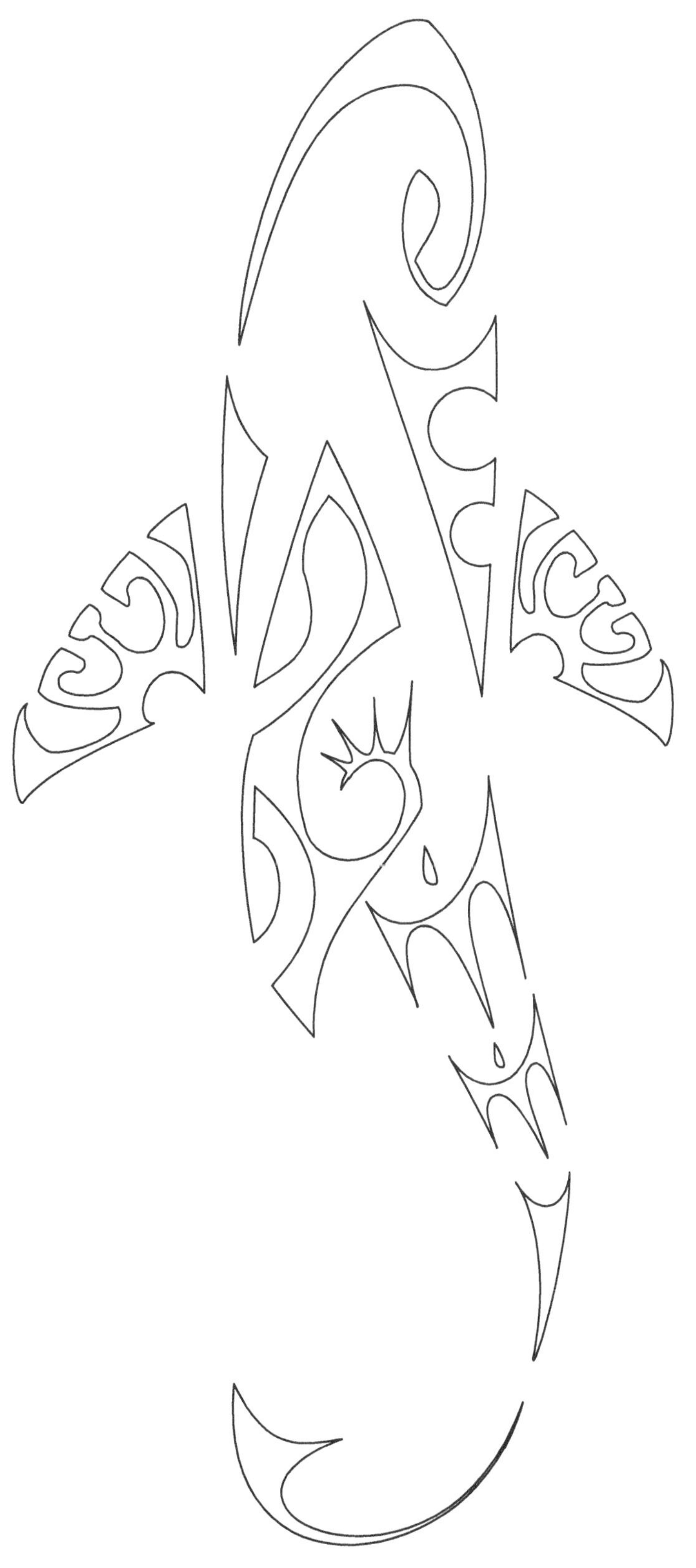

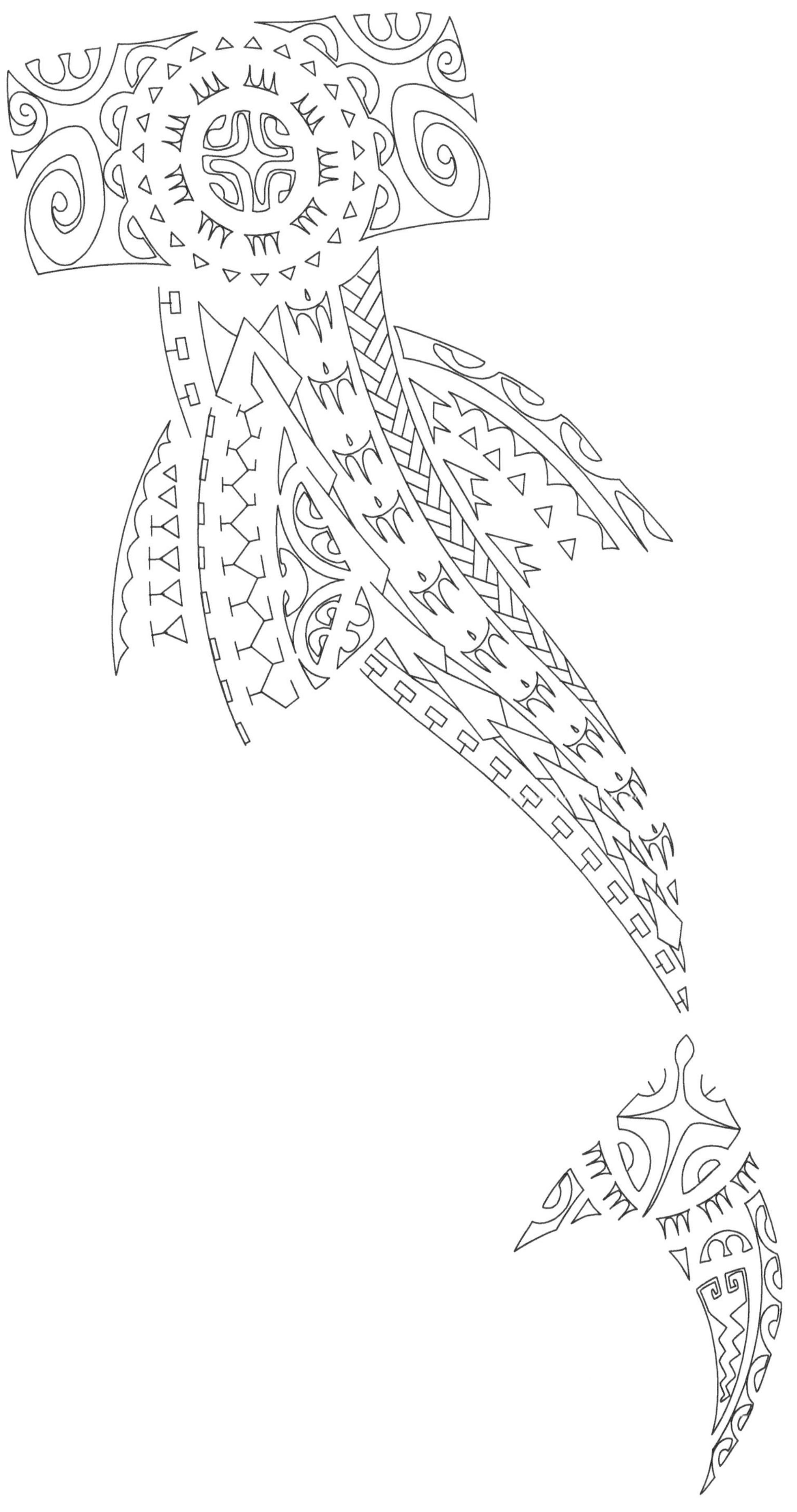

t045

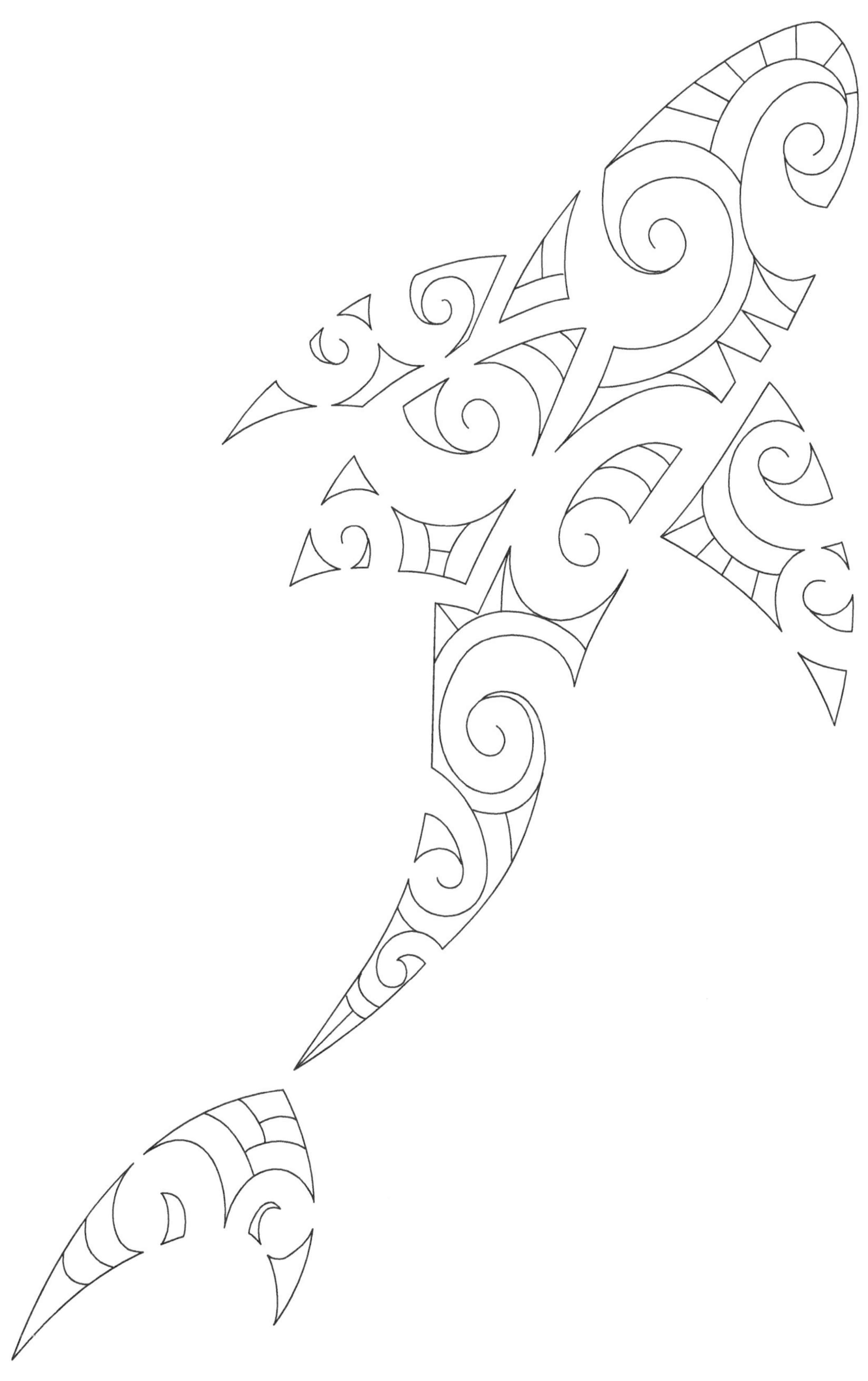

t046

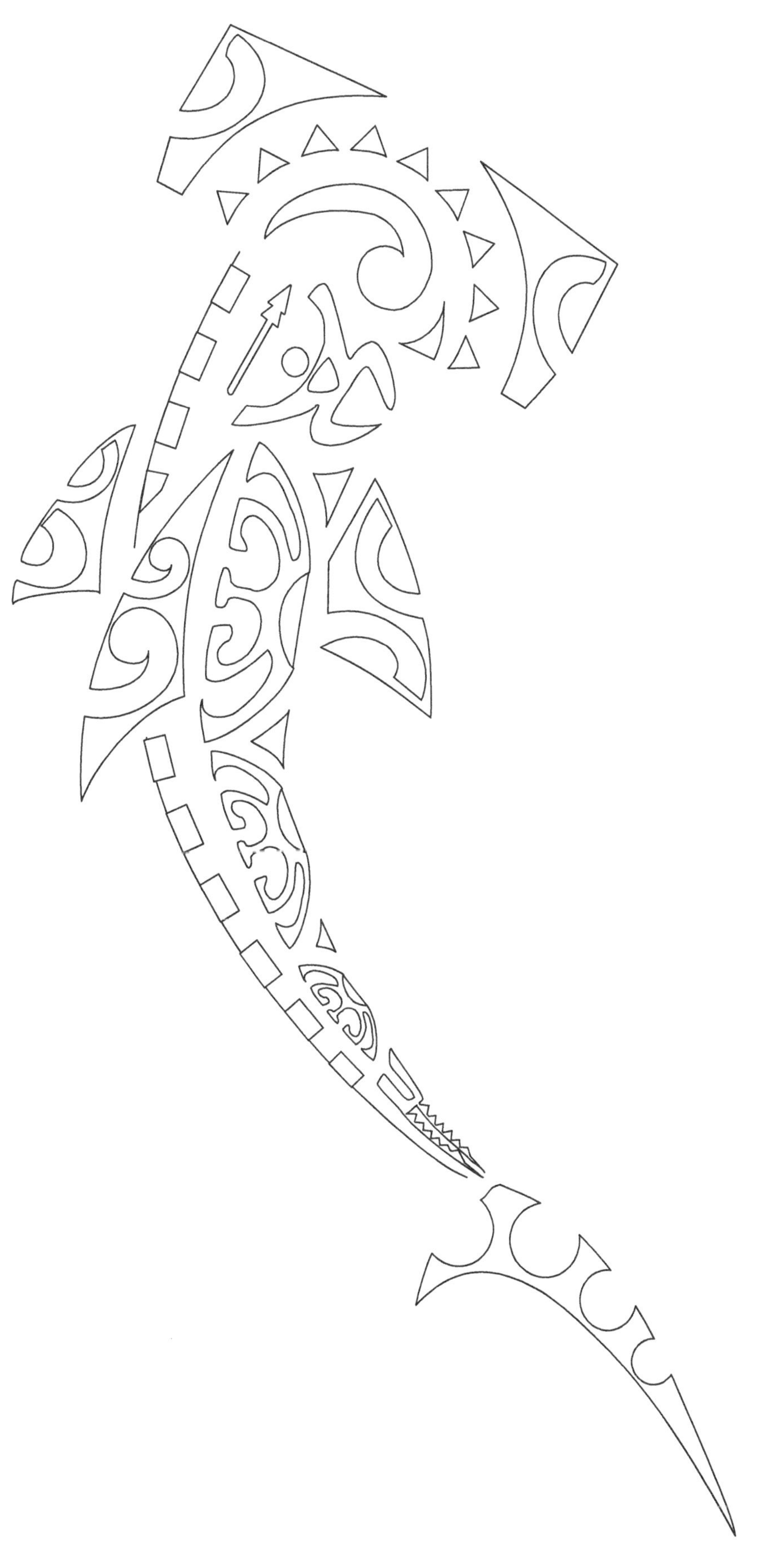

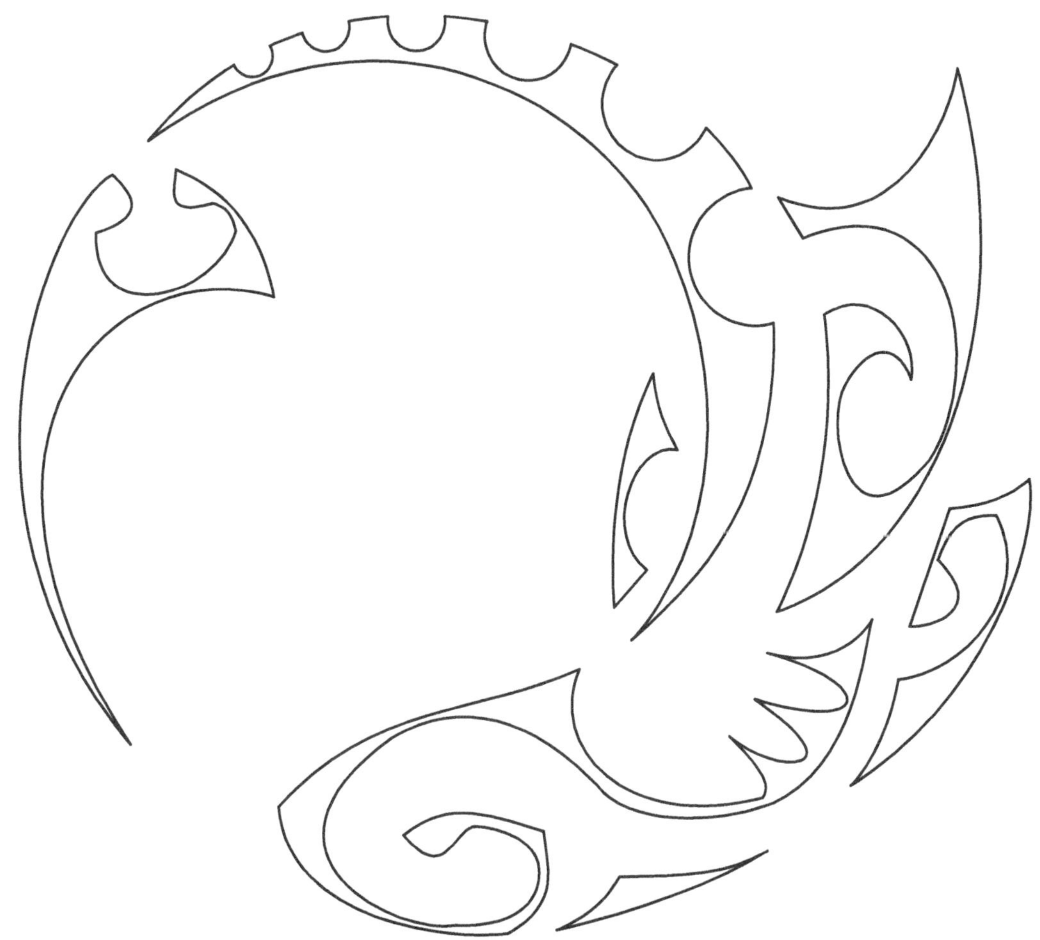

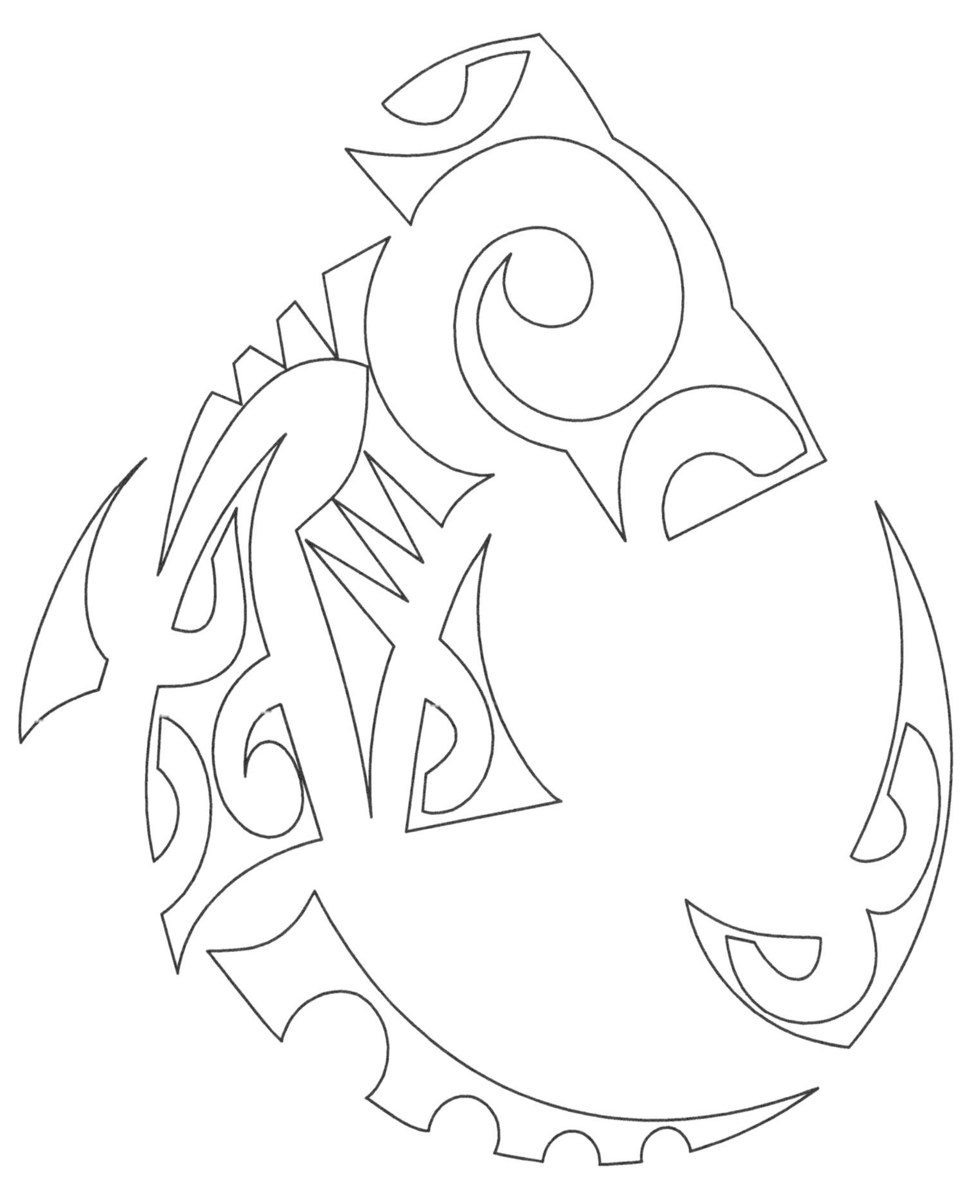

t049

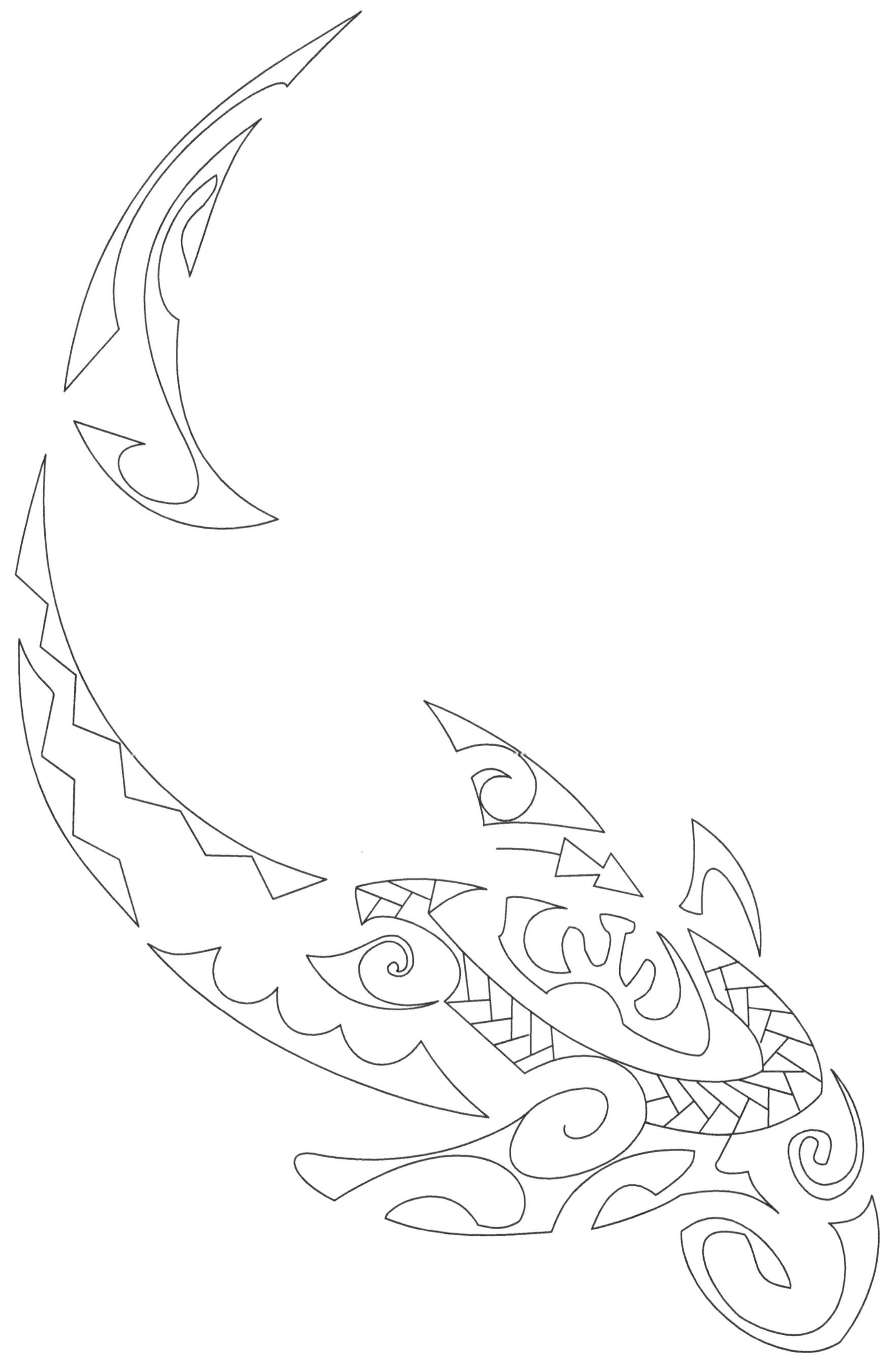

t050

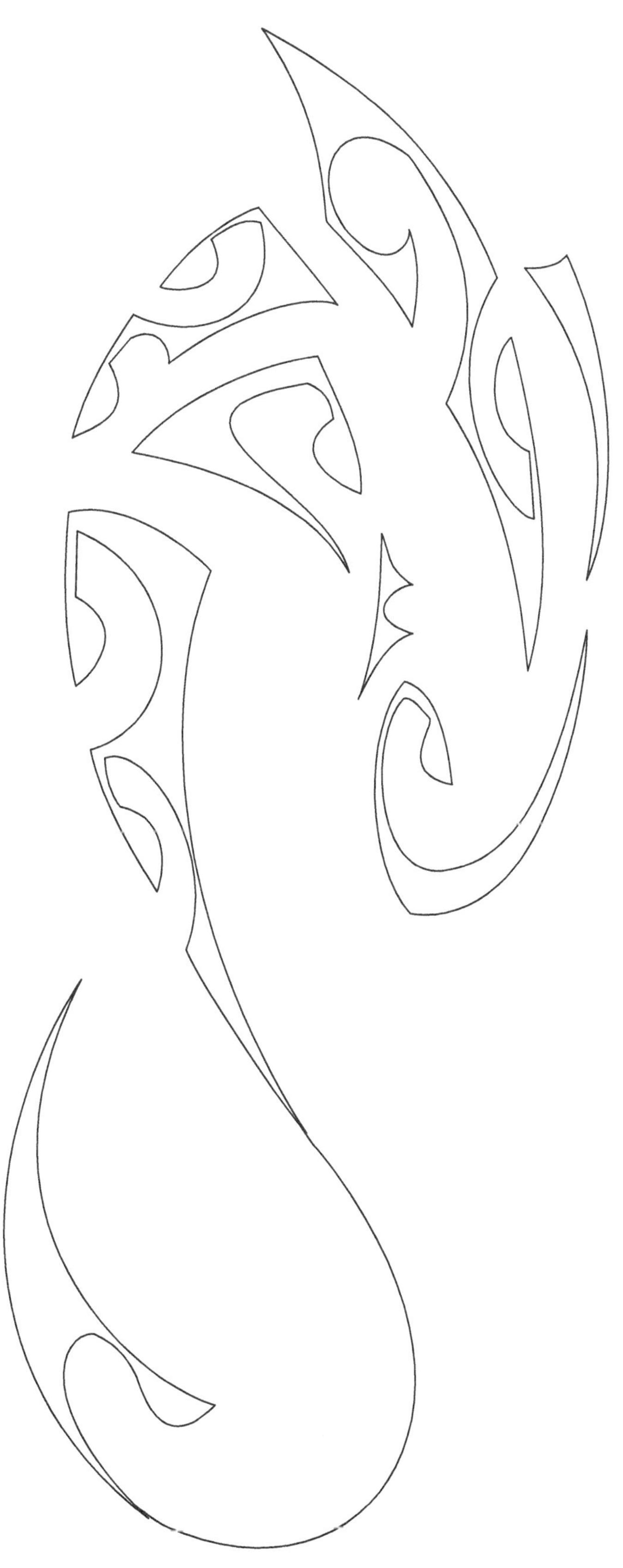

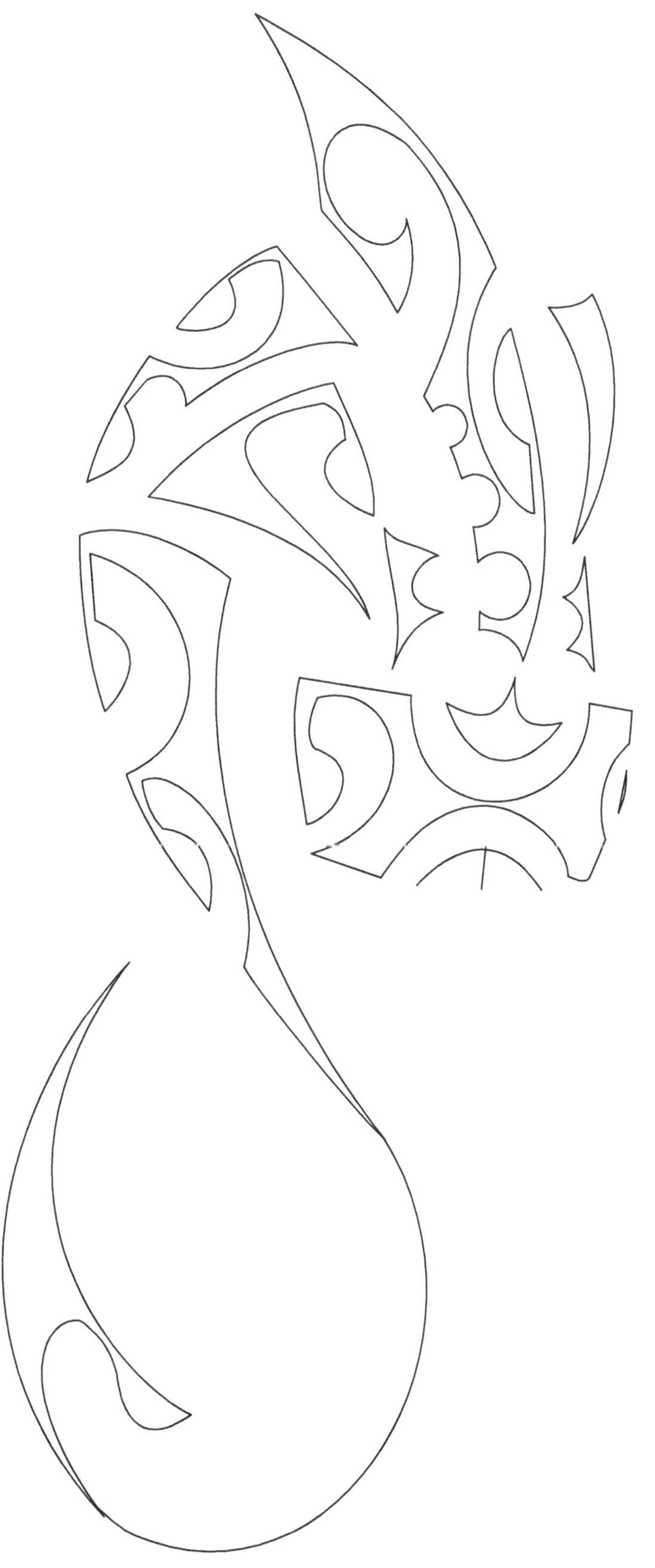

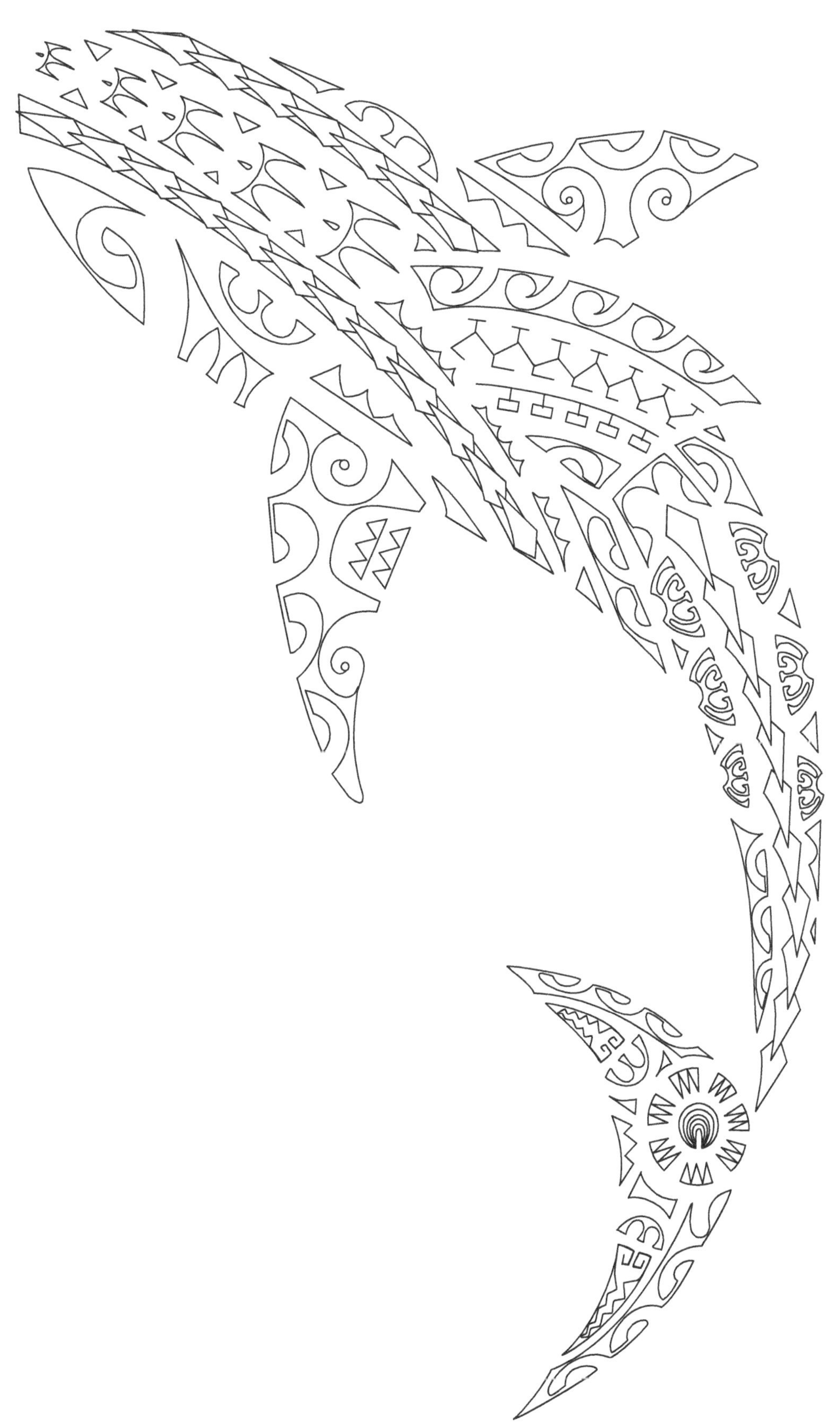

t053

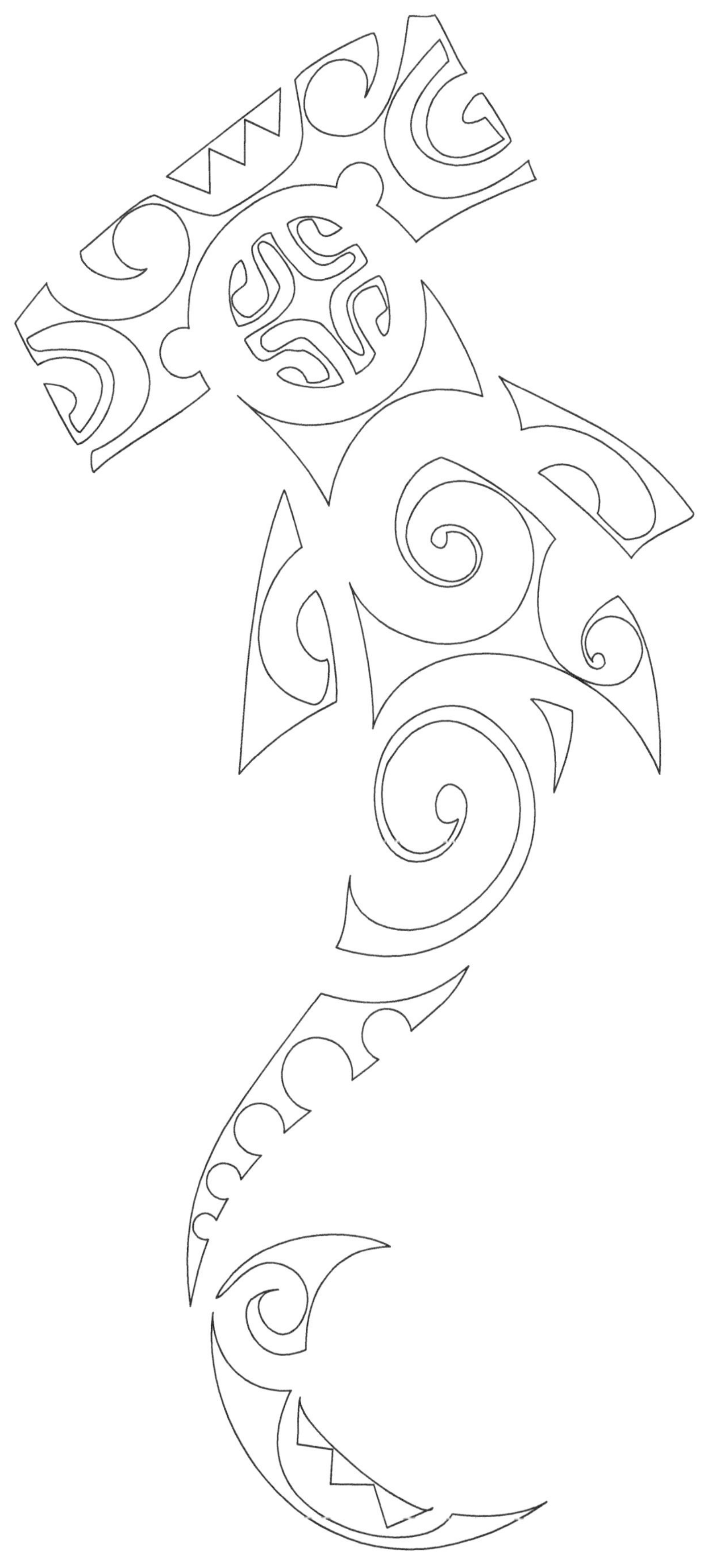

t054

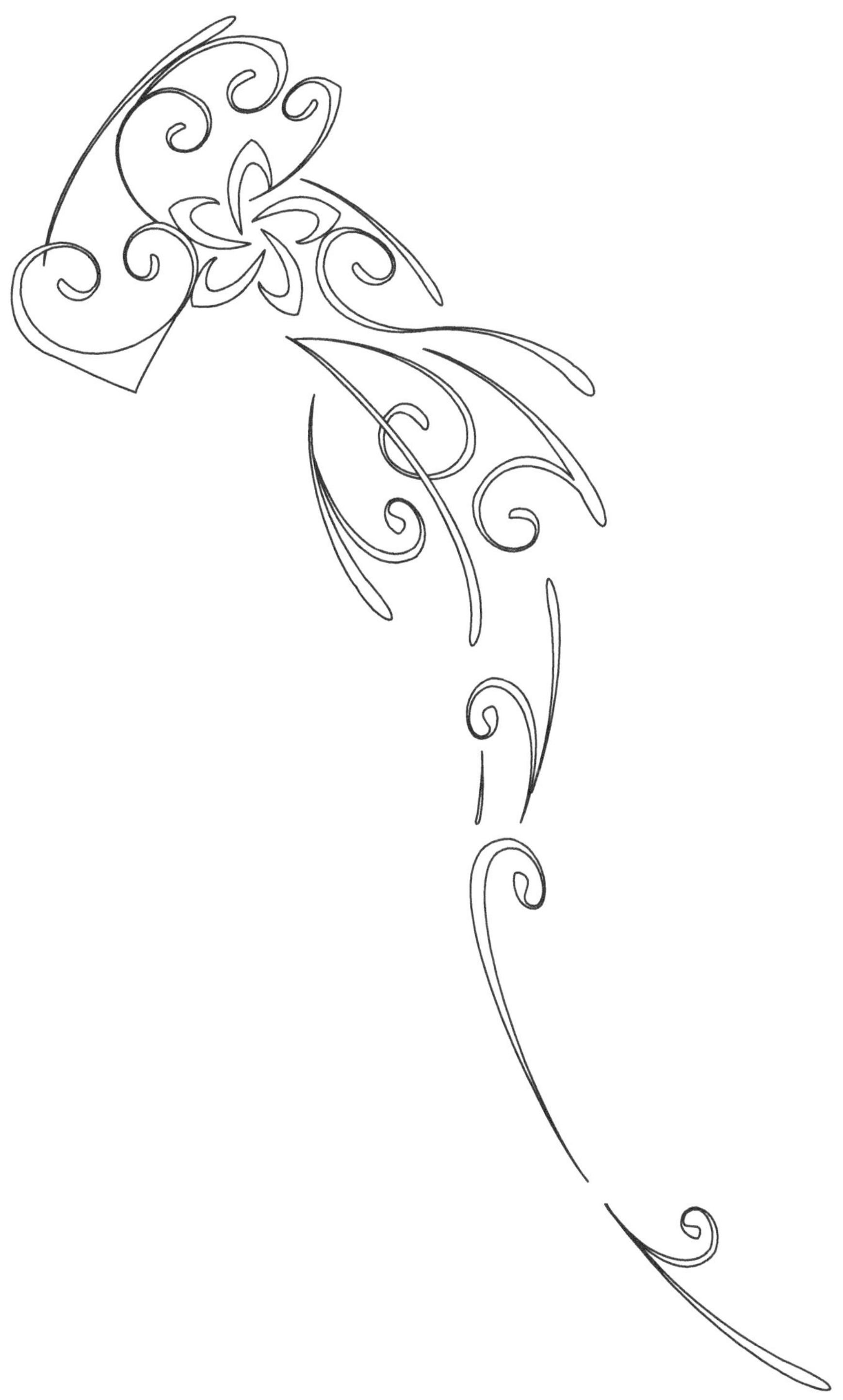

t055

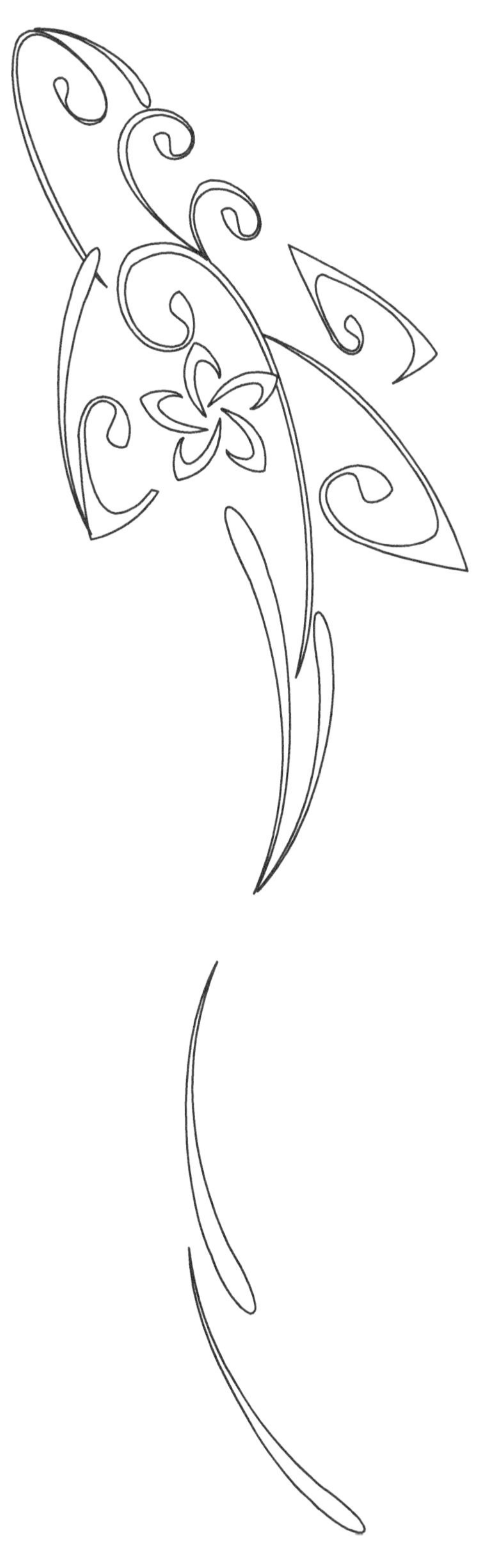

t056

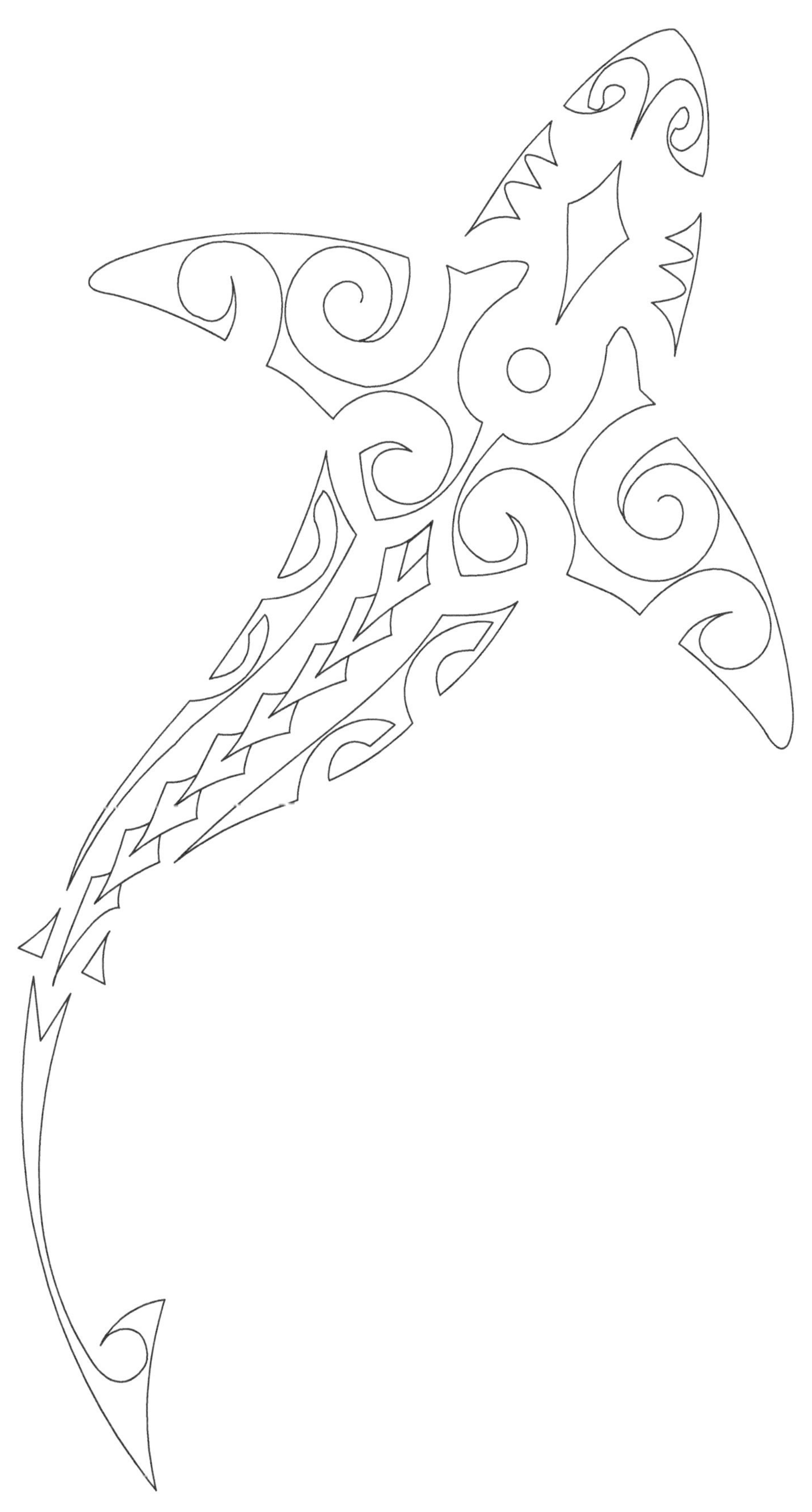

t057

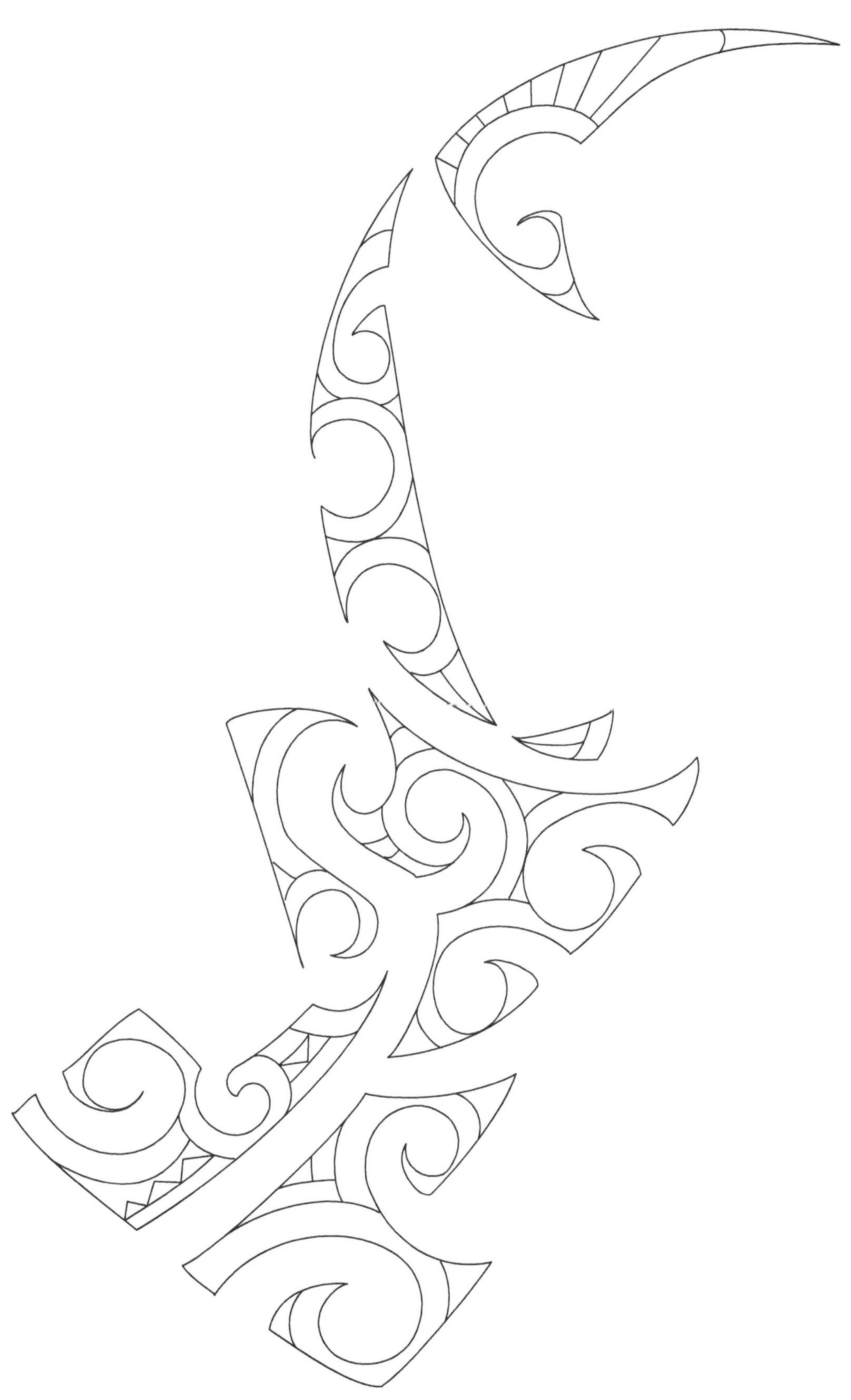

t058

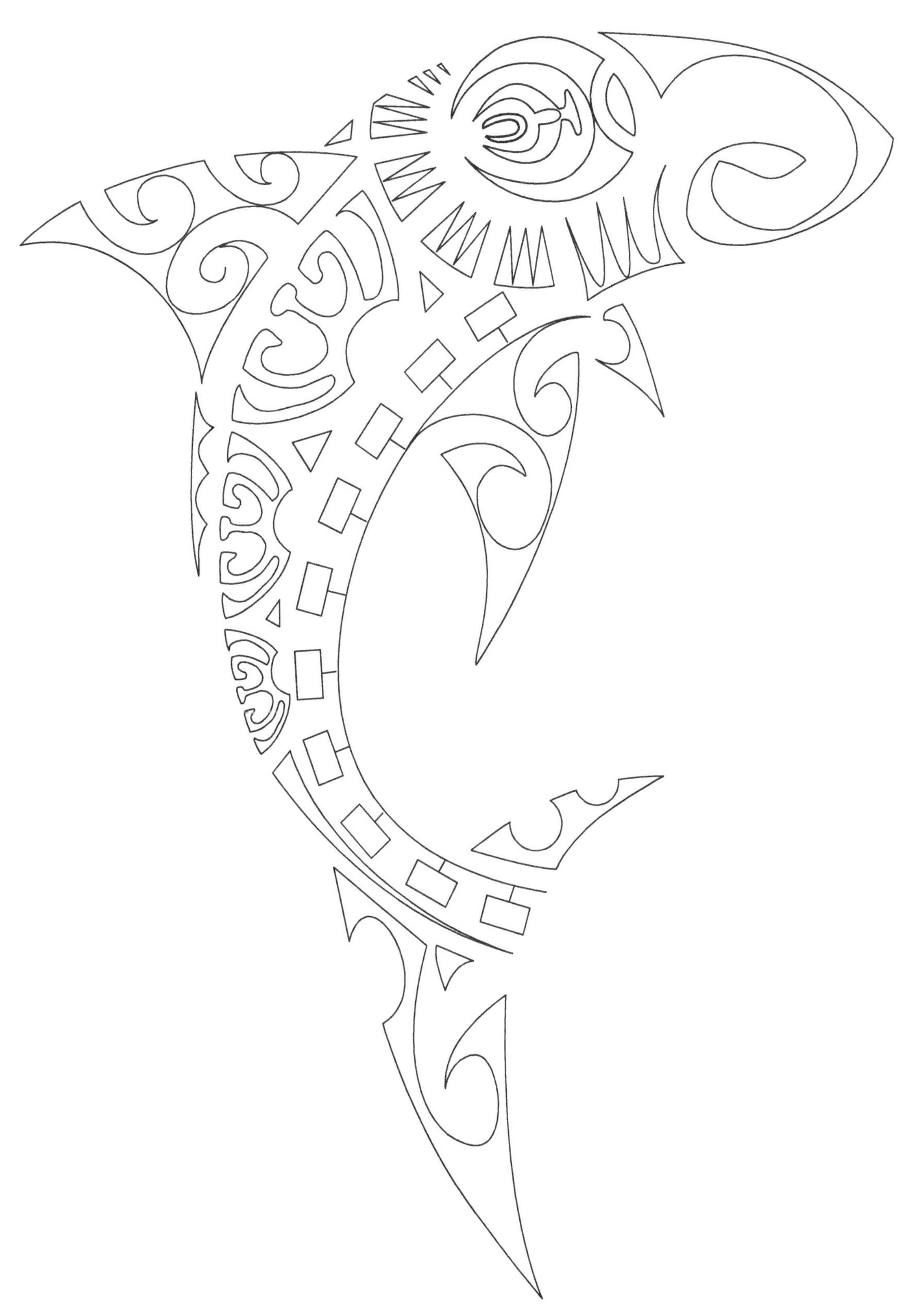

t059

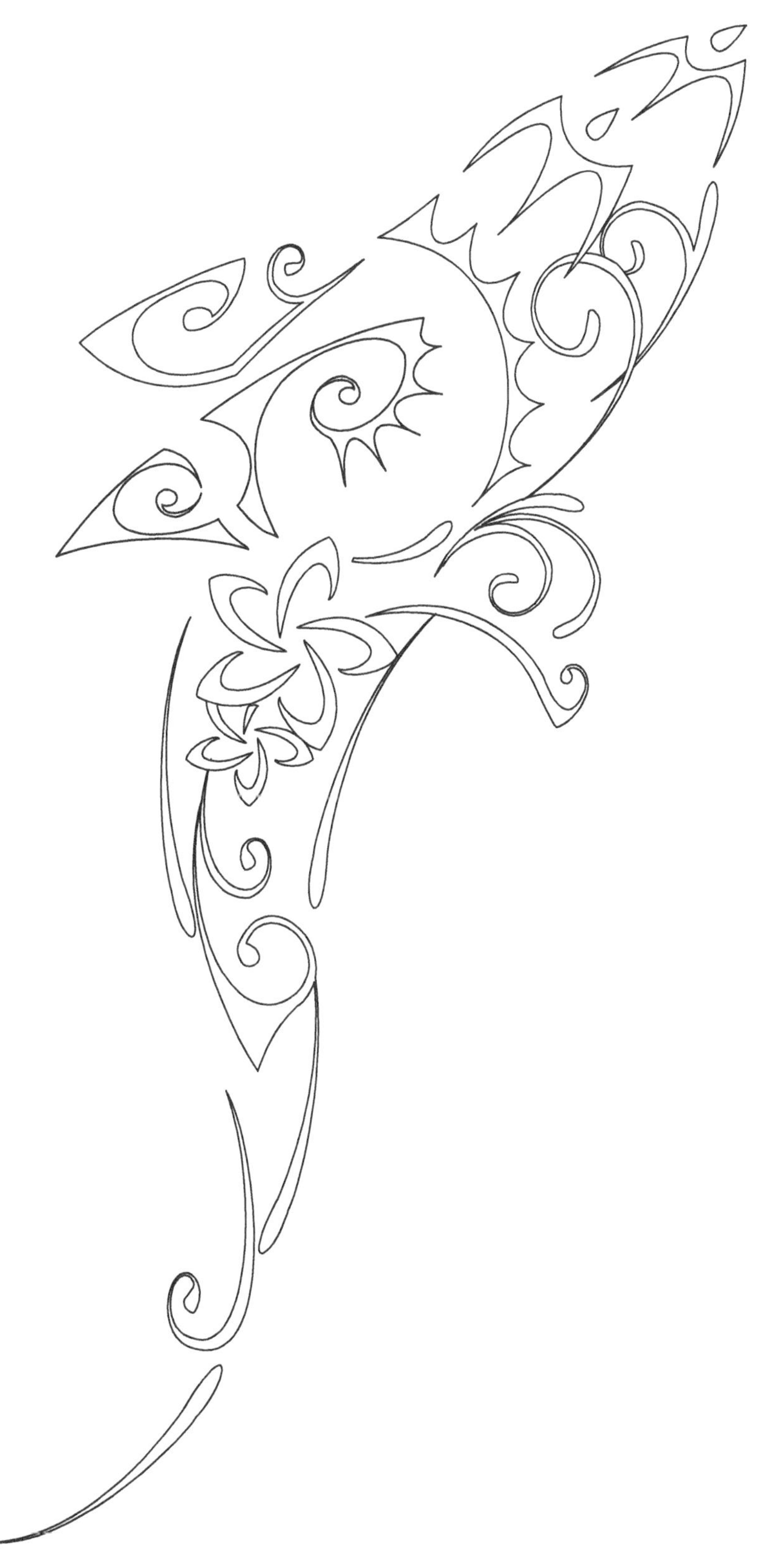

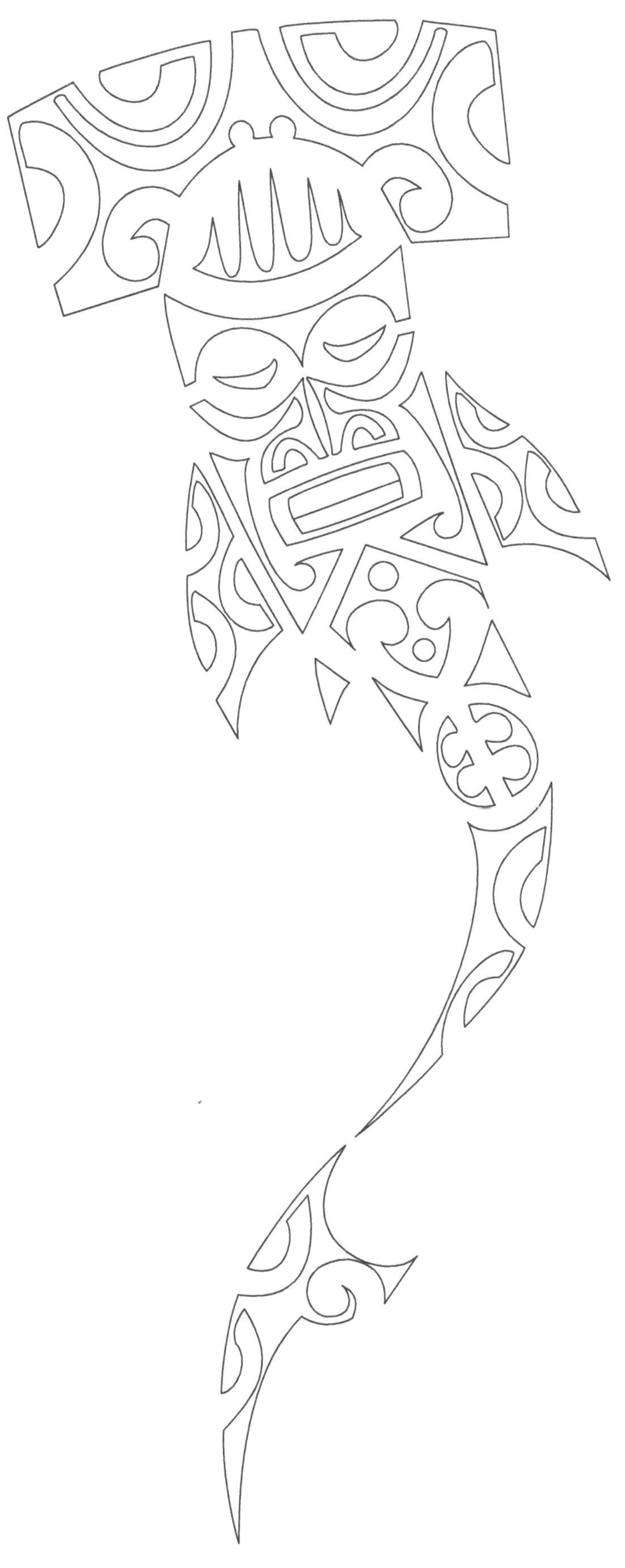

t061

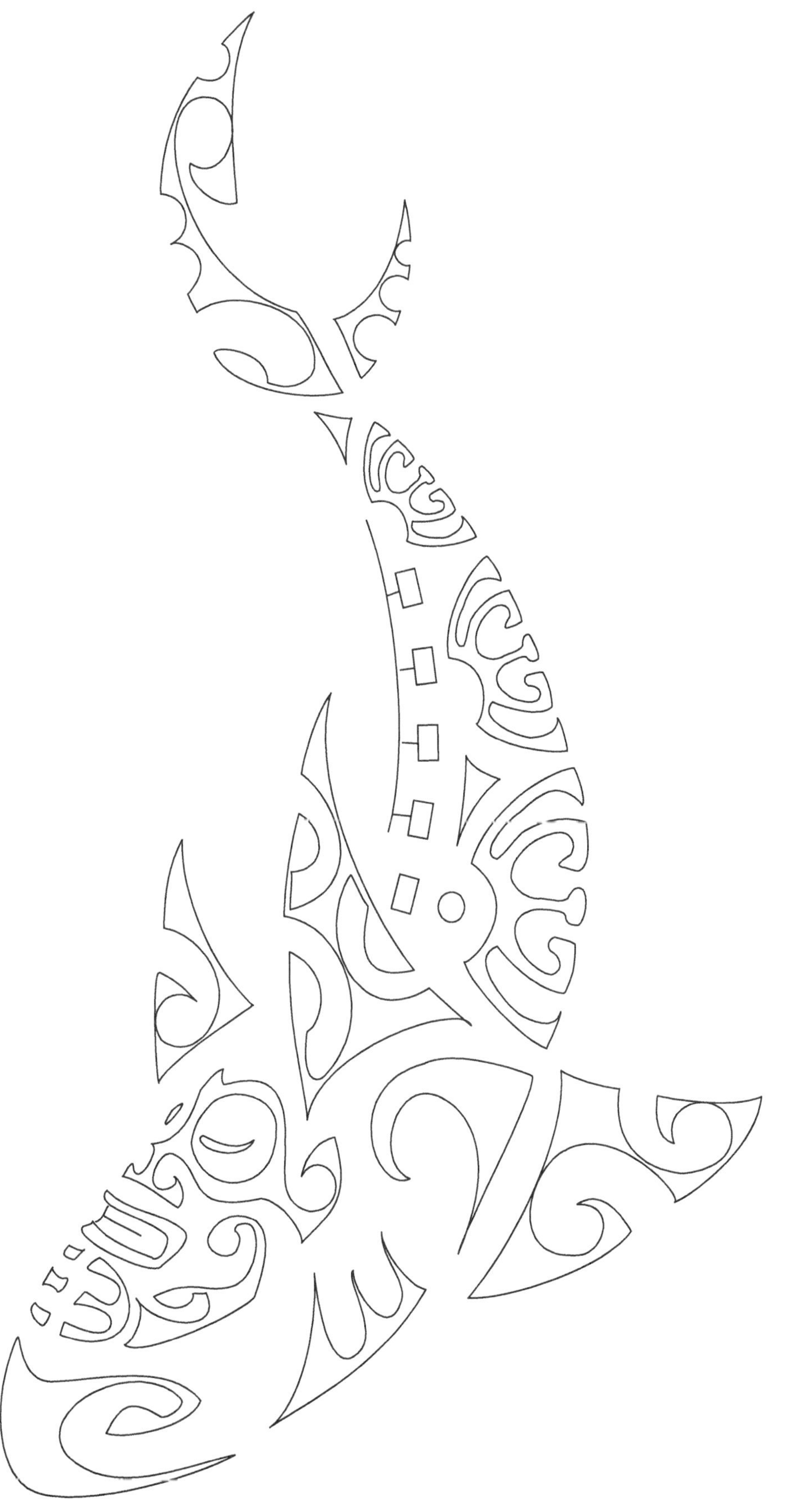

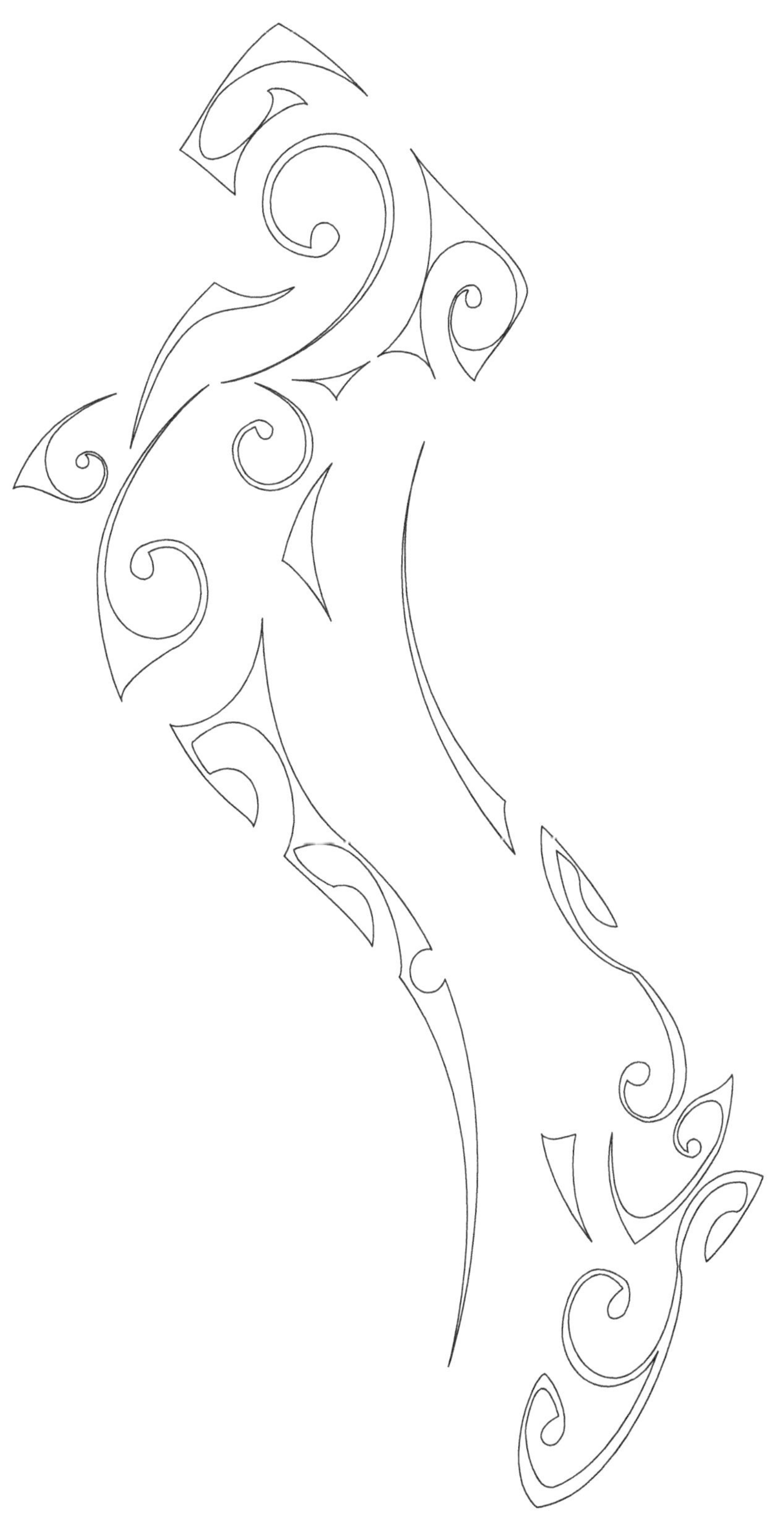

t063

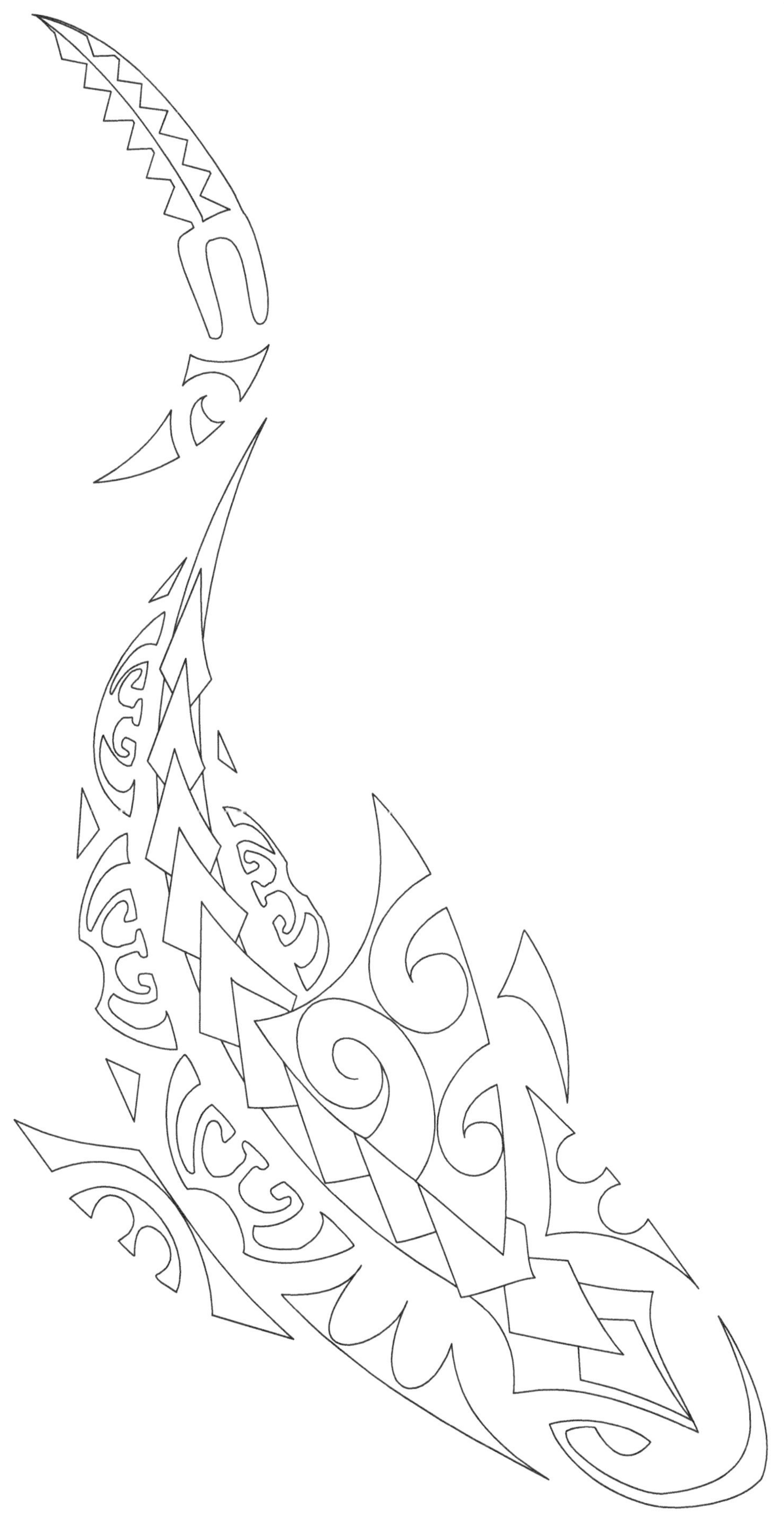

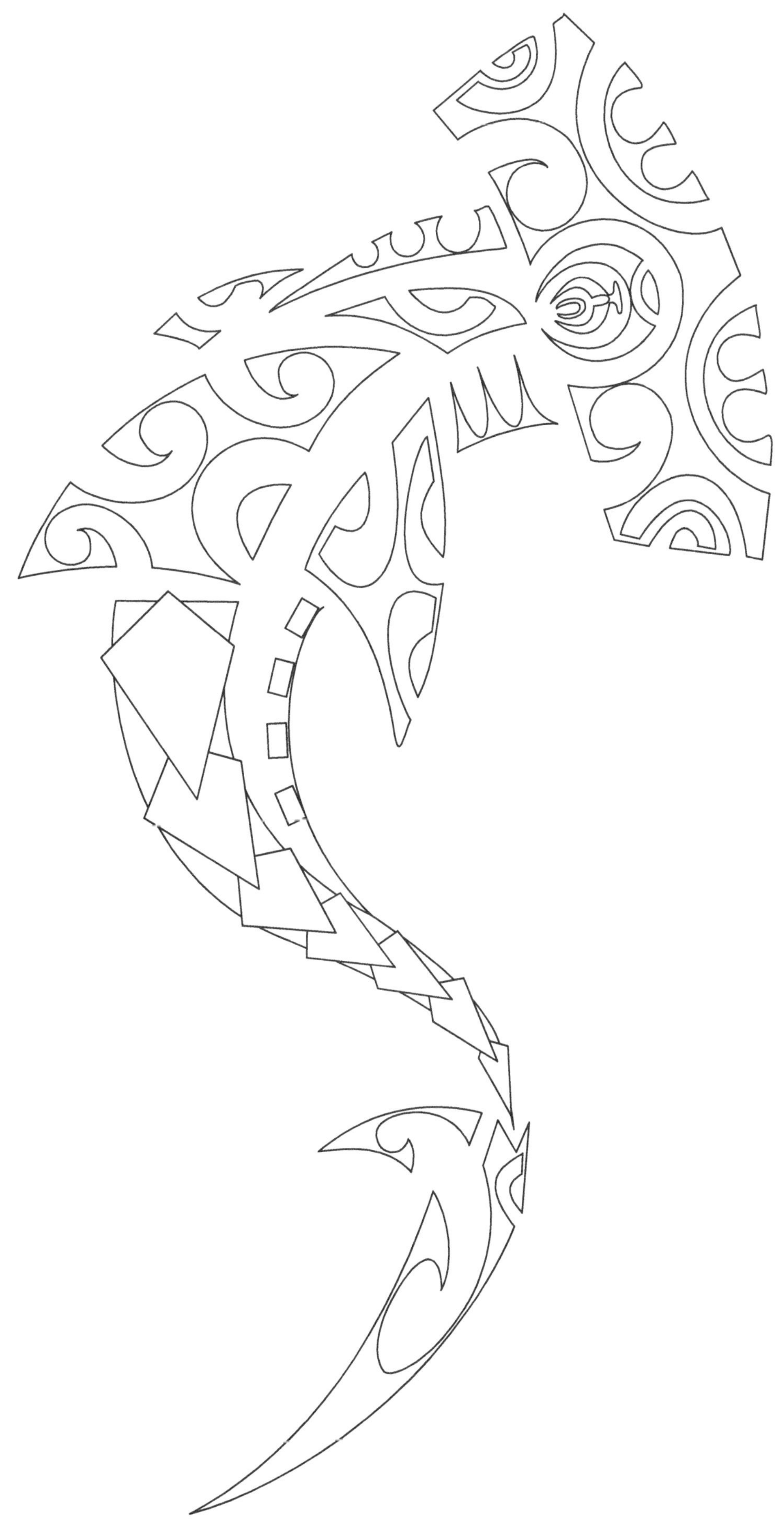

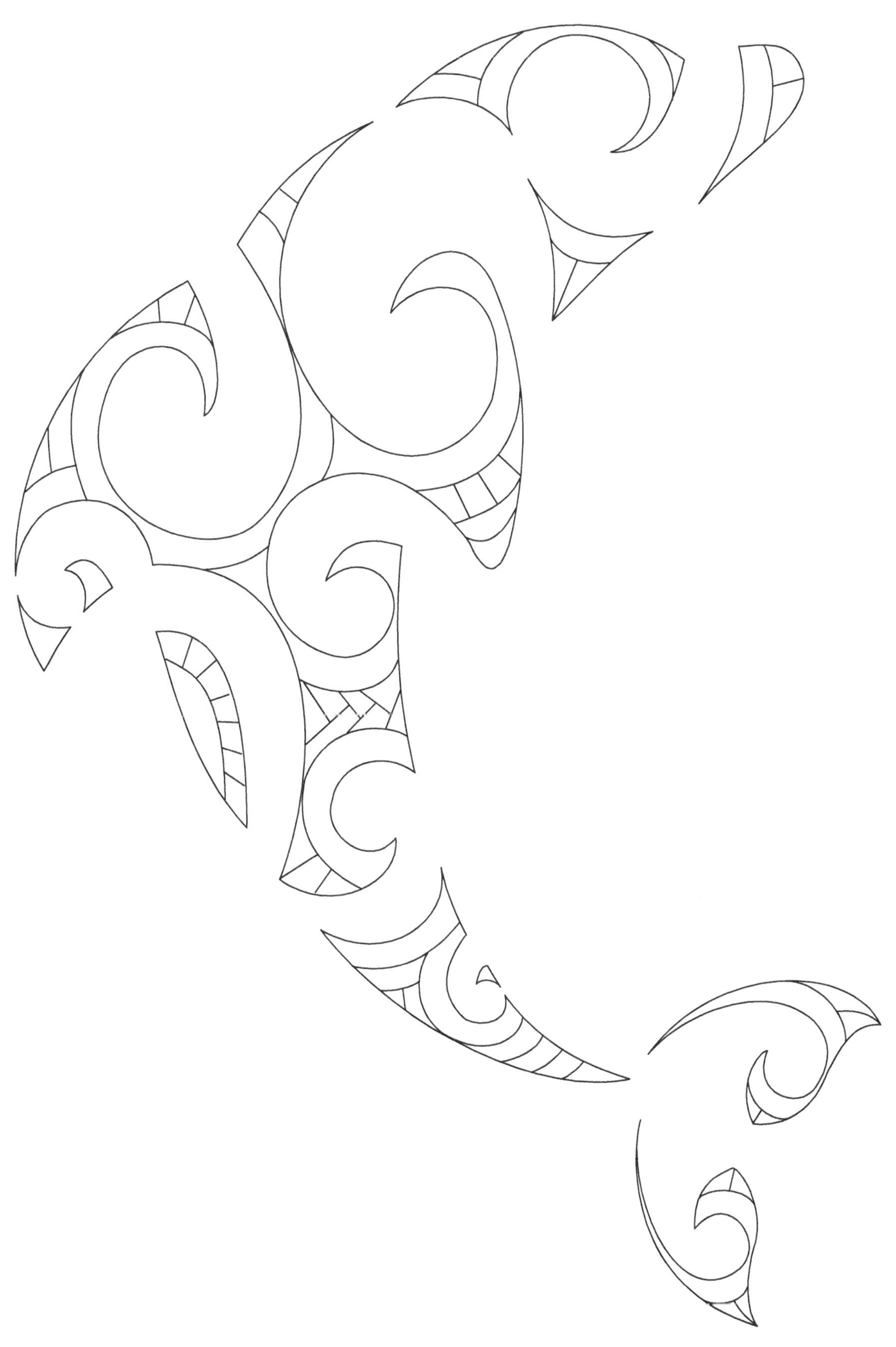

t066

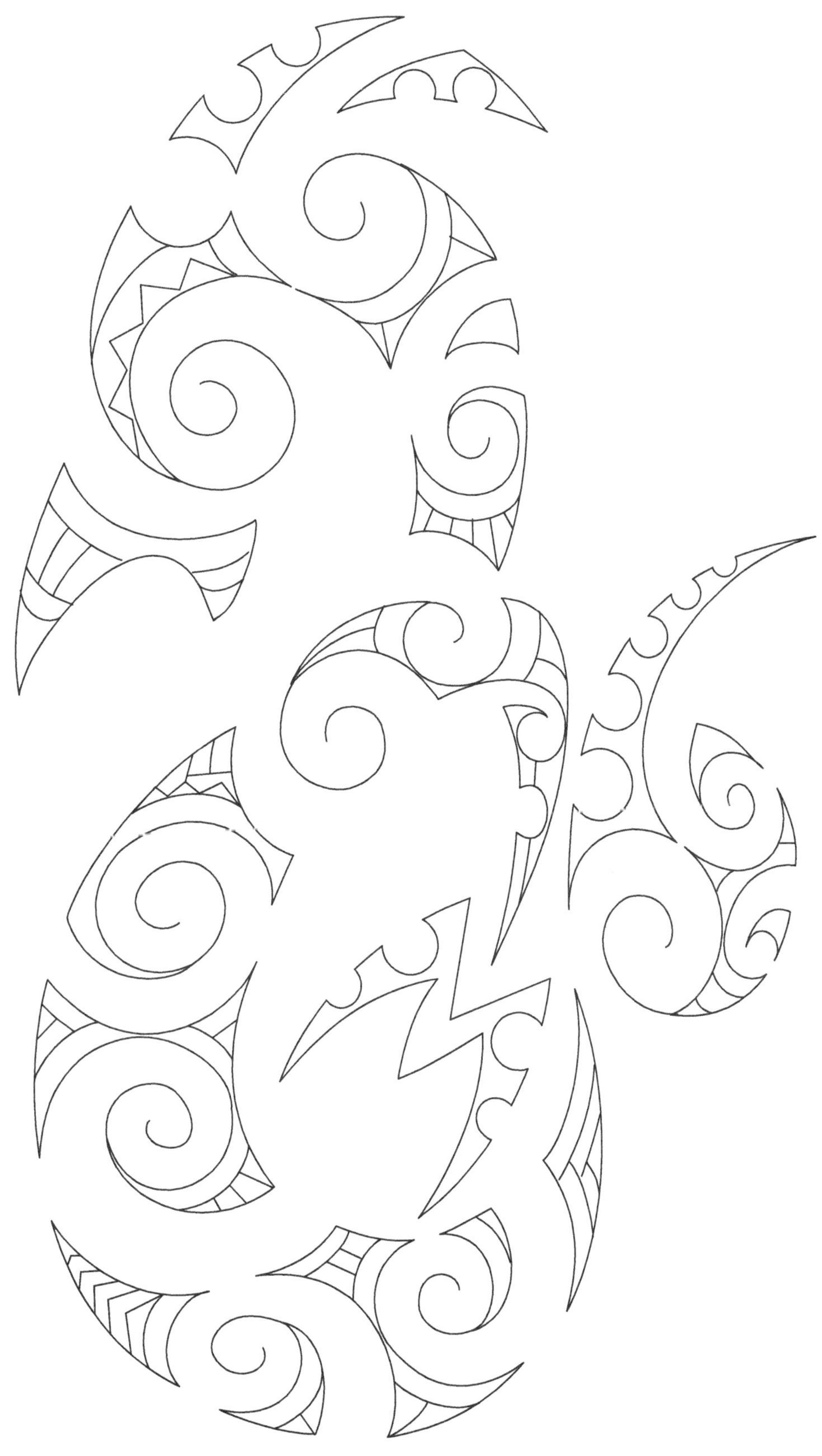

t067

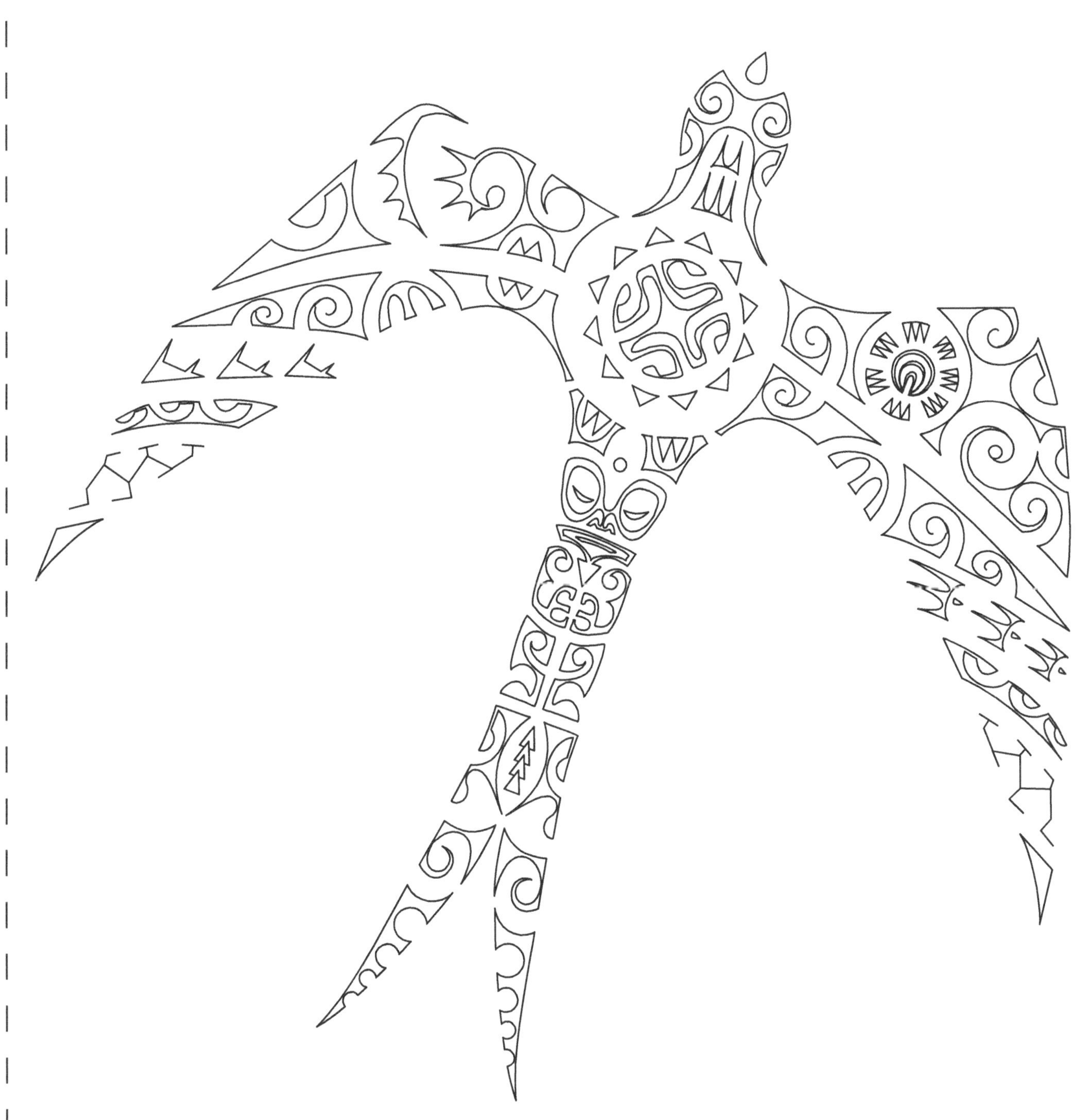

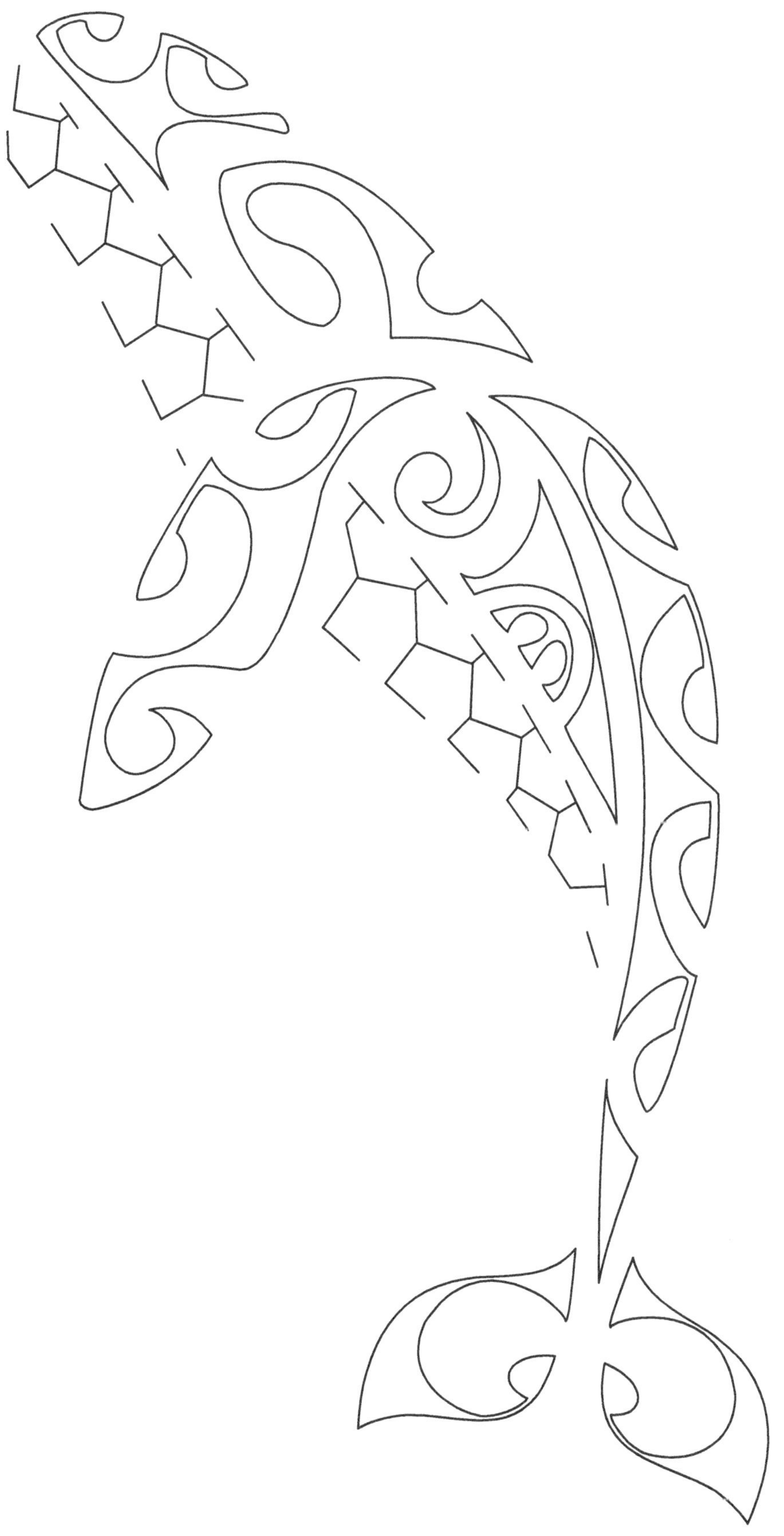

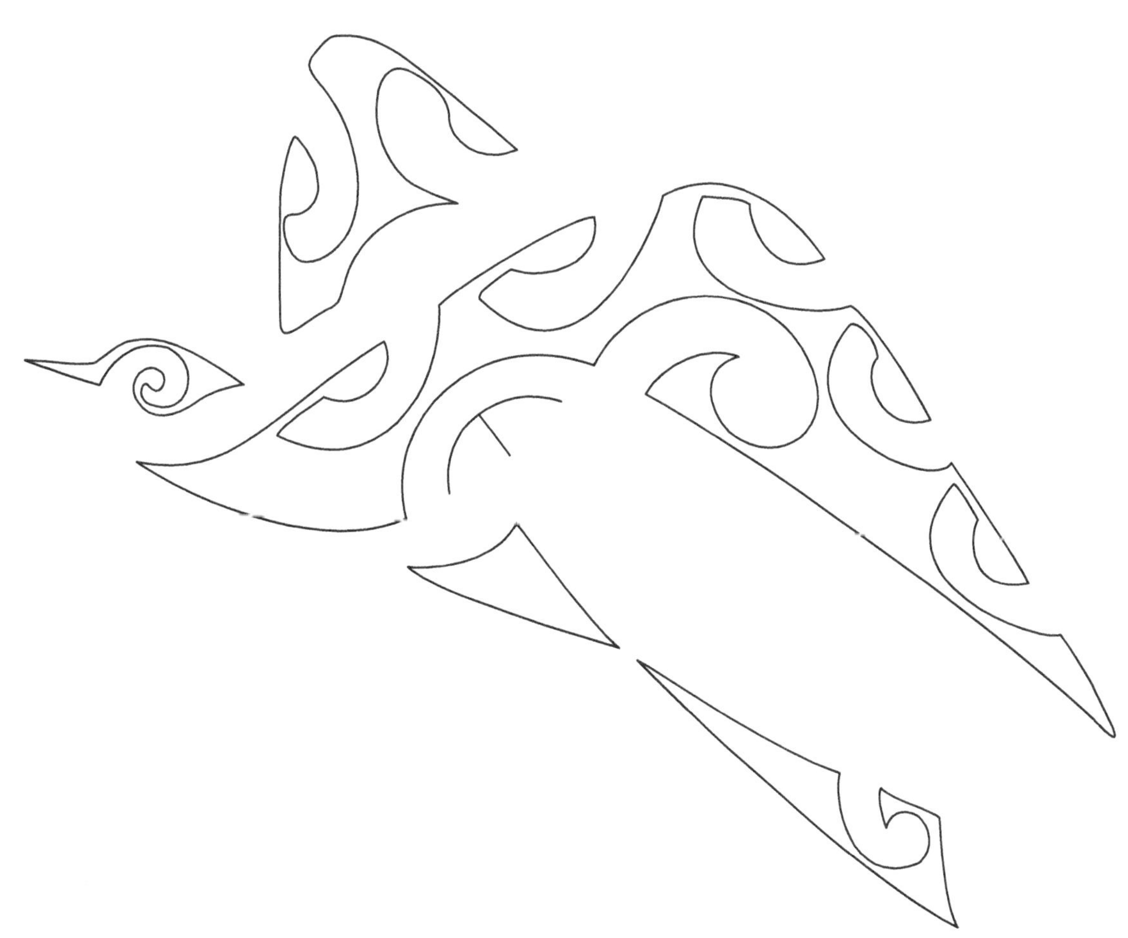

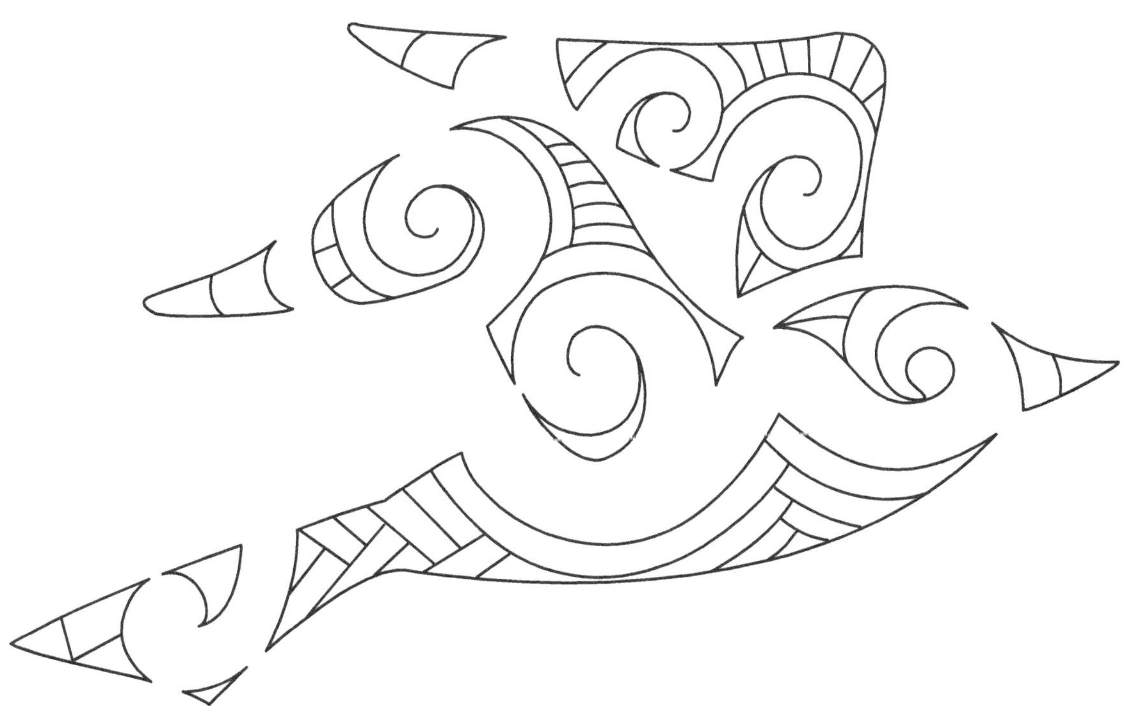

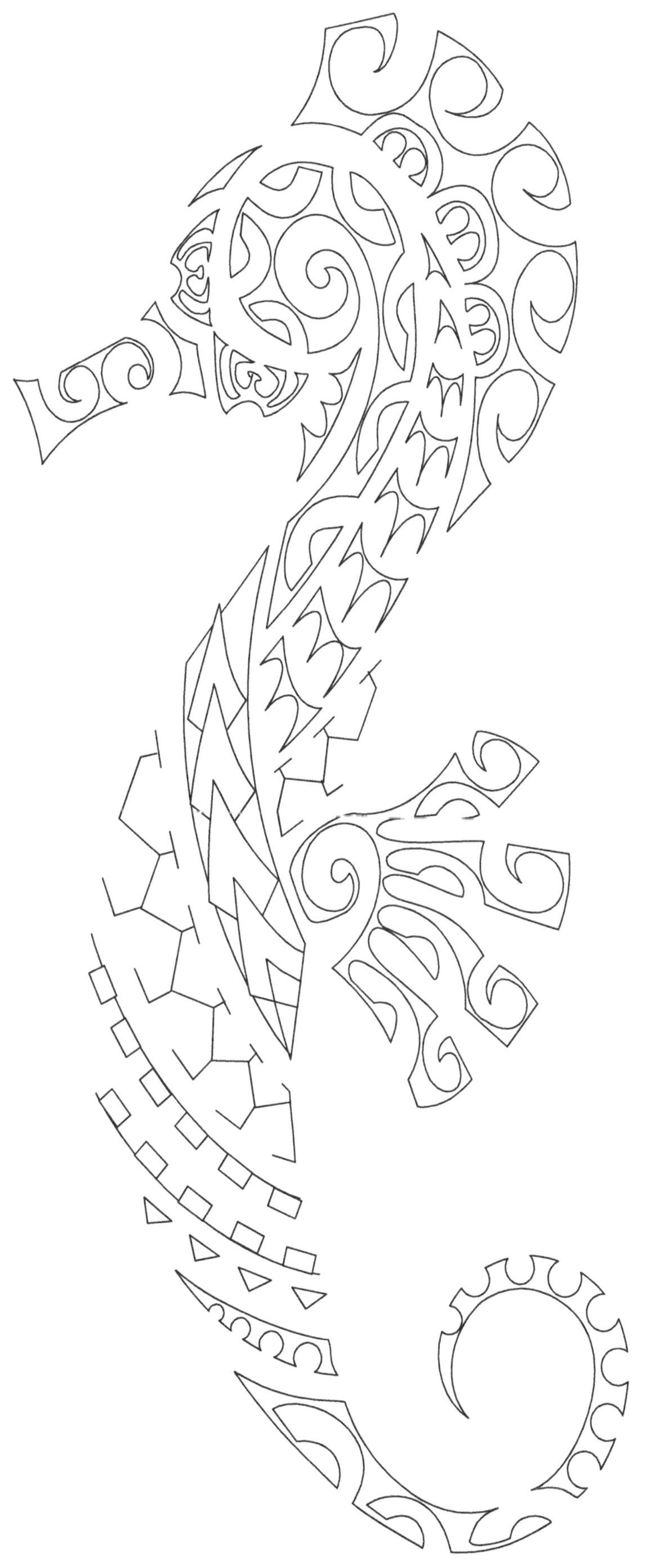

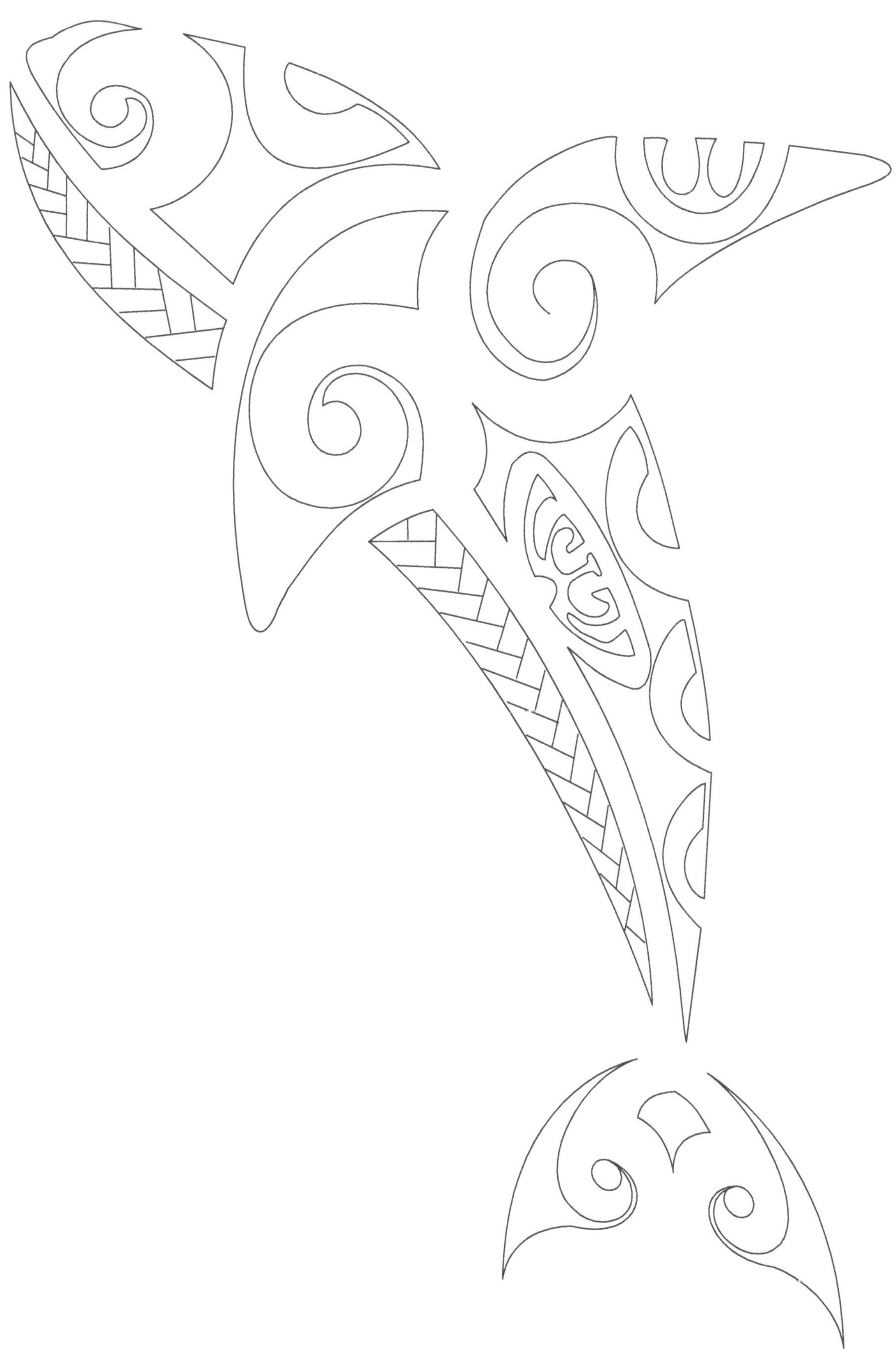

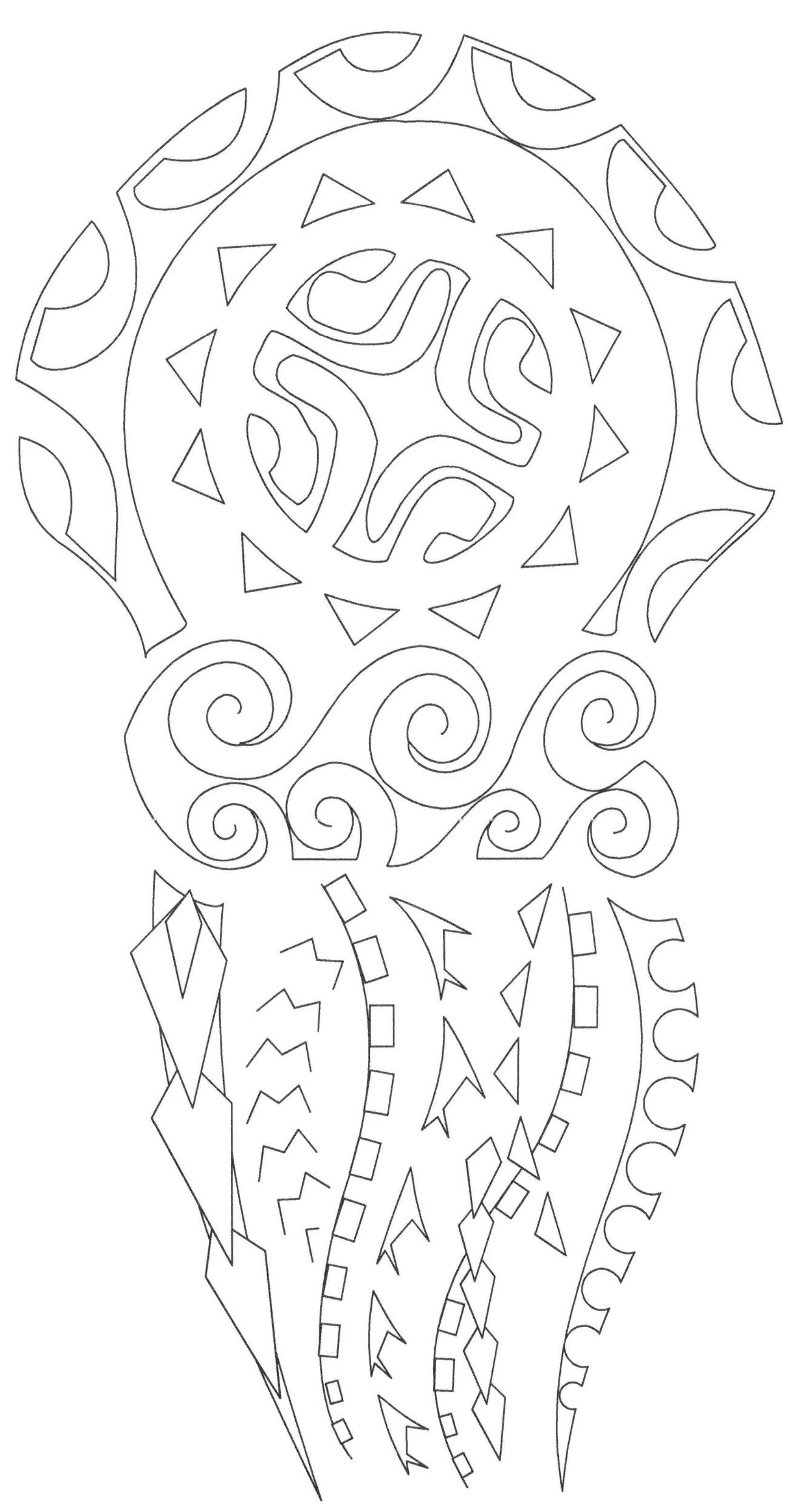

t074

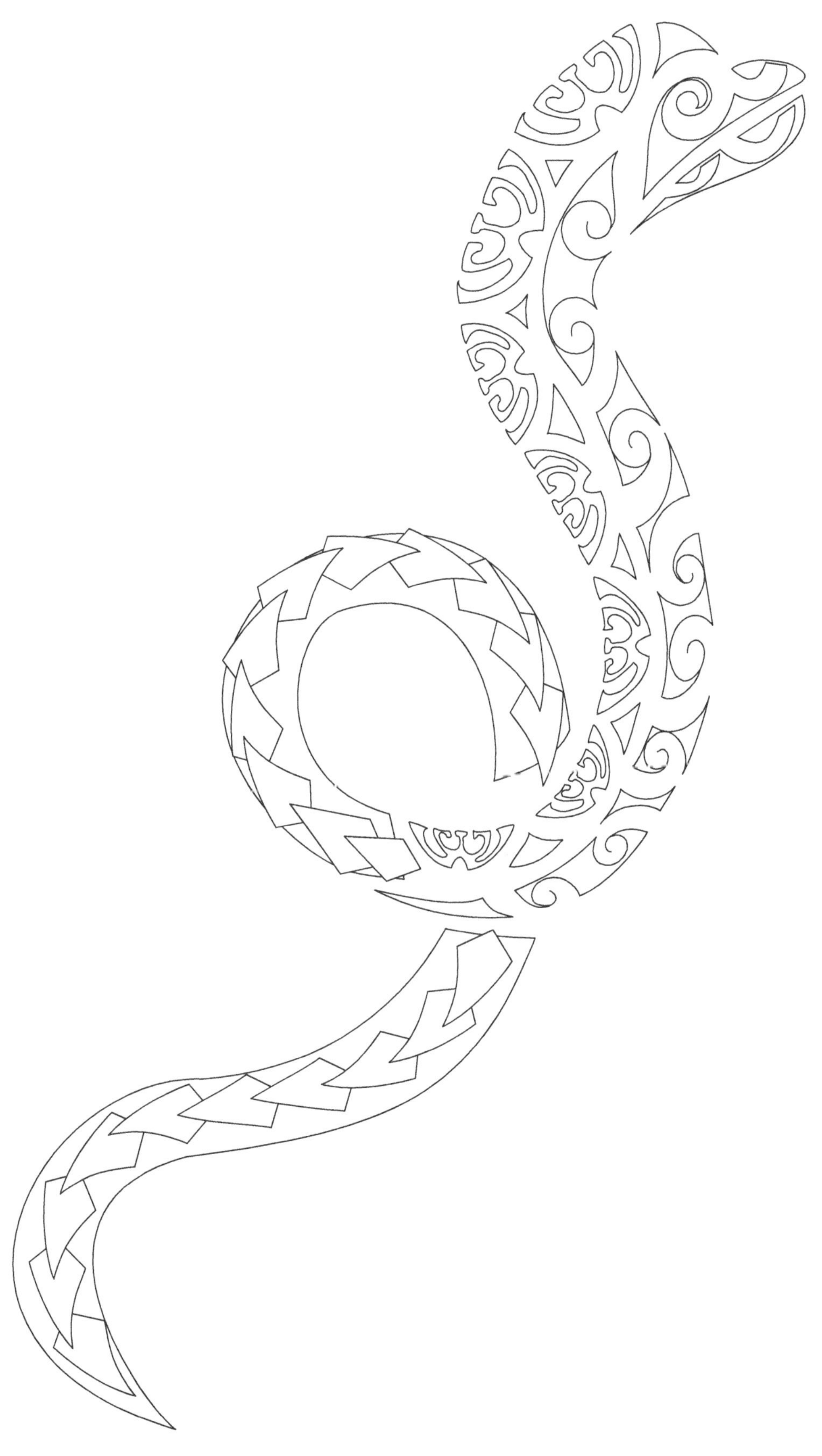

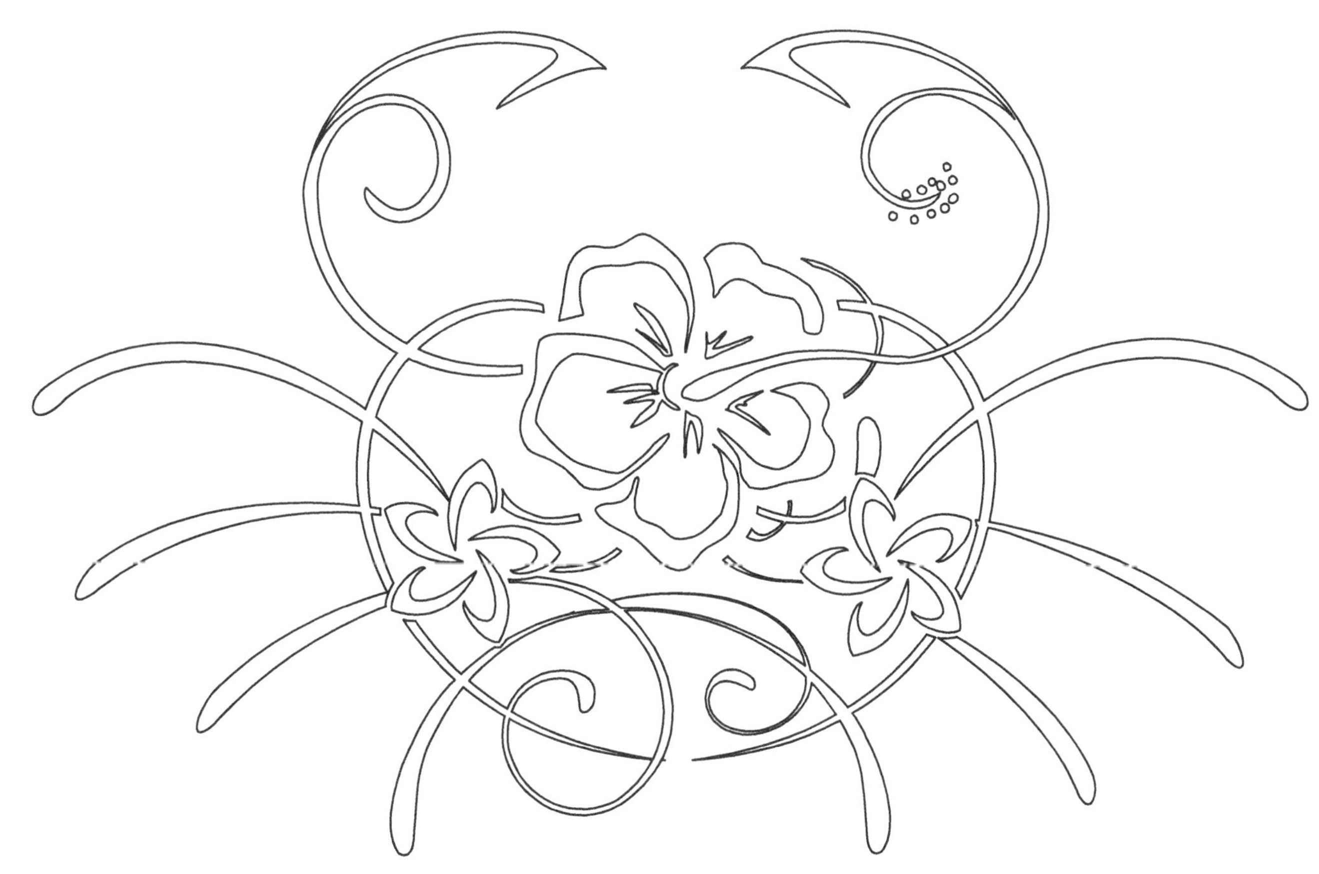

t076

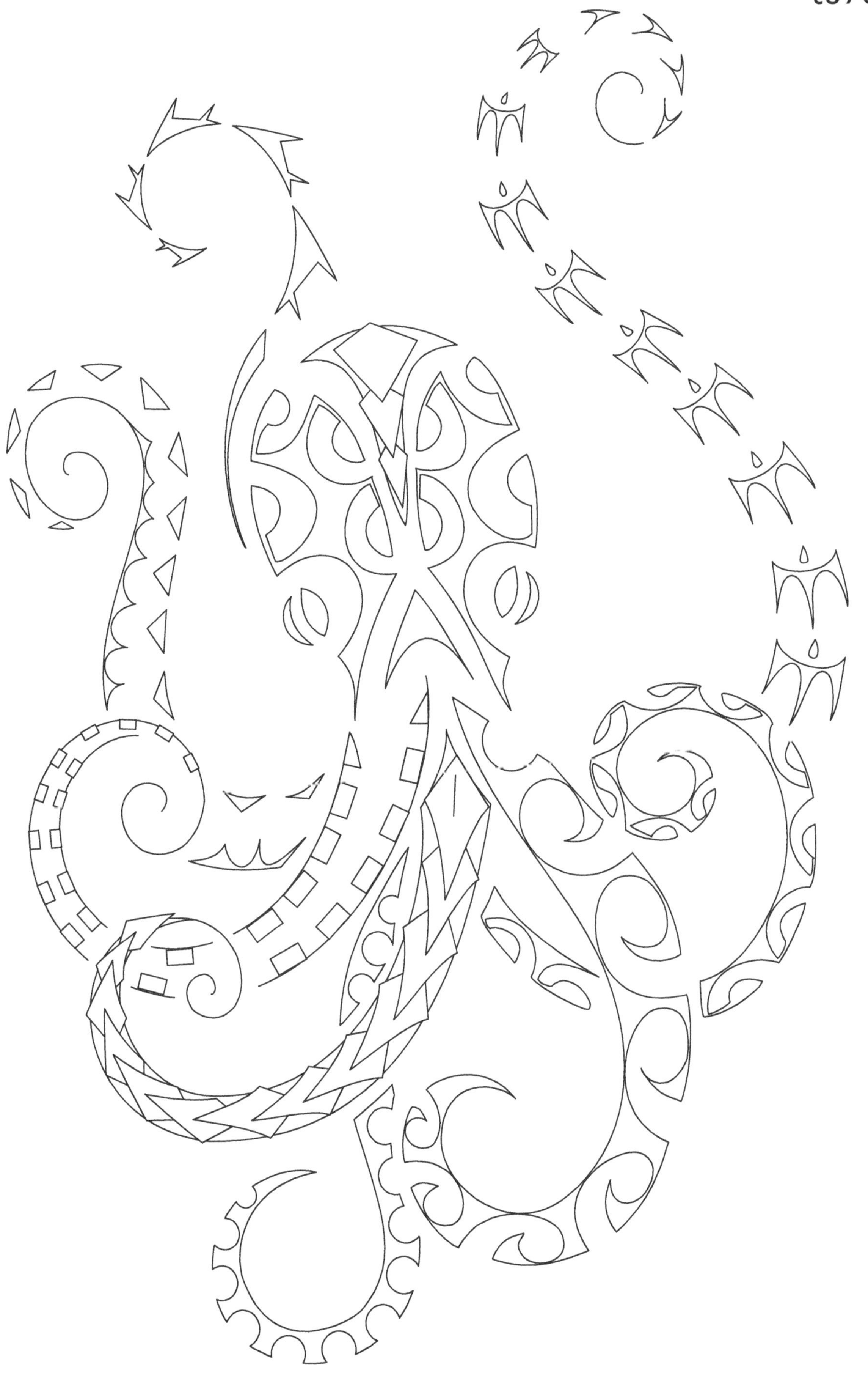

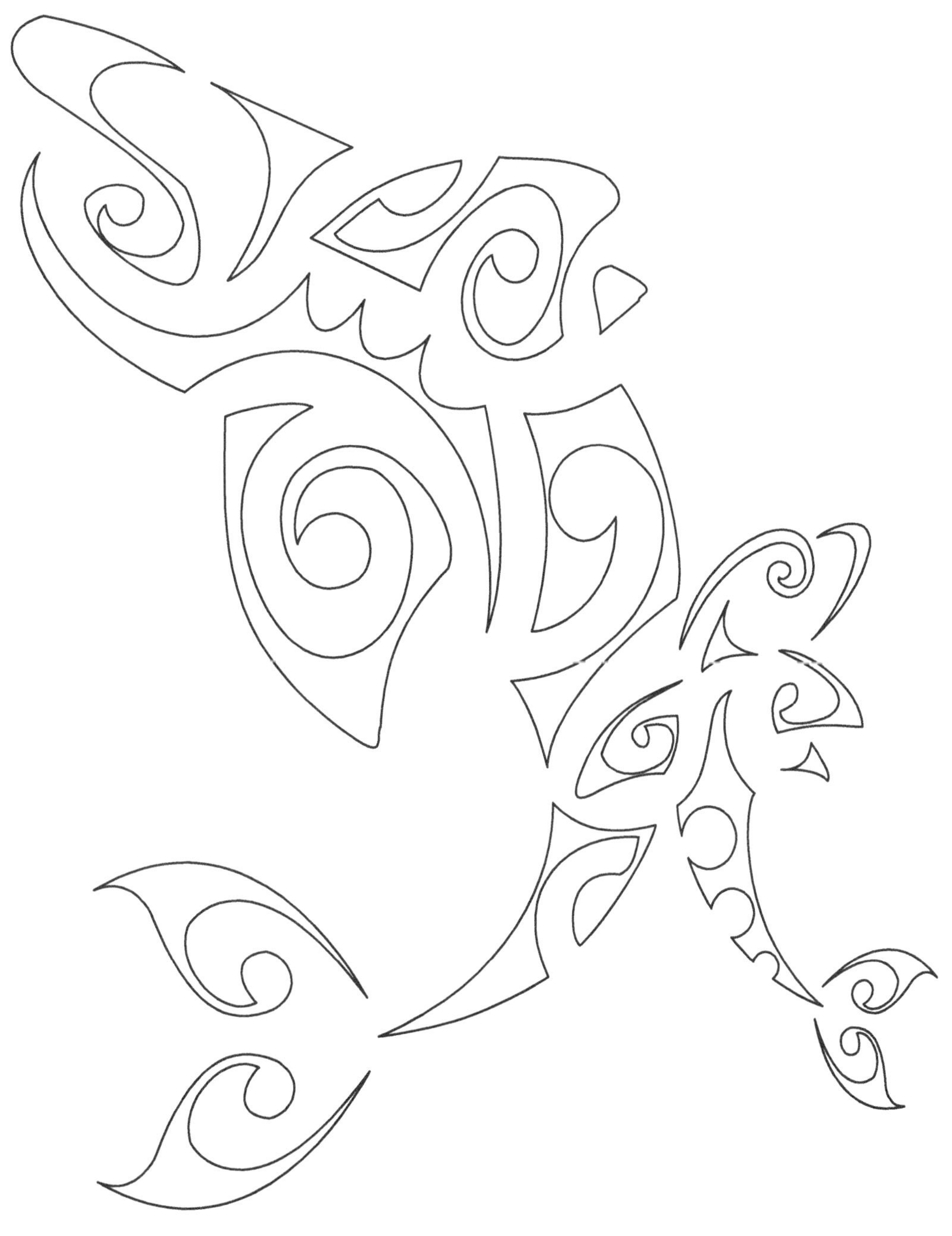

t078

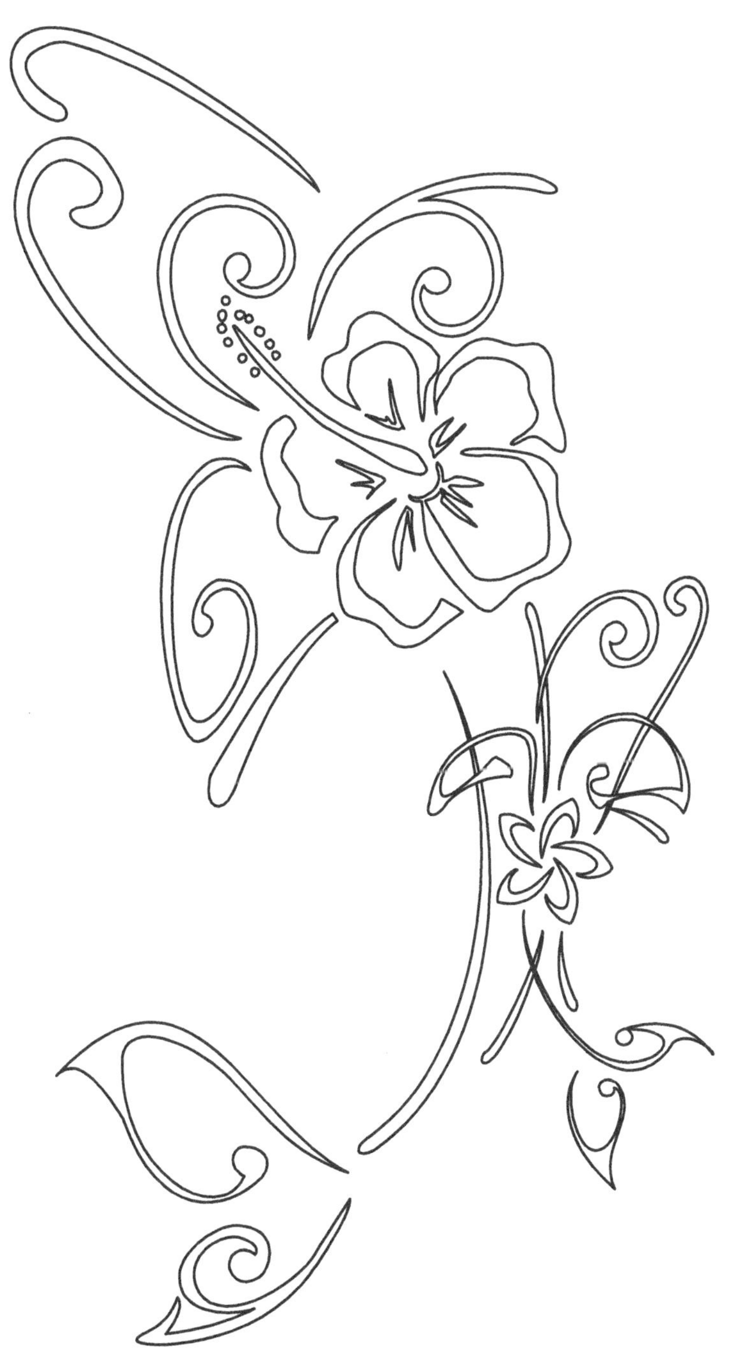

t080

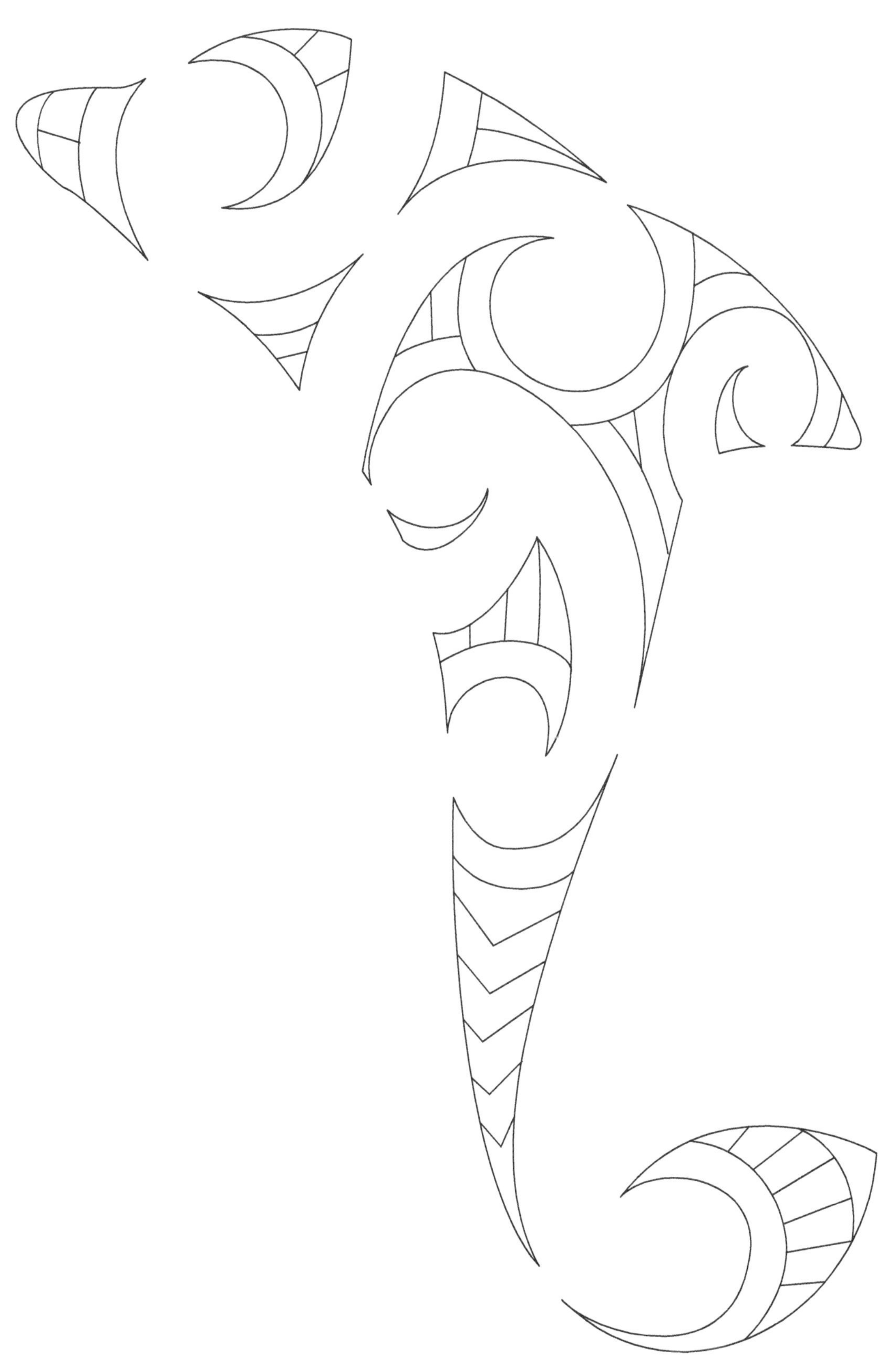

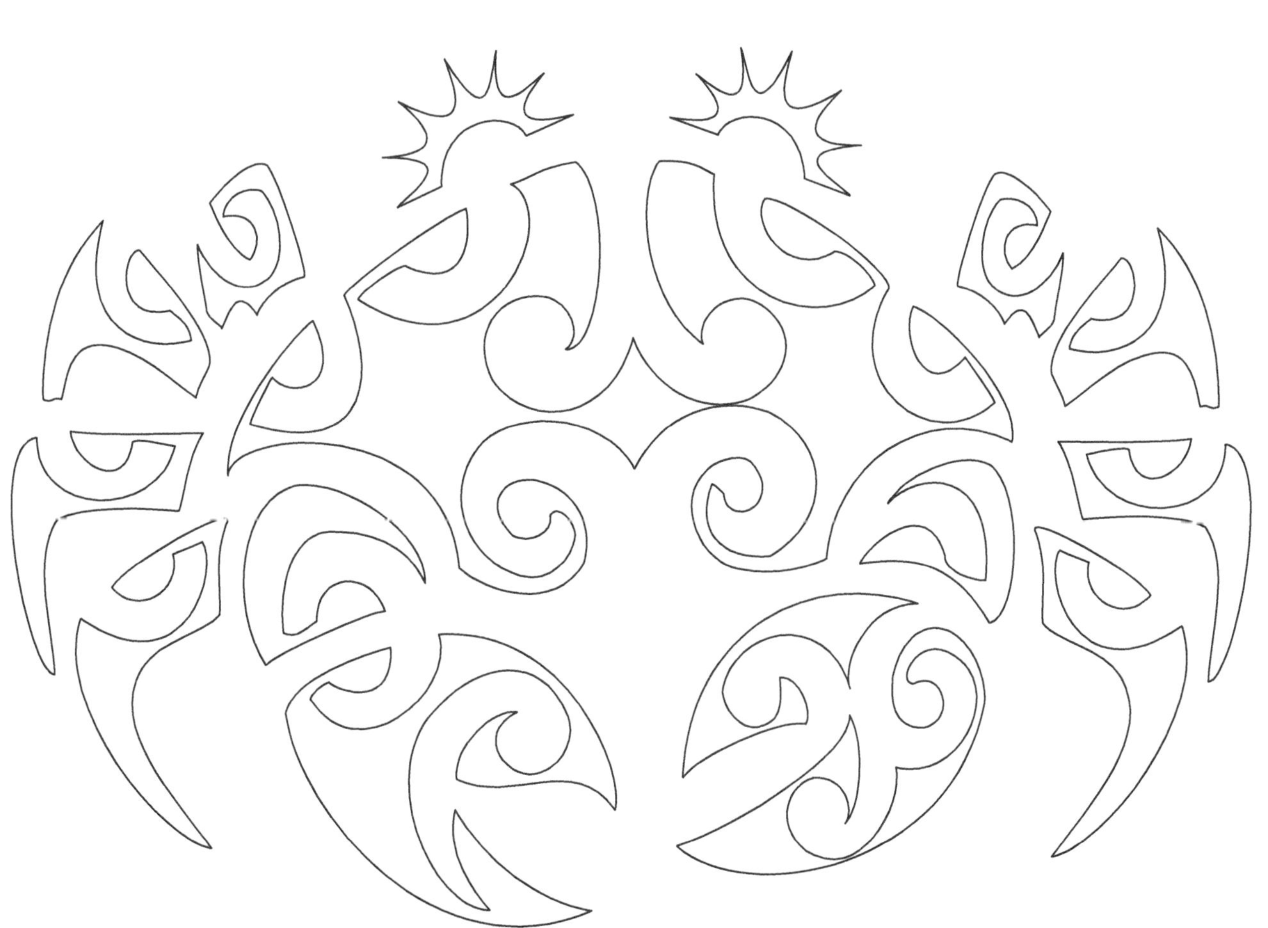

t082

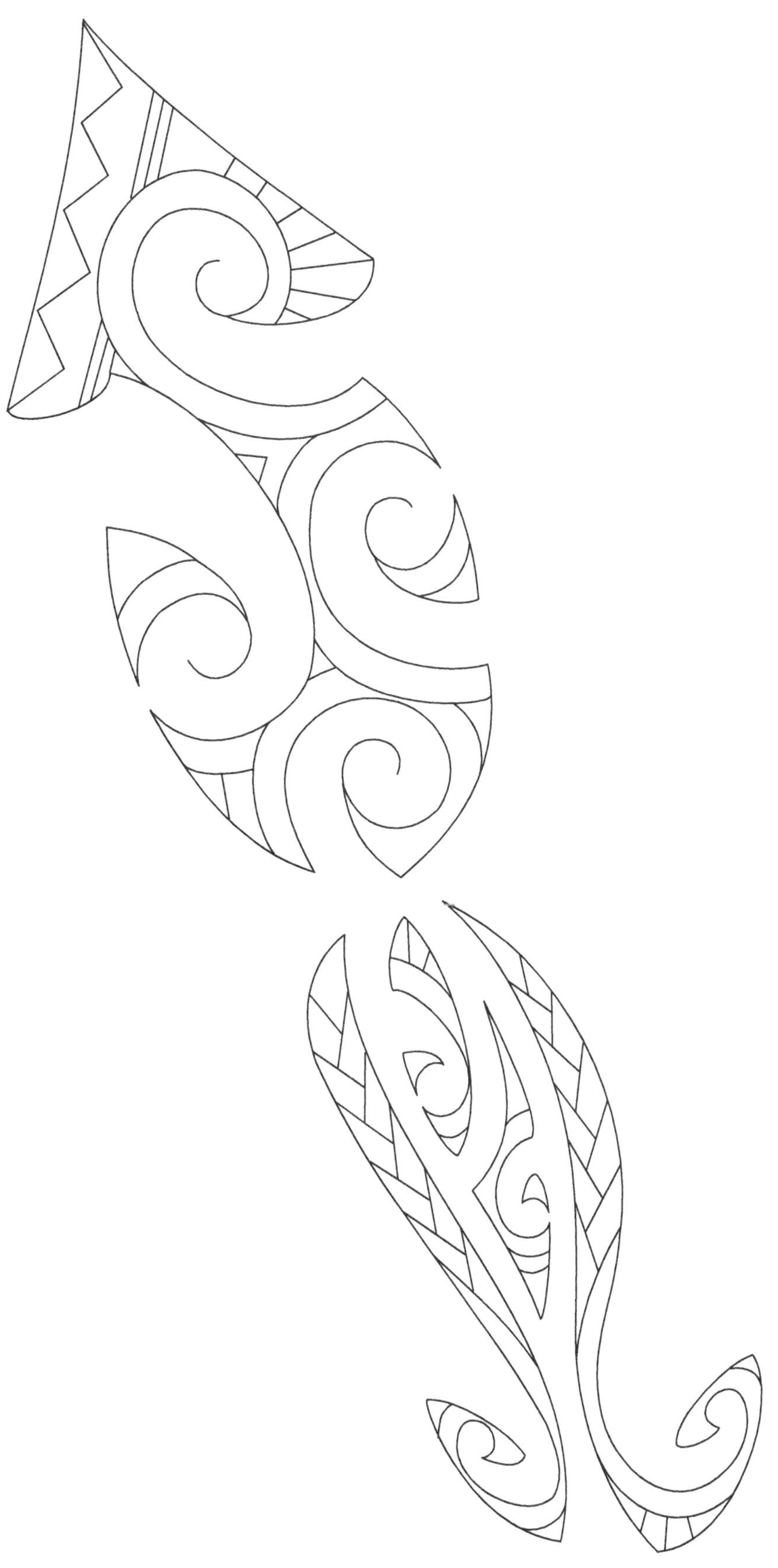

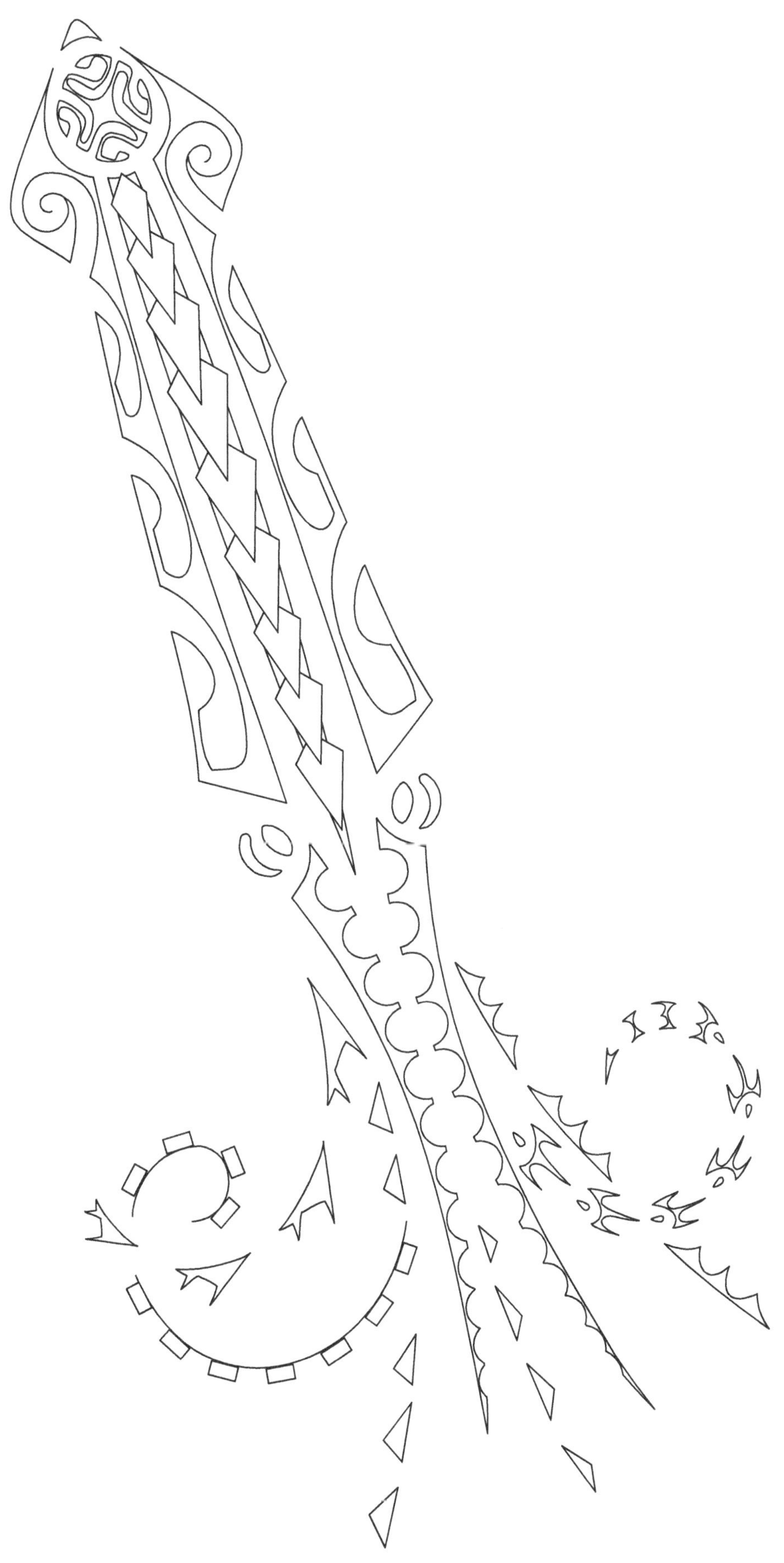

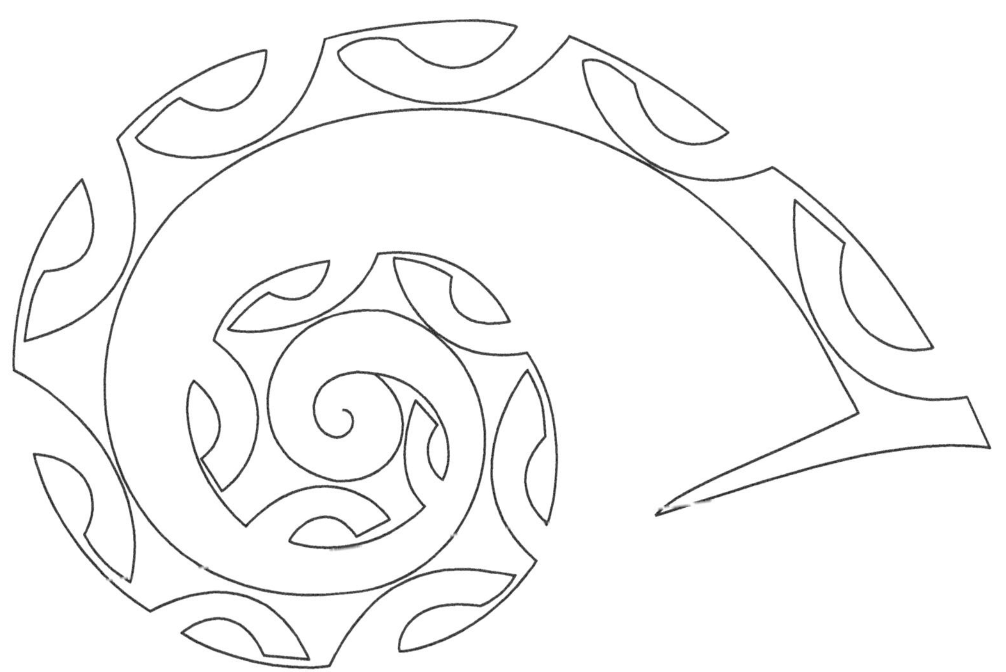

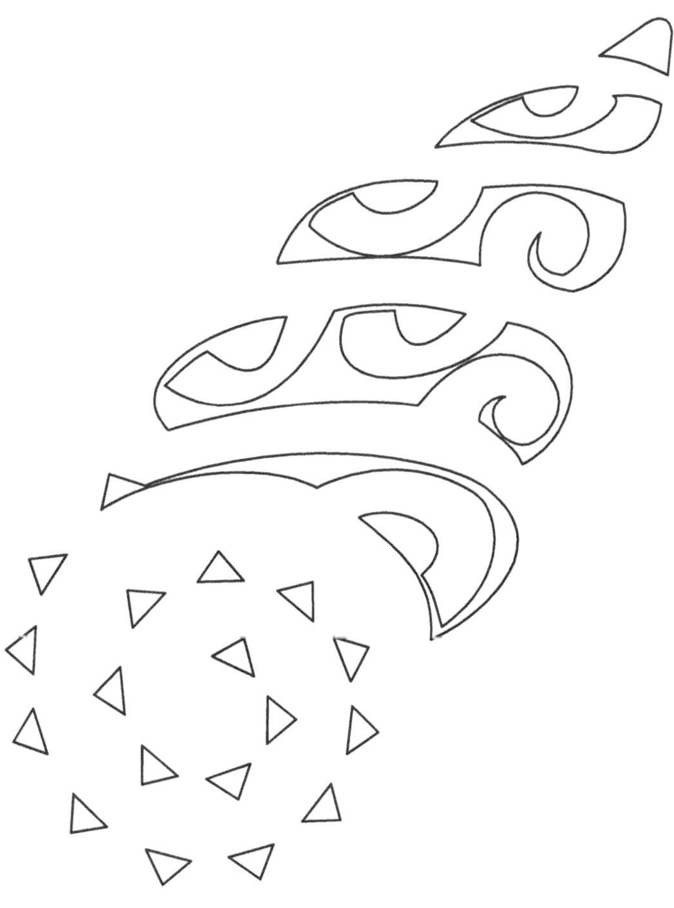

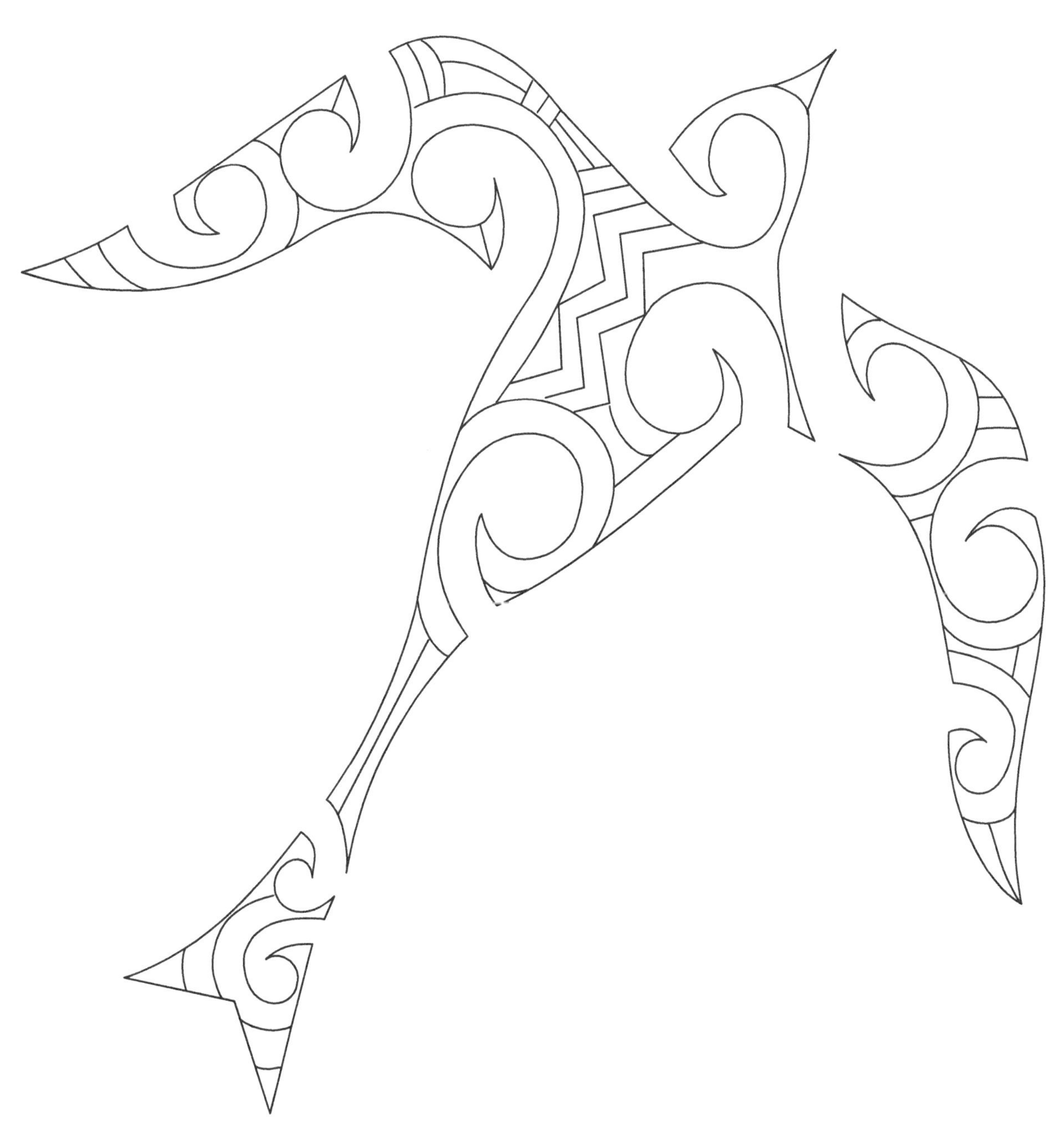

t087

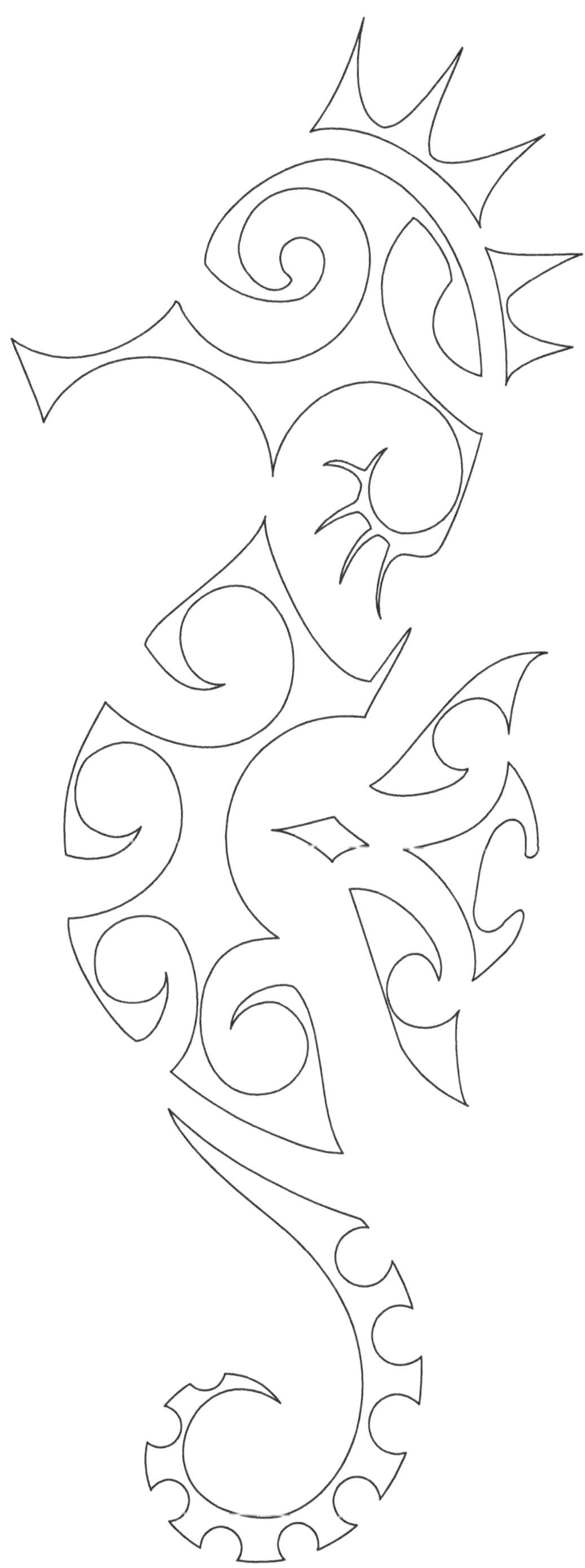

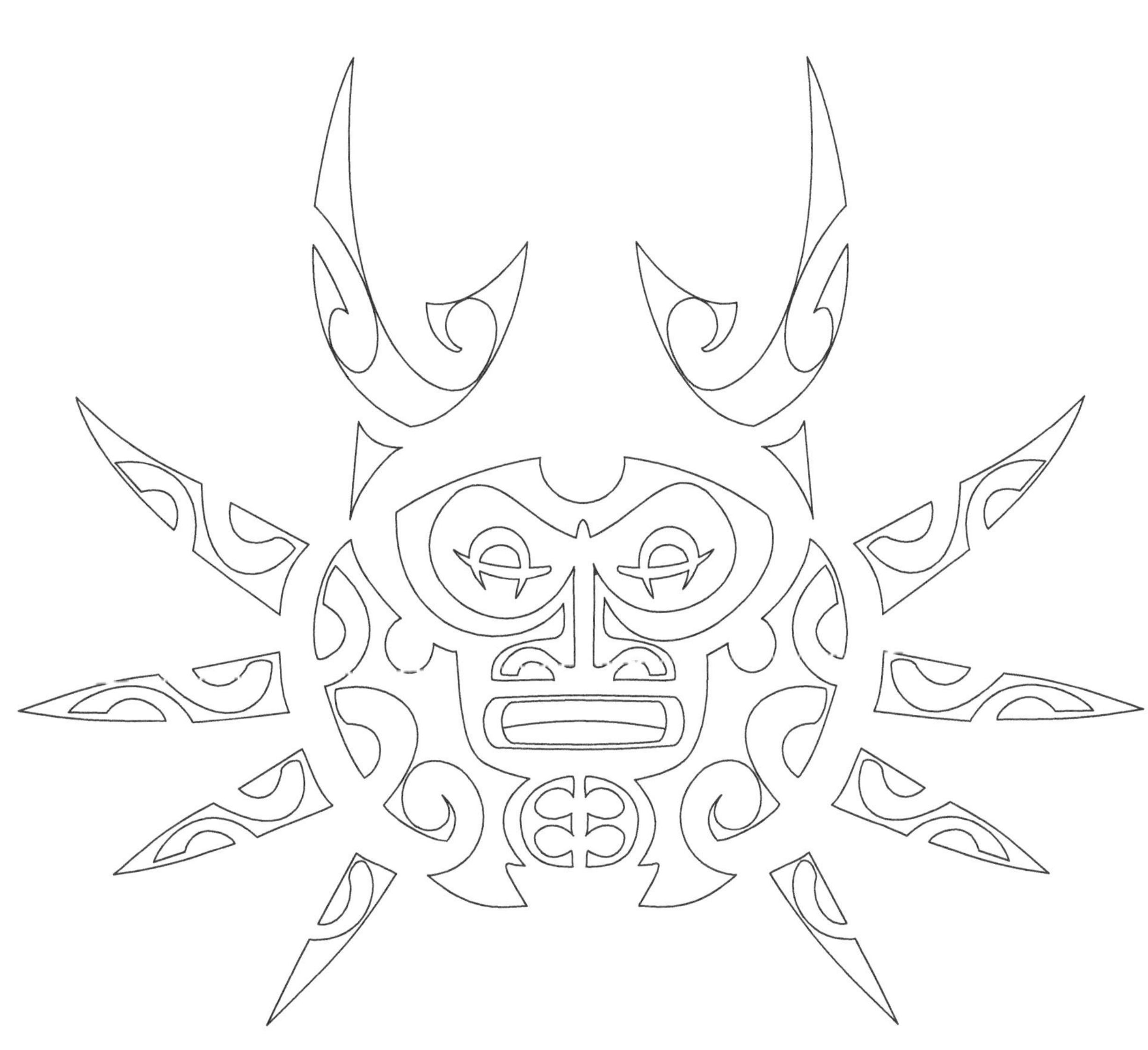

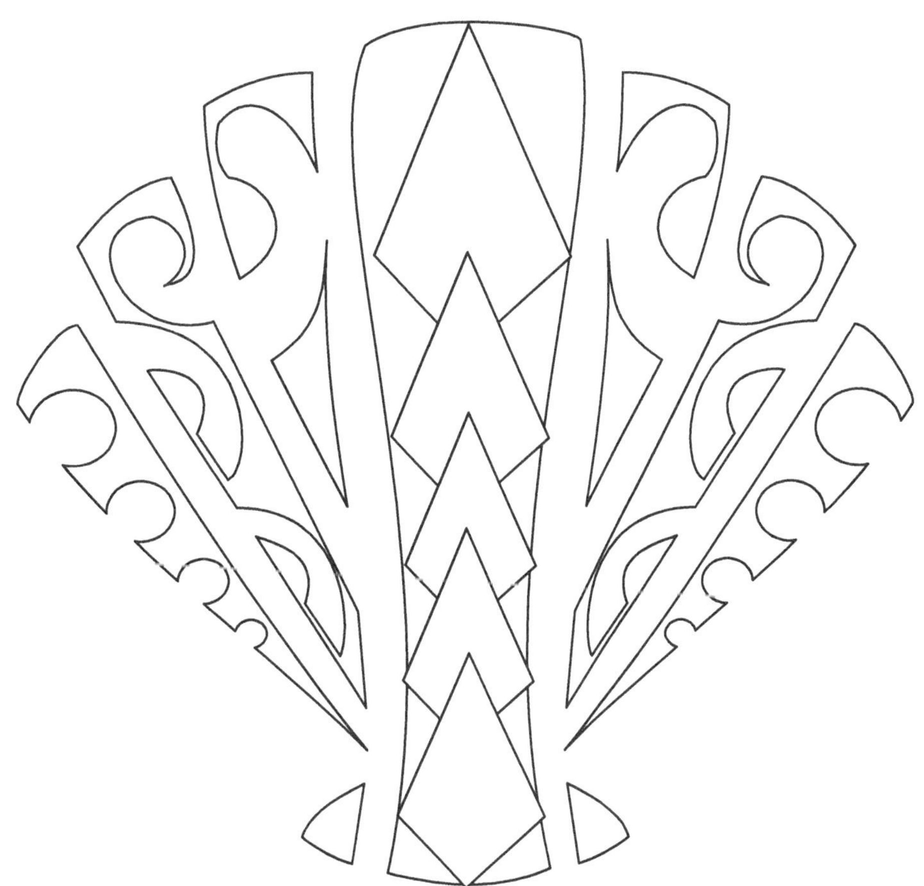

t090

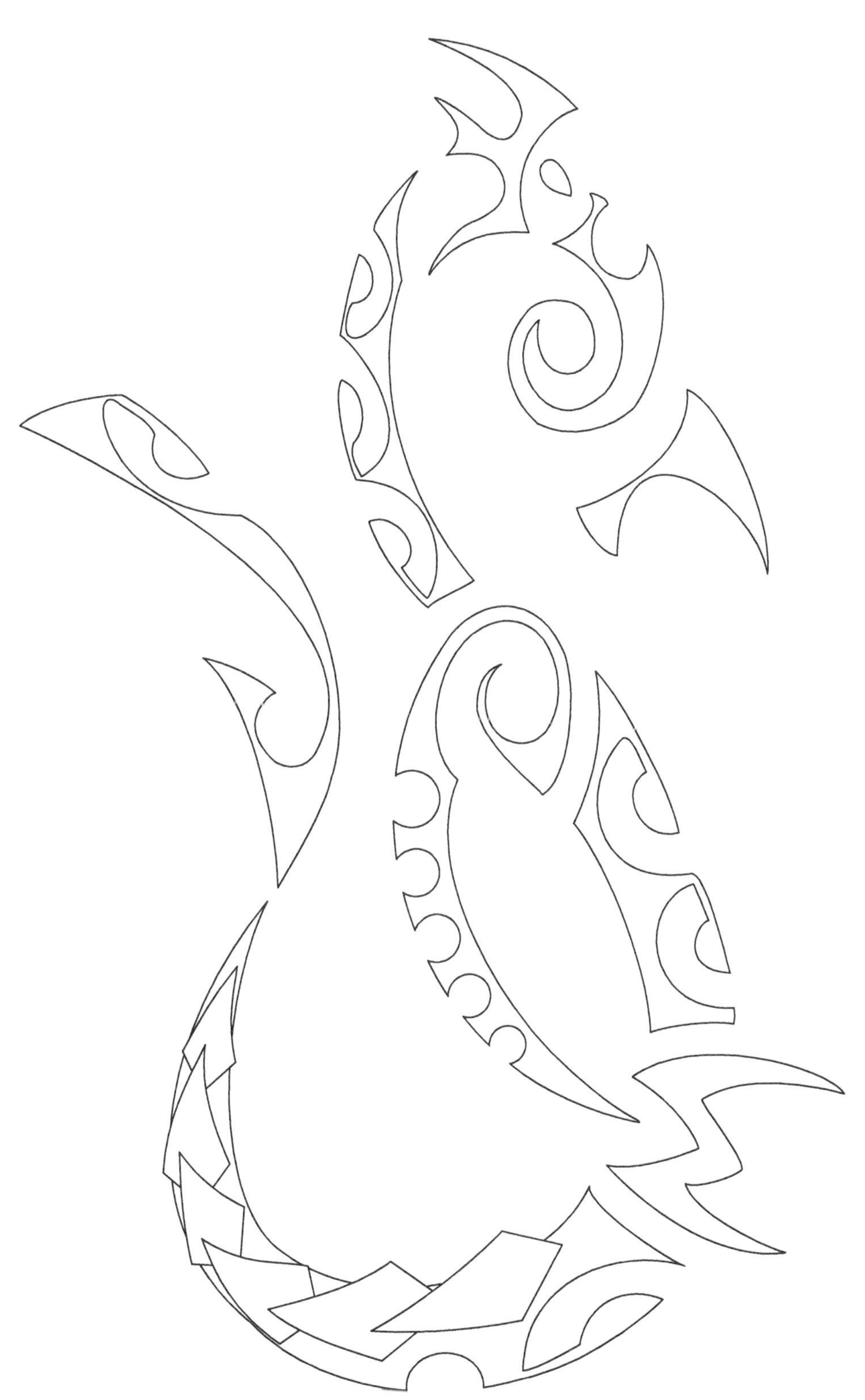

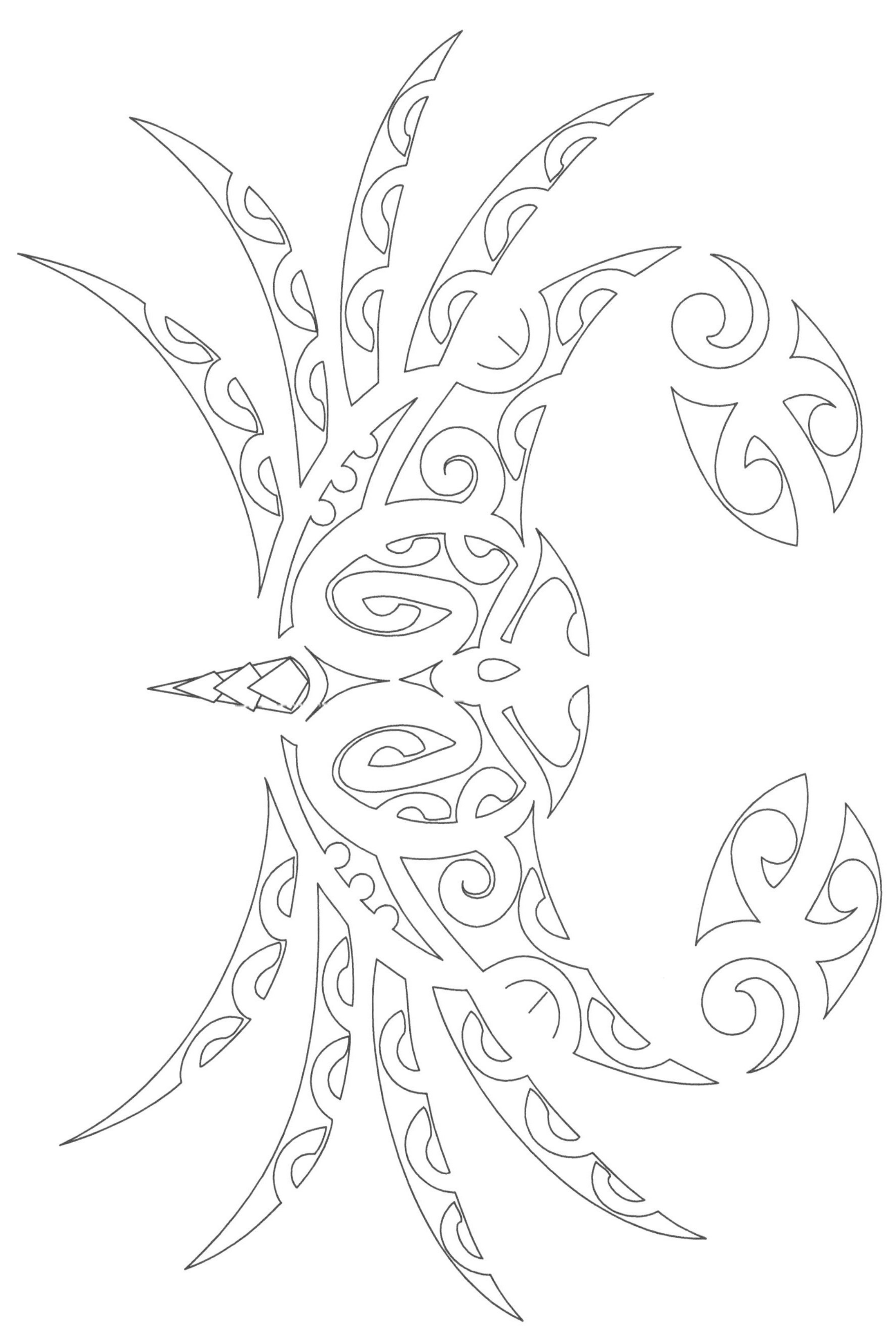

INDEX

All the symbols used to create the designs featured in this book are derived from Polynesian traditions and are clearly explained along with many others in The Polynesian Tattoo Handbook, which is also the source inspiration for the twin app that allows creating personal designs by adding the chosen symbols to a design pad, easily moving, rotating, resizing and assembling them:

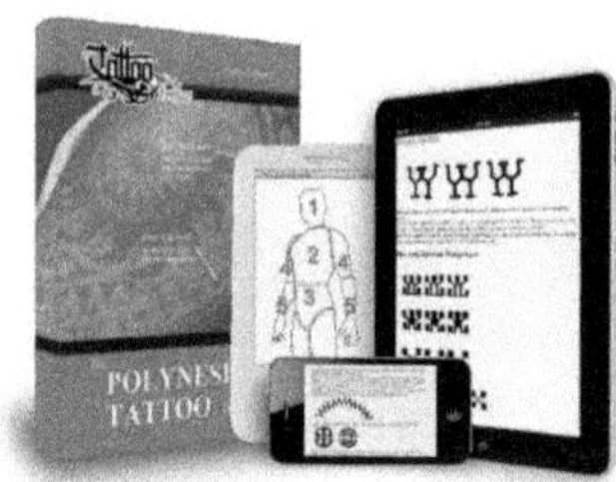

The Polynesian Tattoo Handbook

Get to know Polynesian tattoos and their symbolism. 250+ pages with symbols, their meanings, their placement on the body, case studies and step by step tattoo creation, basic elements and reusable designs. More info on:

www.polynesian-tattoo-handbook.com

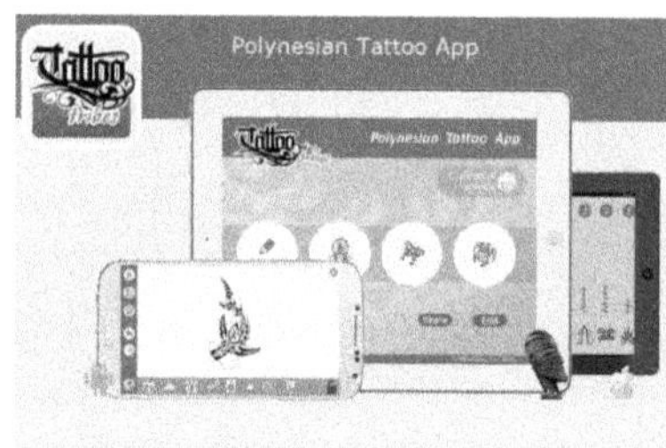

The Polynesian Tattoo App

After you learnt the symbols and how to place them from our book, the App goes one step further and uses them to help you create your own tattoos.

AS EASY AS PLAYING WITH LEGO™ BRICKS!.

app.polynesian-tattoo-handbook.com

www.ingramcontent.com/pod-product-compliance
Ingram Content Group UK Ltd.
Pitfield, Milton Keynes, MK11 3LW, UK
UKHW061707190726
13853UKWH00008B/2444